SCOTLAND
SOUTH
Scale of Miles
0 5 10 15 20 25
NORTH SEA
ENGLAND
FIRTH OF FORTH
Firth of Tay
SOLWAY FIRTH
ANGUS
FIFE
KINROSS
CLACKMANNAN
WEST LOTHIAN
EAST LOTHIAN
MIDLOTHIAN
DUNBARTON
LANARK
PEEBLES
SELKIRK
BERWICK
ROXBURGH
DUMFRIES
SIDLAW HILLS
OCHIL HILLS
PENTLAND HILLS
MOORFOOT HILLS
LAMMERMUIR HILLS
CHEVIOT HILLS
LIDDESDALE
TWEEDDALE
Schiehallion 3547'
Garth
Weem
Fortingall
Aberfeldy
Falls of Moness
Kenmore
Loch Tay
Dunkeld
Birnam
Amulree
Glenalmond
Ben Chonzie 3048'
Almond
St. Fillans
Ochtertyre
Crieff
Comrie
Muthill
Earn
Gleneagles
Auchterarder
Blackford
Allan Wr.
Dunblane
Bri. of Allan
Alva
Stirling
Bannockburn
Alloa
Clackmannan
Kincardine
Culross
Dunfermline
Cowdenbeath
Kirkcaldy
Dysart
Kinghorn
Burntisland
Inverkeithing
Rosyth
Queensferry
Inchcolm
Forth
Grangemouth
Boness
Falkirk
Linlithgow
Armadale
Bathgate
Hillend Resr.
Airdrie
Coatbridge
Whitburn
Motherwell
Wishaw
Hamilton
Braidwood
Lanark
Avon Wr.
Kirriemuir
Forfar
Friockheim
Lunan B.
Alyth
Glamis
Blairgowrie
Rattray
Isla
Coupar Angus
Auchmithie
Arbroath
Carnoustie
Monifieth
Dundee
Broughty Ferry
Tayport
Wormit
Dunsinane Hill
Kinnaird
Scone Palace
New Scone
Huntingtower
Perth
Tay
Abernethy
Auchtermuchty
Leuchars
Cupar
St. Andrews
Boarhills
Kingsbarns
Magus Muir
Cameron
Dunino
Ceres
Fife Ness
Crail
Falkland
Kinross
L. Leven
Leslie
Lundin
Largo
Leven
Cellardyke
Anstruther
Pittenweem
Elie
E. Wemyss
W. Wemyss
North Berwick
Bass Rock
Tantallon Castle
Law
Gullane
Aberlady
Dunbar
Granton
Leith
Portobello
Edinburgh
Colinton
Dalkeith
Rosslyn
Haddington
E. Linton
Gifford
Cockburnspath
St Abb's Hd.
St. Abbs
Coldingham
Eyemouth
Burnmouth
Reston
Soutra Hill
N. Esk
S. Esk
W. Linton
Duns
Blackadder Wr.
Berwick-upon-Tweed
Lauder
Greenlaw
Marchmount
Tweed
Peebles
Biggar
Stobo
Innerleithen
Clovenfords
Galashiels
Earlston
Melrose
Abbotsford
St. Boswells
Coldstream
Kelso
Roxburgh
Belford
Till
Wooler
Bowmont Wr.
Tinto Hill 2335'
Douglas Wr.
Douglas
Culter Fell 2454'
Clyde
Abington
Crawford
Elvanfoot
Tweedsmuir
Yarrow
Yarrow Wr.
St. Mary's Loch
Ettrick Bridge
Selkirk
Teviot
Jedburgh
Tweedshaws
White Coombe 2695'
L. o' the Lowes
Birkhill
Ettrick Wr.
Leadhills
Wanlockhead
Greenlowther 2403'
Hart Fell 2651'
Devil's Beef Tub
Nith
Sanquhar
Denholm
Hawick
Cavers
Borthwick Wr.
Moffat
Beattock
Carter Bar
Alnwick
Aln
Enterkinfoot
Scar
Drumlanrig
Thornhill
Kinnel Wr.
Rede
Otterburn
Font
Morpeth
Moniaive
Craigdarroch Wr.
Auldgirth
Ewes Wr.
North Tyne
Lochmaben
Lockerbie
Langholm
Esk
Wansbeck
Blyth
Torthorwald
Maxwelltown
Dumfries
Ecclefechan
Canonbie
Annan
Ken
Longtown
Lyne
Irthing
Caerlaverock Castle
Ruthwell
Gretna Green
Haltwhistle
South Tyne
Hexham
Tyne
Newcastle
South Shields
Gateshead
Urr
New Abbey
Criffell 1866'
Castle Douglas
Dalbeattie
Kirkbean
Dee
Kippford
Rockcliffe
Auchencairn
Dundrennan
Silloth
Carlisle
Eden
Wigton
Derwent
Alston
Petteril
Caldew
Durham
Maryport

Clan Johnston

John Douglas Johnston
169 Farm Lane

Contents

FRONTISPIECE OVERLEAF: *Black Mount, Argyll*

SCOTLAND'S SPLENDOUR

as seen by

George Blake

W. H. Murray

J. S. Grant

Seton Gordon

Tom Weir

John R. Allan

Moray McLaren

and the SCOTTISH FIELD

COLLINS, 144 CATHEDRAL STREET, GLASGOW, C.4

Publisher's Preface

As Scottish publishers we are proud to present *Scotland's Splendour*, which attempts to capture in photograph and text the charm and beauty of our native land. The seven sections into which the book is divided cover the whole country, and we hope that wherever you may be it will help you to make your own remembered or imagined journeys through any part of Scotland.

Pictures capture the visual splendour at one moment of time, but it is the pen that brings the scene to life when the writer knows his subject and his craft so well that he can put you there beside him. Each of the seven regional chapters is by a leading Scottish author who knows the area intimately and mostly lives and works there. Each has his special interests and outlook, bred of long familiarity with his own part of Scotland. And so the style and emphasis change from chapter to chapter as the traveller moves on through the living, varied Scottish scene.

A word about Scottish place-names. For many there are two or three versions in common use, and we do not claim that ours is more "correct" than the others. We have, however, tried to be consistent where a place-name, or surname, occurs in different parts of the book.

This book is very much the result of team-work, and it would have been impossible, economically and practically, had we not had at our disposal the entire photographic library and colour plant of our country's leading picture magazine *Scottish Field*. We had the full co-operation of its editor, Mr. Sydney Harrison, and his staff in Glasgow, as well as the enthusiastic support of the composing room, blockmaking section and printing department of the Munro Press in Perth. We wish to thank also the many photographers whose work is represented in these pages. Their numbers preclude individual mention but the skill and patience which lie behind each picture should not be forgotten. To our own staff at Cathedral Street has fallen the task of planning and designing, and of striving for accuracy and harmony in bringing text, pictures, captions and maps together. We hope that this combined effort has succeeded, and that *Scotland's Splendour* will give as much pleasure to the reader as we have had in preparing it.

GENERAL EDITOR: J. B. FOREMAN, M.A.

FIRST PUBLISHED, 1960

This book is set in Monotype Baskerville, ten on eleven point and printed by The Munro Press, Perth on Art Paper supplied by The Inveresk Paper Company, Musselburgh, and bound in printed Rexine by William Collins Sons and Company Limited.

GLASGOW AND THE SOUTH-WEST

George Blake

LIST OF ILLUSTRATIONS

THE WEST

W. H. Murray

LIST OF ILLUSTRATIONS

page

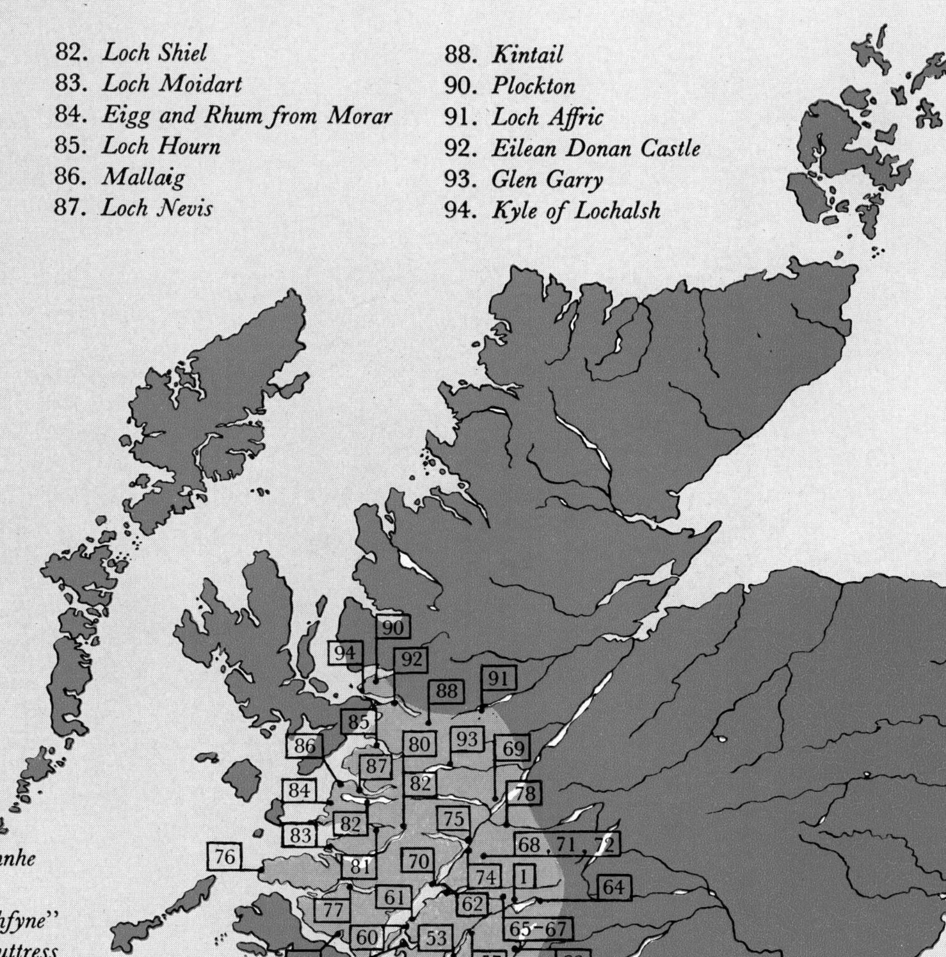

THE HEBRIDES

J. S. Grant

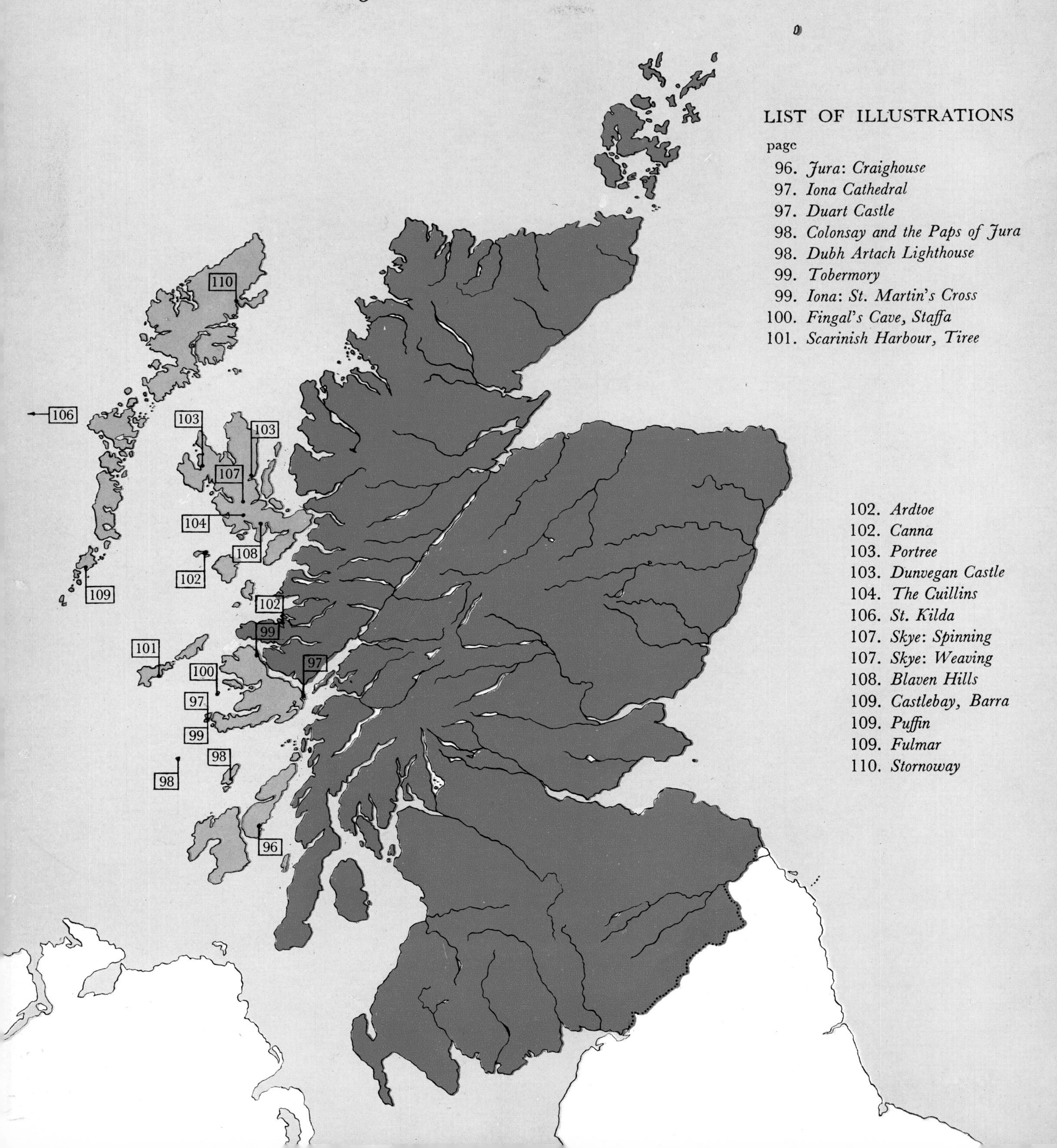

LIST OF ILLUSTRATIONS

SCOTLAND
An impression of the main features drawn for "Scotland's Splendour" by John Mackay
The ATLANTIC OCEAN
The NORTH
SHETLAND
[65 mls. south of true position]
LERWICK
ORKNEY
Skara Brae
KIRKWALL
Scapa Flow
Pentland Firth
Duncansby Head
Cape Wrath
Loch Erriboll
THURSO
WICK
BEN HOPE
BEN LOYAL
REAY FOREST
MORVEN
Loch Shin
BEN MORE
SUILVEN
R. Oykell
Butt of Lewis
FLANNAN ISLES
LEWIS
STORNOWAY
North Minch
HARRIS
Loch Broom
AN TEALLACH
BEN DEARG
Loch Maree
Measach Falls
SLIOCH
SGURR MOR
BEN WYVIS
Dornoch Firth
Moray Firth
N. UIST
Loch Torridon
Loch Dunvegan
SKYE
R. Beauly
INVERNESS
Loch Ness
Falls of Glomach
MAM SOUL
Loch Duich
BEN ATTOW
THE CUILLINS
AFFRIC
GLEN
MONADHLIATH MTS.
STRATHSPEY
R. Spey
R. Findhorn
R. Deveron
R. Ythan
BENNACHIE
R. Don
S. UIST

ERISKAY
Sea of the Hebrides
Sound of Sleat
RHUM
EIGG
Sound of Arisaig
Loch Morar
Loch Shiel
CORRIEYAIRACK PASS
BRAERIACH
LAIRIG GHRU PASS
BEN MACDHUI
CAIRNTOUL
ROTHIEMURCHUS FOREST
GRAMPIAN MTS
Loch Ericht
LOCHNAGAR
BALMORAL FOREST
ATHOLL FOREST
ABERDEEN
R. Dee
BEN NEVIS
BEN ALDER
BEN Y GLOE
R. Garry
FORT WILLIAM
GLENCOE
BUCHAILLE ETIVE
Loch Rannoch
Loch Tummel
BEN Y VRACKIE
R. South Esk
SCHIEHALLION
GLEN LYON
COLL
Loch Linnhe
Loch Etive
BEN LAWERS
R. Tay
STRATHMORE
SIDLAW HILLS
SEA
TIREE
BEINN DOIREANN
Loch Tay
DUNDEE
BEN CRUACHAN
BELL ROCK
STAFFA
BEN MORE
MULL
OBAN
BEN MORE
PERTH
Firth of Tay
Loch Earn
R. Earn
IONA
Loch Awe
BEN VORLICH
BEN LEDI
Loch Katrine
OCHIL HILLS
BENCLEUCH
Loch Leven
LOMOND HILLS
Firth of Lorne
BEN LOMOND
R. Teith
ISLE OF MAY
Loch Long
R. Forth
Crinan Canal
Loch Fyne
Loch Lomond
STIRLING
KIRKCALDY
Firth of Forth
BASS ROCK
COLONSAY
CAMPSIE FELLS
INCHCOLM
JURA
EDINBURGH
GLASGOW
LAMMERMUIR HILLS
PENTLAND HILLS
ISLAY
R. Clyde
MOORFOOT HILLS
BUTE
Kilbrennan Sound
GOATFELL
LANARK
R. Tweed
R. Tweed
KILMARNOCK
GALASHIELS
TINTO
CULTER FELL
DOLLAR LAW
R. Yarrow
ARRAN
THE EILDONS
R. Teviot
Firth of Clyde
AYR
SOUTHERN UPLANDS
HART FELL
St. Marys Loch
GREENLOWTHER
R. Ettrick
HAWICK
R. Doon
CHEVIOT HILLS
Mull of Kintyre
AILSA CRAIG
MERRICK
N
R. Nith
R. Annan
Loch Ryan
Loch Trool
DUMFRIES
NORTHERN IRELAND
R. Dee
CRIFFELL
W
E
STRANRAER
KIRKCUDBRIGHT
Solway Firth
Luce Bay
0
10
20
30
60
miles
S
Mull of Galloway

THE NORTH

Seton Gordon

LIST OF ILLUSTRATIONS

page

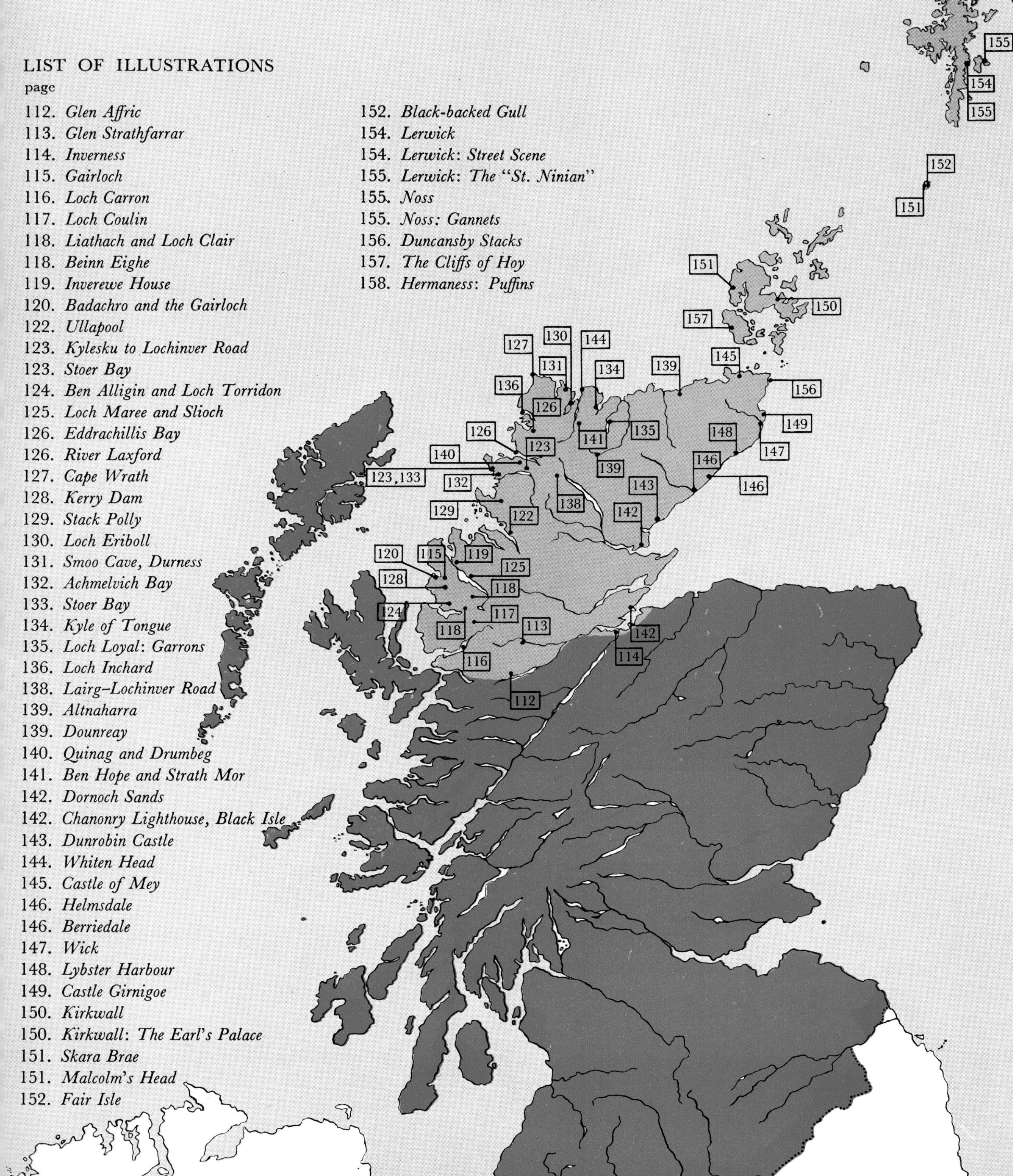

THE NORTH-EAST

John R. Allan

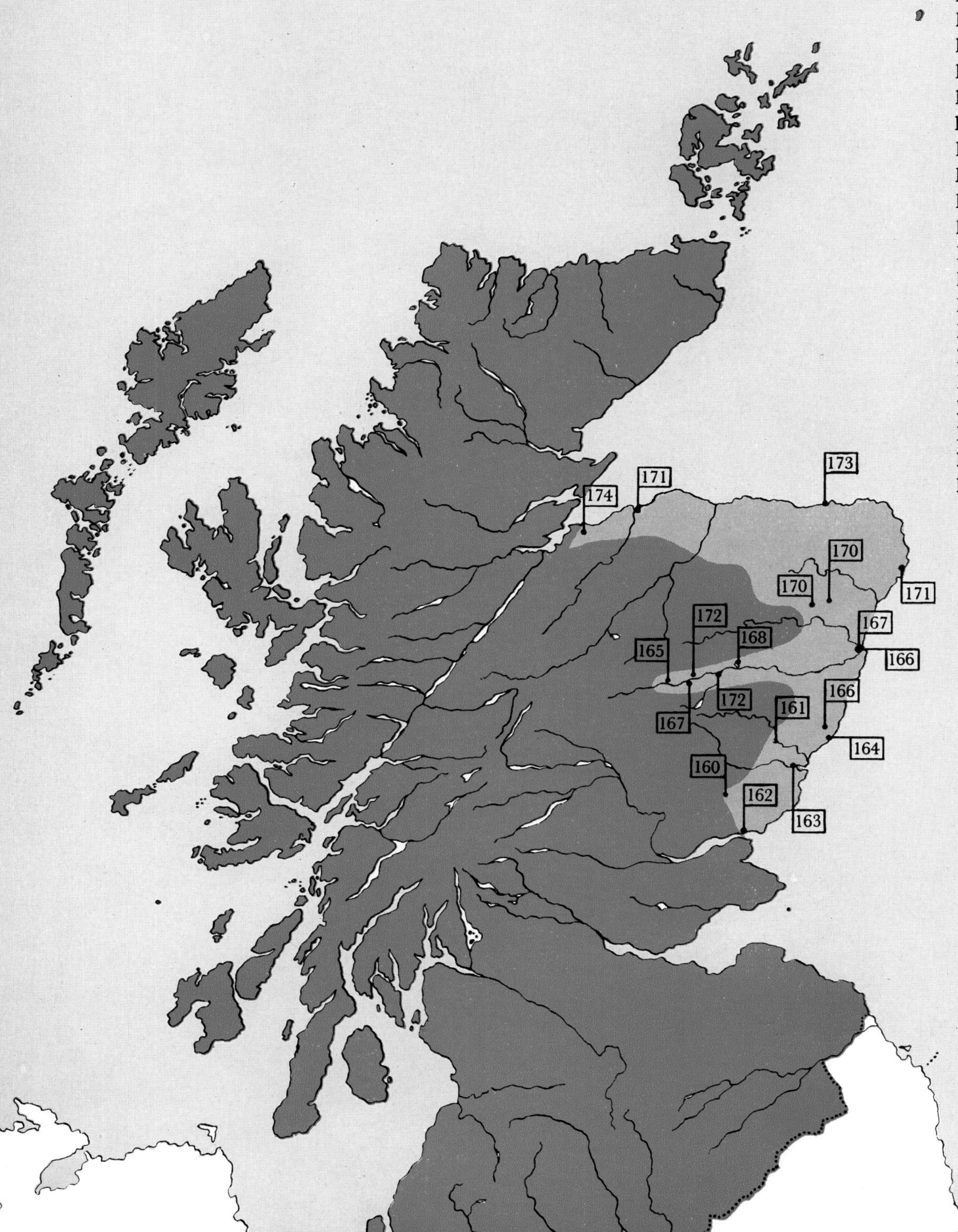

LIST OF ILLUSTRATIONS

THE CENTRAL HIGHLANDS

Tom Weir

LIST OF ILLUSTRATIONS

page

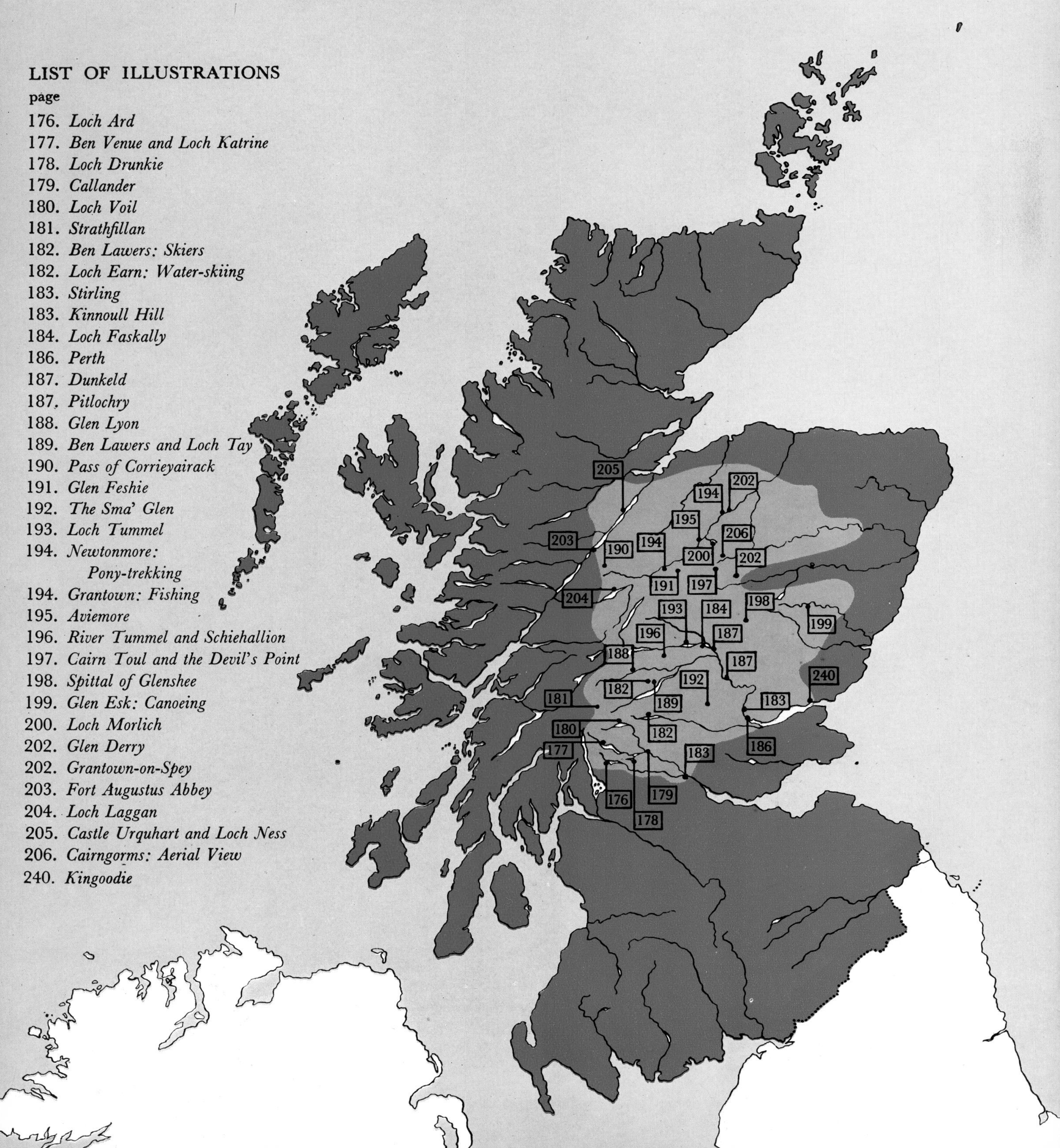

EDINBURGH, FIFE AND THE BORDERS

Moray McLaren

LIST OF ILLUSTRATIONS

The "Queen Mary", running trials off Arran

Was it the size of her, that great cliff of upperworks bearing down upon him? Was it her majesty, the manifest fitness of her to rule the waves? I think that what brought the lump to the boy's throat was just her beauty, by which I mean her fitness in every way; for this was a vessel at once large and gracious, elegant and manifestly efficient. That men could fashion such a thing by their hands out of metal and wood was miraculous. Ships he had seen by the hundred thousand, but this was a ship in a million; and there came to him then as he saw her, glorious in the evening sunlight, the joy of the realisation that this was what his own kindred could do, this was what the men of his own race, labouring on the banks of his own familiar River, were granted by Providence the privilege to create. In that moment he knew that he had witnessed a triumph of achievement such as no god of battles or panoplied monarch had ever brought about.

GEORGE BLAKE: *Rest and Be Thankful*

GLASGOW AND THE SOUTH-WEST

George Blake

The proper understanding of Scotland in both its physical and social aspects is befogged by the unhappy and inaccurate division of the country into Highlands and Lowlands. The phrase is convenient, but it has created in the popular mind a vague illusion that the top half of Scotland is all mountains, bens, crags, stags, grouse, gillies and Gaelic-speaking crofters, while the lower portion is given over to industry, slums and Association Football played by dour men who speak as Harry Lauder did, with a few farmers and razor-slashers thrown in.

The traditional "Highland Line" still exists in outline, though sadly dented nowadays by the impacts of such modern influences as radio, mass merchandising and tourism, but it certainly does not run across Scotland in a straight line of latitude due east and west. It is above all important to understand that the Lowlands are on the whole not at all low in terms of altitude, and that, as we shall see, the south-western region with which this chapter deals runs in places very high, craggy and dangerous. The region has very little to show in the way of proper plains, except along a few alluvial stretches, and nothing so extensive in flatness as that stretch of the English Midlands through the shires of Stafford, Bedford and Hertford that afflicts with a sense of strangeness the Scot travelling towards London.

There is no part of Scotland, one must insist, that has not its landmark of hill within easy sight. The scale is small, the features of landscape are everywhere close-gathered, in the Lowlands as in the Highlands. One odd case of a town within the Lowlands, Greenock in Renfrewshire, is that of one built on slopes so steep that the municipality is at its wit's end to attract light industry, so desirable to-day, for sheer lack of flat ground on which modern-type factories may be built.

Before our long journey through this south-western region of Scotland begins in earnest, it is well to appreciate another falsity in the popular distinction between Highlands and Lowlands. As a direct consequence of the Industrial Revolution the impoverished Highlanders sent their sons and daughters to the growing industrial towns to look for gold and, too often, to find little more than the sordid obscurity of slums. Thus there are 64 pages of Macs in the Glasgow Telephone Directory, from MacAbney to MacWillie, while in Greenock you may attend a service in Gaelic any Sunday and listen to one of the best Gaelic choirs in Scotland. The place-names of Scotland are, indeed, predominantly Celtic down to the Border. So far as the social pattern is concerned, the Irish came in by the thousand, with the Highlanders, to complicate it; to be hewers of wood and drawers of water, to dig canals and build railways—with one odd and still discernible effect: that in a predominantly Presbyterian country there are still pockets of Catholicism wherever the progress of one of the new railways halted for a station to be built and a goods yard laid out.

The Scoto-Irish conflict remains a social problem throughout the south-western region, especially in Glasgow and the industrial area of Clydeside. In all its absurdities and tragedies, however, it has been amply documented, and perhaps we do better to look at the Highlands-Lowlands apposition with the eye rather than with the mind and the emotions, so long as we remember that geography, or topography, is not a remote and separate science but is always at the root of human attitudes, and that pictures, plain or coloured, greatly help to show what is the general nature of a people, and why. It may be seen, I think, that Scotland, especially in this lower left-hand corner of the map, takes much of its character from the generalisation already hazarded—that the Lowlands are rarely low, and that a complex of natural features governs their nature.

Glasgow, the capital city of the region (its natives would probably say, of Scotland) lies in the valley of the Clyde between two ranges of hills. Especially on the northern side of the river it is a city built on hills, with many of its streets so steep that cars are tested on them and ageing men are induced to think of the condition of their hearts at the sight of them. These characteristic hills of Glasgow are "drumlins," moraines left by the passage of the glaciers of long, long ago, and they dictate the character of the city to a remarkable degree.

Thus, each seems to house a separate community as neighbouring islands do: separate, that is, in spirit. Garngad in the north-eastern corner of the city is a vastly different sort of place from Garnethill, the ridge that rises above the main shopping thoroughfare of Sauchiehall Street and has the mass of the Glasgow School of Art, one of the masterpieces of the great native architect, Charles Rennie Mackintosh, clinging to its slopes. Garngad is apt to be tough, Garnethill shabby genteel. Neither is in the least like that western drumlin, its prow like a battleship's, that looks over the Kelvin tributary of the Clyde towards the Victorian Gothic of the university, the vast stone mansions of Victorian merchants (now mostly offices and hostels) seeming to glare westwards towards the shipyards, the ship-channel of the Clyde, and even the tidal Firth, which were the very foundations of their wealth.

Glasgow School of Art, showing the west and south sides of the building. It stands on the steep slope of Garnethill, one of Glasgow's 'drumlins' and was designed by Charles Rennie Mackintosh.

But nobody has ever written satisfactorily of Glasgow as a whole, and this is not the place to inaugurate another attempt on that baffling problem. It is a community more complex, perhaps, than London itself. Many strangers find it intolerably slattern—and it is. Many find its central shopping centres exciting—and they are. Some critics complain of a low level of general manners, and others find the rough and open ways of the Glasgow folk enchanting. (A Canadian visitor said "These people are quite incapable of hypocrisy"). Slums, terraces and squares of beauty and dignity; classical grandeur in the business streets that run uphill towards the fiery sunsets of the west; too many public houses occupying too many corners; furlong after furlong of high tenement buildings; and then the sprawl of vast housing estates needed to relieve the internal pressures, with strange blocks of skyscraper flats on the perimeter—such are one's impressions of a city so much too big in relation to the population of Scotland as a whole that the local authority has latterly been planning in agony to "overspill" its clotted population into places so distant and different as Wick, Haddington and Stranraer.

Glasgow was "the beautifullest little city in Europe," according to Daniel Defoe, and it is remarkable that so much of its elegant ancientry survived the brutal impacts of the Industrial Revolution. Because of its key position in the network of Scottish communications and on the edge of a rich coal and iron belt, Glasgow suffered most damnably from quick exploitation for quick gain, a fate escaped by Edinburgh and Aberdeen, though not by Dundee, among the great cities of Scotland. But still there stands serenely at the Townhead of Glasgow, on the top of yet another hill, the grandest pre-Reformation building north of the Border, Glasgow Cathedral, the lamp in the beautiful crypt gleaming on the tomb of the patron saint, Kentigern or, popularly, Mungo. The remaining riches of Glasgow in stone and lime are adequately listed and explained in the literature

A view of George Square in the heart of Glasgow, looking towards the City Chambers. Aesthetically the cause of much argument from time to time, the statues here are solid tributes to the famous. Among those that surround the central figure of Sir Walter Scott are Queen Victoria, Sir John Moore, James Watt and Robert Burns.

supplied by the Corporation, and they are of much greater interest than may be imagined by those who accept the music-hall view of a fascinating community.

Through the benevolence of landowners and industrialists, and through the wisdom of municipal buying, this city of heavy industry has ample and beautiful space in which to breathe. It needs fresh air, indeed. That heaviness of colour in the sandstone buildings, which gives the occasional visitor a sense of drabness, is a product of weather and industry in unholy conjunction, industrial sulphurs and such fusing with the prevalent moisture to produce acids that darken and even corrode the soft stones of which so many of Glasgow's glum buildings are built. The parks are nature's recompense. The most casual visitor can hardly miss those in the central area—

The Clyde is broad and shallow but has been made navigable at a cost of millions of pounds. It is a river which nurtured pioneers of the Industrial Age, such as James Watt, who harnessed the power of steam and Henry Bell, the builder of the " Comet ". More recently, the " Queen Mary " and her sister ship " Queen Elizabeth " were built by John Brown's of Clydebank, whose shipyard is in the foreground of this picture. But grey industry is only one of the Clyde's faces. Out on the estuary is one of Scotland's splendid playgrounds where an admirable steamer service takes one to picturesque islands or up narrow sea-lochs deep into rugged hill country.

Kelvingrove, Queen's and the tidy charm of the more formal Botanic Gardens—but the richness of the city's endowment is to be realised in unexpected places. Far out to the west of the city, behind a zareba of shipyards, is the Victoria Park, with a character much more surprising than its name: a park with a fossil grove under cover and an adorable rock garden fashioned out of an old quarry. Far out to the east is Tollcross Park, wonderfully wooded and, until quite recent times, the shelter of a herd of deer. The sweetness of peace is in the wooded parks in the southern outskirts of the city, Pollok and Linn and King's, culminating on Glasgow's southernmost boundary in Rouken Glen—a real glen, of which the city gardeners have maintained the natural character.

Glasgow's writ in the matter of parks runs far beyond the city boundaries. The Corporation owns and maintains Balloch Park at the lower end of Loch Lomond. Balloch is a fascinating little place—a thought artificial and characterless with its many hotels, garages and synthetic silk factory in the middle of holiday confusion. Even so, it has the odd graces of a place of pleasure in lovely surroundings, and there is life on the Leven which, flowing out of the loch as a short but copious tributary of the Clyde, carries such a gay flotilla of houseboats, motor boats and skiffs as to give it something of the atmosphere of the Thames above Richmond. This is a place of organised pleasure, the terminal port of the thousands who wish to sail the vast lake, the largest in Britain.

Glasgow's ownership of a stretch of the "bonnie banks" is right on every count. Access from the city is easy and cheap by a frequent train and bus service. To be sure, it is an old and rather stale joke that Glasgow is a good and easy place to get out of, but the Glaswegian can fairly retort by asking what other large conurbation has such wonderful escape routes. Perhaps he nowadays takes Loch Lomond and even the majestic mass of Ben Lomond for granted. In its lower reaches, indeed, the loch seems just an awful lot of water. William Wordsworth, nostalgically remembering his tidy little Lakes, complained a thought petulantly of the "large proportion of diffused water" and required "a speedier termination of the long vista of blank water." But Coleridge was being difficult, and the inn at Luss was abominable, and perhaps it was raining. How could a poet have ignored the charm of the islands before Luss, the serenity with which the Ben presides over the scene? Today we marvel that these shores remain so unspoilt—a testimonial to the good sense of the chief landowners, the Colquhouns of Luss—and may tremble to think what might have happened to them in, say, the Isle of Man.

The upper, narrower end of Loch Lomond is out-

Sauchiehall Street with its famous tramcars, which are now rapidly disappearing, is Glasgow's most exciting thoroughfare and one of its busiest shopping centres.

side the scope of this essay, but that does allow us to travel as far as the point where, most dramatically, the fresh water of Loch Lomond comes very near to meeting the salt water of Loch Long. The isthmus between the two is little more than a mile long; over it the Vikings hauled their boats to sail down to Balloch and harry the Vale of Leven. The short run from Tarbert to Arrochar brings the traveller abruptly face to face with the true West Highlands in the steep faces, rising sheer from seaweedy shores, of Ben Ime and Ben Arthur, the latter known as The Cobbler since the tangle of rocks at its summit suggest, against the skyline, 2,891 feet up, the figure of an aged craftsman bent over his last.

In the early years of this century Arrochar lost much of the character of a Highland hamlet when the naval authorities set up a torpedo range in Loch Long, but around it is still one of Scotland's wilder playgrounds. The range of the Arrochar Alps makes a rare set of nursery slopes for climbers. It was here, during the depression of the early 1930's, that a number of young shipyard craftsmen, rebelling against the tedium of hanging about street corners and Labour Exchanges, took to the hills. This group

GLASGOW UNIVERSITY

The five-hundred-year-old University of Glasgow has twice been uprooted—once from its original site in Rottenrow, and then ninety years ago from the High Street to Gilmorehill above the River Kelvin. The present building, designed by Sir George Gilbert Scott, has a unique filigree spire surmounting the tower on the central block,

THE RIVER LEVEN AT BALLOCH

Balloch with its hotels, garages and synthetic silk factory in the midst of determined holiday confusion, tends to be slightly artificial. On the Leven, houseboat meets motor boat and skiff in lovely surroundings. Here is an attractive resort for tourists and a convenient base for sailing on Loch Lomond, the largest sheet of fresh water in Britain.

In the once aristocratic east of Glasgow is the Cathedral, the only undamaged survivor of great Gothic churches in south Scotland. Behind is the huge Royal Infirmary building, in front the Necropolis.

became a mountaineering club so highly skilled that its members are still called on to take part in rescue operations—for these mountains are merciless to the inexperienced and the foolhardy.

Loch Long is a fjord of striking character. The hillsides come down sheer to its deep waters. Cut into the eastern slopes is that most picturesque of British railways, the old West Highland line that winds northwards to cross the Moor of Rannoch towards Fort William and, ultimately, Mallaig across the sound from Skye. The western slopes are rugged, wooded, almost trackless. The main loch has an offshoot in Loch Goil, rather a sombre sheet much used by the Royal Navy for experimental work, and here, behind the village of Lochgoilhead, one finds—rather improbably—another of Glasgow's far-flung possessions. This is the rugged, mountainous estate of Ardgoil, given to the city early this century by a member of the Cameron Corbett, now Rowallan, family. It is a jagged, alpine chunk of territory, almost offensively picturesque, and as the service of Clyde coast steamers has been curtailed since the two wars, access to it is not easy. Glasgow Corporation has developed it along forestry lines, and since it marches with the huge plantations of the Forestry Commission to the south of Loch Goil, there is hereabouts the makings of a magnificent National Park.

Wild as the nature of Loch Goil may be, however, the traveller must observe with some surprise that the little places along its shores contain a large proportion of largish houses of the Victorian villa type. This is a regional phenomenon that needs understanding.

The Clyde was the cradle of the steamboat and it opened up the splendid Firth to the industrial population of the hinterland. Rich men built mansions "at the Coast", solid men in the middle orders of society built their solid villas, and poor men took lodgings in seaside cottages or were content with the occasional day's sail "doon the watter." (At one period of intense steamboat competition about the 1850's the Glasgow worker could sail all day from Glasgow to Rothesay and back for a shilling). The rush to the sea, out of the smoky places, became a fever; it created at once a trade and a legend. It helped to make the Firth one of the yachting centres of the world. It assisted, quite directly, the evolution of the modern steamship.

The chain of "resorts" along the shores of the inner Firth is almost continuous, their names familiar throughout Britain at least. At the mouth of Loch Long are Blairmore, Strone, Kilmun, with Cove and Kilcreggan on the opposite shore—almost cases of ribbon development. Round the short but pretty Holy Loch the tale is resumed in Ardnadam and Sandbank, merging into Hunter's Quay, Kirn, Dunoon and then Innellan, all on the Cowal shore, that chain ending in Rothesay on the Isle of Bute. The theme continues, though patchily, up the cosily romantic Kyles of Bute and does not end even before it has reached the heroic Isle of Arran. All these little places have several distinct features in common. They all seem to be clinging by their eyebrows to rocky slopes. They all command splendid views over one of the world's most magnificent estuaries. They are all inveterately Scottish, even where the local authority has sought to create a Blackpool of the North; the Highland blood must out to defy extreme sophistication. The larger of them,

Well up Loch Long, one of the deepest fjords in Scotland, Loch Goil branches off into the mountainous west. At the top of the loch lies the peaceful village of Lochgoilhead.

The " British Duchess ", an oil tanker of 42,000 tons, the first arrival at the new jetty of the Finnart Ocean Terminal on Loch Long in June, 1959. From this deep-water anchorage the oil is pumped across Scotland for refining at Grangemouth. This view from Finnart (" fionn-ard "—" beautiful headland ") looks west across the hills between Lochs Long and Goil.

unhappily, suffer the curse of the industrial tradition in the shape of rather shabby tenement buildings and narrow streets in a huddle at the local pierhead, hardly living up to the sandstone dignity of the Victorian merchant's "Clydeview" or the cottage, "Rivetbank" or the like, in which some shipyard craftsman of the same era invested his savings.

These resorts are, moreover, alike in their fate. The Victorian positions have been reversed. Most of the fine villas are institutions or boarding houses nowadays, the smaller dwellings given over to summer lets. The steamer services are not so copious as they were, and the development of the long-range bus has altered the pattern. Those resorts which nowadays advertise their charms systematically used to depend on the exodus of the Clydeside worker, but now look for patrons from industrial England. The Scottish worker, his conditions vastly improved within the last century, finds what he wants in Blackpool, Douglas in the Isle of Man and Whitley Bay, if not on the Costa Brava.

This new mobility of the masses has vastly altered the plan of living throughout the whole of this south-western district of Scotland; and it could be said that the changes brought about by increasing ease of transportation are nowhere more obvious or dramatic than about the great expanses of the Firth of Clyde. One is tempted to dwell at perhaps too great length on this wide sea area, so diverse in its interest and so important in its various bearings on the lives of the people on the mainland. Here the islands alone have already furnished the material for a small library of books.

The economies of all these islands depend in varying degrees on what is nowadays called the tourist trade. If the Lesser Cumbrae is not much more than a stance for a lighthouse, its Greater sister, some modest farming apart, looks to attract the summer visitor through the pleasant, delightfully old-fashioned resort of Millport, and this townlet has a special point of interest in the marine biological station out at Keppel, under an eccentric cliff of red rock. Bute is largely Rothesay, "the Madeira of the North," but not by any means all. Rothesay is part and parcel of all the Glasgow holiday legends, slightly vulgar, endlessly interesting, if only as a steamer junction. But Bute has also a wealth of things, from brochs to Druid circles, to enchant the archaeologist, and it has in Mount Stuart, the seat of the Marquesses of Bute, one of the most ornate of Britain's aristocratic mansions. It is hardly so interesting, however, as the old ruins of Rothesay Castle, through which the heir to the throne inherits a Scottish dukedom. Apart from knobbly lumps of high land at its northern and southern extremities Bute is a sweet and gentle island—"douce" and "bien", to use two good Scottish epithets. Its farms are large and craftily managed, and Ayrshire cows from these farms are often prize-winners.

Bute is, in fact, rather Lowland in general character; whereas Arran, well out in the fairway of the Firth, is a Highland place. This is a great, arrogant lion of an island with a noble skyline, adorable bays, ravishing glens and such a wealth of natural interest that it is the happy hunting ground of geologists and botanists. Arran profits from holidaymakers, in increasing numbers on day trips from the mainland, but it is all contrived with very little of the spoliation that has afflicted the Isle of Man so sadly. The settlements—Brodick, Lamlash and Whiting Bay on the eastern coast, Blackwaterfoot and Loch Ranza on the western—are only reasonably "developed". Those who make holiday regularly on the island are bound by a sort of tacit oath to decency; and the people who habitually use it—climbers, anglers and quiet family parties—favour the preservation of peace and the simplicities.

It is remarkable of both Bute and Arran that excesses of exploitation have been checked by the benevolent authority of the reigning landed families in both cases, the Crichton-Stuarts in Bute, the Hamilton-Montroses in Arran. It was gratifying that in early 1959 a mighty effort by the National Trust for Scotland saved Brodick Castle from the dereliction that would otherwise almost certainly have followed the impact of death duties: a wonderful thing that the heiress put into the Trust's care a huge expanse of high ground that embraces the noble cone of Goatfell and much of the craggy, dangerous region of ridges that give Arran its alpine aspect, like the scene of a rather horrific but essentially romantic legend in the Teutonic manner.

Glasgow has indeed its innumerable ways of escape from its own congestion. The comfortably-off, as elsewhere, do escape nightly to such pleasant dormitory towns as Bridge of Weir and Kilmacolm on the edge of the Renfrewshire moorlands, or to Helensburgh and the villages round the Gareloch on the

LOCH LOMOND FROM INVERUGLAS

The peacefulness of this scene towards the narrow, northern end of Loch Lomond contrasts with the greater activity of the wider, southern end near Balloch. This picture is taken from a point almost directly opposite Inversnaid and gives a typical view of Ben Lomond (3,192 feet). The area is a favourite week-end haunt of hikers and campers.

At Greenock, just before the Clyde changes course to flow south, the prospect is still one of industrial activity. Here are sugar refineries, engineering works, shipyards and also the only non-tidal dock on the Clyde.

northern shores of the Firth of Clyde, the tendency being always towards the sea. Gourock, a sort of western extension of Greenock, with its own blinding views of the Cowal hills under the technicolour sunsets of the west, also sleeps its quota of commuters. Nowhere in this region is it easy to escape from the signs of Glasgow's pervasive influence, but those who have some regard for peace should not ignore the curious triangle of high ground with Greenock-Kilmacolm-Largs as its points.

This is heathery, sheep-farming country; a lost bit of the world amid so much coming and going, pleasantly studded under the open sky by the sheen of reservoirs for the ablutions and refreshment of the hordes in the towns below. The whaup cries incessantly up here and the Blackface ewes mourn for their lambs, and the district bears the suitable local name of the Back o' the World. Some reconstruction of hill roads has made it feasible for cars, but a man does best hereabouts to go prayerfully on his feet.

The map shows that this knob of high ground is as an island. The tides of modern traffic sweep about its bases, along the fine road by the coast from Greenock southwards or by one or other of the valleys that lead south-westwards out of Glasgow towards the Ayrshire coast. These latter roads are Glasgow's short cuts to the sea and to the view of Arran, always filling the eye along scores of miles of shore. The main route to Kilmarnock out of the city carries the bulk of motor traffic over high, moorland country. That which comes out of Paisley through Johnstone and Dalry is an important railway approach to the ports of Ardrossan and Irvine, and it was the line by which the canal-builders of the late eighteenth century fondly hoped to reach the sea. They had got no farther than Paisley when the locomotive overtook them, and their only memorial is in a name—that of Paisley (Canal) Station—for their cutting was filled in to make a permanent way for the triumphant rival.

So the natural communications between the industrial region of Clydeside and the Clyde coast are short. One route comes in from the steel-and-coal belt of Lanarkshire through the odd townlet of Strathaven—pronounced Stráy-ven—to cross the covenanting moorlands and reach Kilmarnock through the Irvine Valley where they still make the long, sweeping lace curtains, to this day in heavy demand from North America and Northern Ireland. All converge on Kilmarnock, a tidy town with a nice variety of industry and, for the local authority, a continuous headache in the form of traffic problems.

North Ayrshire presents in its physical aspects the material for a Ph.D. thesis by a young geographer-sociologist. It is the strangest mixture of bare, mountainy country and shabby little pockets of exhausted industrialism. A green and pleasant land enough, though nowhere exciting in the scenic sense, it has its sound agricultural basis, but the small coal-mines and cotton-mills of yesterday are almost all run down or abandoned, and one sometimes feels that such small towns as Lochwinnoch, Beith and Dalry wear the air of old ladies who have seen better days. But this region of Ayrshire comes to contemporary life with a bang in the Kilmarnock-Ardrossan-Irvine complex, where your pet golf course may march with the sad dunes of an explosives works or, as at Troon, one half of the town on a peninsula is given over to such industrial arts as shipbuilding and the other to the mansions of city stockbrokers and a golf course in the championship class: swift transition from the workaday to the elegant.

As far down as Ayr—the shape of Arran always looming over the scene—this stretch of coast is a strange mixter-maxter of industry, beaches, golf links, shipyards, roadhouses, swimming pools, a great airport at Prestwick and high-powered horticulture—with a busy coalfield in the background. The old battle of amenity versus expediency is hereabouts being fought out with more intensity than in any other part of Scotland.

"Royal" Rothesay, capital of Bute, has two aspects. In winter quietly gracious, in summer a bustling resort.

Ayr, the centre of the Burns country, is a popular seaside town with a small harbour at the mouth of the river.

The importance of the Clyde coast steamer service has not been emphasised without a purpose: nor the symbolic importance of the splendid Isle of Arran stressed idly; for when the motor-coach arrived in the 1920s to offer the people cheap and comfortable transport to the sea over relatively short routes, this Ayrshire coast began to take from the pleasure steamers a large proportion of their trade. The decline of the old Presbyterian standards and the chaotic vagueness of the laws governing the sale of drink in

Glen Rosa, one of the most beautiful glens in Arran, is typical of the quiet and unspoiled nature of the island. The glen opens on to Brodick Bay and is flanked on the east by Goat Fell.

When May comes to the upper Firth of Clyde, bright little yachts like the Pleiades, sailing at Blairmore and Strone, can be seen showing their keels at every puff of wind.

Scotland on Sundays helped to transform the riparian scene almost overnight. The catering trades jumped at their opportunity, and all the way down the Ayrshire coast from Largs, through Saltcoats and Irvine and Troon and Prestwick to Ayr, there is much dancing and deray on any fine summer weekend, vastly surprising to those who remember the douceness of the Scots Sabbath fifty years or so ago.

That may be for better or worse; we are not here judges of morals, only observers of a scene. Mr. Billy Butlin has established one of his camps on the Heads of Ayr. Even south of Ayr, on the glorious coast road that runs along the shores of the Firth, over headlands and through wooded passes, to Stranraer, the stigmata of the out-thrust from industrial Clydeside are seen in the shape of hutment colonies, caravanserais, cafeterias and what you will. Good luck to them and their patrons, indeed! The trouble is that they are apt to be slattern, the city bringing its own untidiness with it into lovely places.

The hinterland is not exciting, even if so much of it is the fabled Burns Country. It is pleasant, pastoral, prosperous. The banks of Doon are bonnie indeed, but anybody who has read the poems of Burns without sentimental adhesions knows that his eye was microscopic, and that his vision, however piercing, lacked lateral range. It is of much interest that, though he lived so much of his life within sight and sound of the sea, he rarely used it for his poetic purposes. A beautiful young woman, a budding flowerlet, the bend of a river—any of these, on the other hand, was enough to set fire to the lyric fuse.

The Burns Country is easily covered by bus from Ayr. There may be some, however, who will flout convention by taking more pleasure in such antique glories as the ruins of Crossraguel Abbey, where Knox had a famous disputation, on the inland road from Ayr to Maybole, by seeking out the background

" Glen Sannox " largest of the Clyde car ferries, runs from Ardrossan and Fairlie to Arran during the summer.

of Johnson's Boswell at Auchinleck or, even at Ochiltree, seeking to recapture the atmosphere so poignantly rendered by George Douglas Brown in *The House with the Green Shutters*—no easy task. Ochiltree is within the Ayrshire minefield, and though that is a decently managed centre of industry, the council houses of our modern age seem to have robbed it of character.

Despite the blobs of vulgarity all the way down the main coast road from Ayr to Stranraer, the influences of industrial Clydeside weaken rapidly as the county town is left behind. The Carrick province of Ayrshire is a splendid bit of country with a splendid coastline. The farms have the look of white mansions, and their cattle are the best of the milk breeds. It is a green, bold country along the coastal strip, and the road seems to zoom and bound above sandy bays and over noble headlands. The southward journey is agreeably diversified by what may fairly be called a series of optical illusions. It is always good fun to lay bets with the stranger about the puzzle of the Electric Brae that leads down to Culzean Castle—a fraud of a hill, the mere alignment of its hedges

Etterick Bay, on the west coast of the island of Bute, with its stretches of sand, is a children's paradise. The Arran hills are in the far distance, across the Sound of Bute.

and ditches creating the curious impression that one is going uphill while in fact freewheeling down, and vice versa. There is the illusion that the peaks of Arran are always somewhere over your right shoulder. And the cone of Ailsa Craig out in the fairway of the Firth—a geological oddity and a wonderful natural reserve for seabirds—appears to play peep-bo, always popping up in the traveller's view, no matter how many bends and glens he may have negotiated in the meantime.

This coastline has a lot of good things to show, indeed. Under a steep slope off the main coast road, Dunure has the ruin of a castle of the Kennedys, the overlords of the district, and it has a little harbour of great charm. The fishermen of Dunure, with their neighbours at Maidens a mile or two down the coast, were pioneers of the ring-net method of fishing, and their boats (mostly built in Fife) are lovely craft, the more so for being perfectly adapted to their task of working in pairs, one stationary while the other circles to draw the fatal ring round a shoal of herring. Maidens lies more open to the sea and the sun than Dunure, and the fact has influenced its development of recent years. The bungalow and the caravan intrude increasingly, but the vast railway hotel at Turnberry has been there for a long time, the golf course has been an aerodrome during two wars, and there is something perdurable in the farms, Shanter among them, that stand in their blinding whitewash against the red soil and curiously light green of the rising ground behind.

It is between Dunure and Maidens that the wise traveller stops to see one of the sights of Scotland, Culzean Castle. This noble Adam building of the eighteenth century is the answer to a hack journalist's prayer, for it contains a flat for the exclusive use of President Eisenhower during his lifetime, a Scottish compliment to the commander of the Allied Forces towards the victorious end of the Second World War. Culzean (pronounced Kil'-ane) is sufficiently magnificent in its own right, in its gardens and in its position on a knot of cliffs above the pounding seas. The Kennedys—Earls of Cassilis and later Marquesses of Ailsa—had it built in 1777, and the sweep of the central staircase is something to see. Culzean Castle is now maintained by the National Trust for Scotland and attracts more

The house in which Robert Burns was born was rebuilt from an original clay "biggin" by the poet's father. It was restored in 1880 and now has thousands of visitors annually.

visitors each year than any other of the properties in the Trust's care.

The only sizeable town on this stretch of coast is Girvan, and that is an odd little town indeed. It is very long, its dwelling-houses seem to be all of the single-storey type, and one is puzzled to know whether it is really a summer resort or a fishing port. It is in fact a small regional capital, if rather lacking in architectural distinction. Hereabouts the first of the earliest potatoes on the market are dug out of the red soil and harvested by brightly-clad gangs of Irish workers; the regional vegetables in the shops are always of the highest quality, for this is a warm, well-cultivated part of the world. The harbour shelters another division of the Clyde ring-net fleet and a lifeboat; and from this cosy little port it is usually quite easy to get a passage over to Ailsa Craig, weather permitting.

The Craig is a very curious lump of rock indeed. Apart from the obvious interest of the lighthouse installations and the bird life on the western cliffs, it seems odd that a feasible track should wind up to the summit, 1,114 feet above the sea, with a ruined keep and a small loch on the way. Out of the walls of a sort of gallery rounding the northern shoulder of the rock, a family concern quarries the granite blocks which, turned and polished on the Ayrshire mainland, are sold all over the world as curling stones.

Ailsa Craig is never out of the eye of the traveller by the coast road down to Stranraer, as we have noted. That road has fine stretches, as through the rocky defile called Kennedy's Pass between Girvan and Ballantrae, where the road runs so close to the sea that the car driver must often use his wipers to brush the spray from his windscreen. Ballantrae itself is a pleasant village at the mouth of the charming River Stinchar, the curious shape of the hill called Knockdolian always in view. Robert Louis Stevenson got the title of a novel from the euphonious name of the village, and he asserts somewhere that he was 'stoned' out of it for the eccentricity of his appearance as a walking tourist. One hopes he went on to enjoy the walk southwards among the wonderful, great trees and then the brief charm of Glen App.

So to the sea again, this time in the form of Loch Ryan, a short and rather shallow sheet of water that until quite recently gave shelter to both oyster-beds and flying boats. At one of the gates of the Western Approaches, it had to accommodate during the Second World War a busy supply base at Cairnryan, and that did not improve the amenity of a pleasant stretch of Wigtownshire coast. At the head of the loch, Stranraer is a tidy little town with a curiously Irish look, as if it could be exchanged overnight with Donaghadee and nobody much the wiser. It has its

In Kilmaurs, an attractive little town north of Kilmarnock, the Tolbooth still has "jougs"—relics of the pillory. Some of the houses date from the seventeenth century.

One of the finely-moulded plaster ceilings in Culzean Castle, Ayrshire. It has been restored in pastel tints.

maritime concerns indeed, but its economic function is to be the capital of a singularly rich dairy-farming area. As for the Irish association, it is of interest to remember that there was always much coming-and-going across the few miles of the North Channel between Ulster and this province of Galloway. The predominant, rather uncouth, surnames of the region have Irish flavours—MacCulloch and MacDowell, even MacClumpha and MacGuffog.

Hereabouts are the great dairy farms, capable of carrying on rich pasture upwards of a hundred milch cows each. Each large farm used to make its own cheese in a nightly ritual of fascinating interest, and though the operations of the Milk Marketing Board have tended to centralise the process, the signs of decent prosperity are to be seen all over this lush, green region. The creamery country, so to call it, extends considerably eastwards along the Solway Firth, but its general character is well expressed in the Rhinns of Galloway, the hammer-headed peninsula that looks across the North Channel to Ireland.

Here are large farms on the hereditary lands of the Agnews of Lochnaw; the villages are quiet and douce; a ruined castle or two and the odd old church show it

AILSA GRAIG

At the mouth of the River Clyde stands the lonely, conical islet of Ailsa Craig, known as Paddy's Milestone, halfway between Glasgow and Belfast. On the island are granite quarries supplying fine curling stones. The cliffs house gannets, gulls, guillemots and puffins.

CULZEAN CASTLE

The most frequently visited of National Trust properties, Culzean Castle stands on the cliff tops between Ayr and Girvan. It was designed by Robert Adam, and the interior was recently restored in the colours which Adam originally intended for it. The castle contains a flat reserved exclusively for President Eisenhower.

to be a long-settled place with something of the character of, say, Sussex. The chief townlet is Portpatrick, which was planned to be the Scottish terminus of cross-channel steamers, but the big seas coming in from the Atlantic smashed up the expensive harbour works, and the terminus was transferred to Stranraer, so that Portpatrick has developed instead as a quiet holiday resort with a good golf course. The traveller with an eye for landscape and seascape will perceive in the Rhinns a character—the Atlantic *motif*, it might be called—that persists down the westernmost parts of Great Britain, through Wales and Cornwall, even into Britanny itself—the wild, noble thrust of rugged cliffs above the tumbling seas and sandy coves and yet the white farmhouses on their edges, facing the storm.

The lighthouse high on the Mull of Galloway means for the mariner one of the gateposts of the Firth of Clyde and also the approach to the Solway Firth. Before we make that diverting turn eastwards, we must look at the huge, high, under-populated mass of country that, in fact, fills most of the total area of this south-western region of ours. We have dawdled so far through industrial regions and along the coastal strips, and yet in sheer square-mileage we have only been on the fringes. It is time to return to the first proposition: that the Lowlands are rarely low, and that much of the land surface is very high, rough, bleak, knobbly and potentially dangerous to the careless walker on lofty hills.

The Rhinns of Galloway terminate in the Mull of Galloway, where the 200-foot lighthouse commands the North Channel on the west and Luce Bay on the east.

The map shows clearly that the country which runs inland from the Ayrshire coast over to the Clyde valley rises to great heights. Not far eastwards from Ballantrae as the crow flies is a range of which the tops are all about the 2,500 feet mark, culminating in The Merrick at 2,764 feet. Another range between the valleys of Doon and Nith runs up to 2,000 feet on the average. The hills are high again between Nith and Clyde, with Queensberry at 2,235 feet, and that within ten miles of the main line between Glasgow and London. The village of Wanlockhead in this region stands at over 1,300 feet above the sea. These hills have not the ferocious look of the Cuillins of Skye or of the Glencoe peaks. They are less rocky, better clad with vegetation and expose their shoulders to a gentler sun, but they are still formidable and always beautiful.

This is sheep-farming country almost exclusively. I have tramped over miles of peaty moorland to the cottage of a shepherd, whose small son might not see anybody but his parents from the beginning of one winter to its end. The shepherd knew every one of his flock of over a thousand Blackface sheep by its face, as you and I recognise our friends and acquaintances. His cottage was within a vast bowl of upland, perhaps twelve miles in diameter, and if you asked him what were the bounds of his bailiwick he answered simply, "the skyline." He thought nothing of a week-end walk of fourteen miles each way to the nearest town and back.

So here is a range of wild country quite insufficiently recognised as such, never mentioned along with the "stags at eve" of regions farther north, though it has been latterly discovered by the new generation of hikers and by motorists with a turn for exploration at decent speeds. It is thus remarkably unspoilt—very much less spoiled than many Highland areas. It seems to have a reasonable chance of survival in aloofness in an age when so many people seem to want to press towards the same places along the same roads at high speeds.

One or two of the north-south roads through this region are inevitably busy, quite apart from the enormous load of traffic carried by the main Glasgow-Carlisle road through the valleys of Clyde and Annan. That which runs all the way from Kilmarnock to Dumfries passes through a busy section of the Ayrshire coalfield. That is not such an oppressive aggregation of pithead bings as one finds in the Clyde Valley or the English Midlands, and when, following the Nith, a beautiful river, it starts to fall down to sea level in the Solway Firth, it passes

Looking from the grounds of Kirkcudbright Academy towards the Old Tolbooth at the end of the High Street. Kirkcudbright, which stands pleasantly at the estuary of the River Dee, was made a Royal Burgh in 1455.

through lovely pastoral country and by great country houses, ruined castles and the remains of the abbey at Lincluden. The place-names of this region are odd and interesting—Enterkinfoot, Drumlanrig, Auldgirth, Torthorwald . . .

The road out of Ayr to Castle Douglas also runs for a time by the collieries of the coastal district, but it becomes magnificent past the stretch of Loch Doon and so to the clean, upland village of Carsphairn, the hills rising to more than 2,000 feet about it, and it becomes adorable when it begins to fall down through New Galloway and along the shores of Loch Ken. The third road of the series, from Girvan over the hill to Newton Stewart, is dramatic all the way, the country lonely and austere, and Barrhill is an interesting example of the upland village with an almost exclusive interest in sheep—not that it is quite so charming as Barr on a quiet road on the Fergusson of Kilkerran lands, behind Girvan itself.

It would be quite idle, and only confusing for the reader, to attempt to follow every road in this enchanting region. Any motoring map shows the complexity of the main system, and the Ordnance Survey shows the tracks feasible on foot. There is not one of either sort that is not worth following with the certainty of rewards in store. Two or three of the transverse routes should certainly be explored, although one of them is a cul-de-sac. This leads off the Girvan-

Newton Stewart highway to Loch Trool, a beautifully serene, remote sheet of water with something of a Swiss air about it. (The observant traveller will note that the Forestry Commission has been busy throughout this region for a good many years past). Two other passes over the hump between the Nith and Clyde valleys are rewarding, both starting near Sanquhar on the Nith or near Abington on the Clyde. One is Dalveen Pass, a gem for connoisseurs of the austere and statuesque; the other climbs under the shadow of Green Lowther through the high villages of Wanlockhead and Leadhills, where lead was in fact profitably mined until quite recent times and, before that, pure gold.

One would not, perhaps, wish to see one of the few tracts of pure peace left in Great Britain becoming too "popular", but there are some of us who feel that it should be enjoyed by discerning folk more fully than it is. The explorer would do well to choose a central base like Newton Stewart, New Galloway or Thornhill, and the rest is easy by car, cycle or even bus. The man on foot will see it best of all, but the moor and mountain tracks can be dangerous, especially when the mist comes down.

GLEN TROOL

A monument at the north end of Loch Trool commemorates the victory of Bruce over a small English force in 1307. Loch Trool is one and a half miles long, narrow, and broken by wooded promontories. The hills around rise precipitously and afford a fine view over the National Forest Park established in the glen.

GLENLUCE ABBEY

Near Luce Bay stand the ruins of the early twelfth century Glenluce Abbey, which originally covered an extensive area. The vaulted chapter house is one of the few surviving intact in Scotland, and the interlocking red clay water-pipes are perhaps unique. Pieces of lead piping and some glazed tiles also remain.

The old royal castle of Kirkcudbright has completely disappeared but the ruins of McLellan's House, which was begun in 1577, stand near the centre of the town. It is an L-shaped building, with an impressive Great Hall.

The northern coast of the Solway Firth looks across to the Cumberland hills, and the Isle of Man also can be seen in fair weather. Here is an estuary of tricky tides and shifting sands, and this has been suggested as one reason why the coastal towns have never developed as popular resorts. It is certainly desirable to take and heed local advice in matters concerning bathing and boating. Mr. George Scott-Moncrieff has made the equally interesting suggestion that the relative quietness of the Solway coast is due to the fact that when the railway was being built to complete a short route to Ireland through Portpatrick, the conservative landowners forced the builders to run their line along the high ground behind and leave the good farmlands and townlets of the coastal strip untouched. The industrial workers of Clydeside certainly do not penetrate the region in large numbers, though the vogue of the touring motor-coach has brought a new trade.

Inwards from the rather bleak expanses of Luce Bay it is a romantic coast of small, rocky islands and small fjords, with a backdrop of knobbly hills, pleasantly described by Scott in *Guy Mannering* and *Redgauntlet* and S. R. Crockett in *The Raiders.* It was a coastline much used by smugglers and other lawless men and the local legends are rich. It may seem strange to the traveller that so many graveyards in the small ports seem to be filled with the tombstones of deep-sea mariners. The Solway Firth was indeed a busy shipping base, as far up as Annan, in the great days of sail, but its winding channels tend to silt and could not accommodate the steamship as it grew in size and power. It is quite an occasion today when a coasting vessel puts into, say, Kirkcudbright on the rising tide.

Kirkcudbright is one of the gems of a necklace of pretty and interesting towns, each so clean and tidy, on the Solway or in the immediate hinterland. Wigtown, however, is perhaps excessively dominated by its modern Town House, and Gatehouse of Fleet, once a port of some magnitude, seems slightly to suggest decay. Dalbeattie, with overbearing granite quarries, has least to commend it to the lover of civic beauty. Castle Douglas lacks mellowness a little, but its situation on Carlingwark Loch is attractive, and there are ruins of interest about, notably those of Threave Castle. Newton Stewart seems oddly gentle by the quiet waters of the Cree; and the peninsula that culminates in Burrow Head has Whithorn for its capital, an agreeable place with a broad main street and good houses set out with decency, and a ruined Priory to add the right touch of ancientry. The best of Galloway on the small scale is certainly in the village called Isle of Whithorn, though it stands on a little peninsula of its own in the lee of Burrow Head. Here are grace and charm and peace. Its men have their fishing on the Solway tides, but the places drowses, as it were, an elegant row of little houses, mostly white but some painted dark red, built above a sea wall. Here, in 397 A.D., St. Ninian came to convert the Picts to Christianity and build his *Candida Casa,* its site now covered by the ruins of the small Norman church that replaced it.

The pleasant places along the Solway shore suffer from the powerful tide of the Firth which sucks the inlets nearly dry and leaves expanses of grey-brown mud that are apt to afflict the spirit not used to the spectacle. This happens in the estuary of the Dee at

Crossmichael is a pleasant and typical little Kirkcudbrightshire village on the shores of Loch Ken, three and a half miles north-west of Castle Douglas.

The Old Bridge of Dumfries, for foot passengers only, was built in the thirteenth century by Devorguilla Baliol, founder of Balliol College, Oxford.

Kirkcudbright, the prettiest town of all. Nor has that lovely place been improved of recent years by the setting-up of industrial buildings on the shore opposite the townlet. But when the tide fills the channel again and sparkles in the pearly light that always seems to hang over Solway, like a kind of concealed illumination, then the place is transformed. And what a fine little town it is!

Its central part by the harbour is dominated by a castle not too hopelessly ruined, and properly called Maclellan's House; it has a tolbooth, almost perfect in the traditional Scottish style, with a sturdy spire and the customary "forestair." It has blocks of fine eighteenth-century houses along its streets, and the classical air most surprising in that corner of the world. This town has, not unnaturally, housed for many years a colony of distinguished artists. Lord Cockburn of the *Memorials*, though not without some strictures on the sleechy mud inevitable in the estuary of the Dee at low tide, fairly allowed of Kirkcudbright that "from several aspects it is the Venice of Scotland."

This essay has avoided elaborate reference to ruins, legends, and the romantic in general, because the intelligent traveller will quickly read up the stories of the districts he has admired. It is nevertheless well in a place like Kirkcudbright to appreciate its associations with the American naval leader, Paul Jones, who was born in the district; nor would one wish the explorer to miss the shell of the Priory near at hand. All such matters, however, are dealt with adequately enough in the conventional guidebooks. The stranger to the region might find it more rewarding to keep his own eye open for the oddities and charms of domestic design in the small places, the local kirk so often a blessed relief from Victorian Gothic.

But it is now time to turn northwards towards Glasgow again, and that route must take us through Dumfries, a town of first importance in this southwestern region. On the whole, it is most agreeable to follow the coast road from Dalbeattie, passing the pleasant small resorts of Kippford and Rockcliffe and going round into the county town under Criffel, the hill that dominates the estuary of the Nith. Nor should one fail to halt at New Abbey to look at the fine, sad ruins of Sweetheart Abbey.

The Nith widens to a broad estuary with its own douce charm, wild geese in the marshes at its mouth, salmon fisheries, fine farms and pleasant villages on its shores. The showpiece of this estuarine district is Caerlaverock Castle, an ancient seat of the Maxwells, with a singularly fine Renaissance facade.

The Dumfries region is specially memorable as the scene of Robert Burns's movements during the last, sad years of his life. His last farm, Ellisland, is six miles north of the town, and in the heart of the town is the house in which he died. St. Michael's

Burns spent the last years of his life in Dumfries, and the Globe Inn was a favourite howff. In it are the chair, punch bowl, jug and ladle which he is said to have used.

churchyard contains the ornate monument under which his remains were laid after being exhumed from their original resting place in gruesome circumstances. Appreciation of the monument must be a matter of personal taste. The irreverent may be more interested to observe the enormous mass and weight of the tombstones the decent burghers of Dumfries, living in a region where red sandstone was copious and cheap, put over their dead. Likewise, those of us who are earthy-minded may find the personal relics preserved in the two taverns Burns

THE FIRTH OF CLYDE

Below Dumbarton the River Clyde becomes the Firth of Clyde, and south of Gourock it expands into a great, broad estuary, with glorious views, between Bute and the Ayrshire coast. The Firth is famous as a yachting centre, and for the pleasure sailings which carry thousands of holiday-makers " doon the watter " to the resorts along its shores.

Maxwelton House on the banks of the Cairn was the birthplace of Annie Laurie. It incorporates part of the Old Castle of Glencairn, and was built in the seventeenth century.

favoured, the Globe Inn and the Hole in the Wa', somehow more evocative than all the laborious work of the sculptors.

Burns nicknamed Dumfries "Maggie by the banks o' Nith," but that seems too comfortable a description of the modern community, rather curiously poised in its nearness to England and its separation from the main stream of north-south traffic. A few years ago it was split—the separate burgh of Maxwelltown on the west bank of the Nith, Dumfries proper on the east. But the "Queen of the South" is a fine town in its own right, the broad river giving it its special quality. The Nith flows in volume through it, peopled by a flotilla of swans which cruise from one bank to the other as offers of food are forthcoming. The Old Bridge, for foot passengers only, was one of the creations of Devorguilla Baliol, that remarkable thirteenth-century lady who set up Sweetheart Abbey at New Abbey in memory of her husband, John Baliol, father of the Scottish king, and founded Balliol College, Oxford. In the Whitesands, on the eastern bank of the Nith, Dumfries has the most wonderful natural parking place, a terminal seething with the life that comes to a junction town with buses, long-distance lorries and cars. And for a last brush with history, the panelled dining-room of the County Hotel was the chamber in which Prince Charles held a council on his miserable return from Derby in December, 1745.

Now, however, we must continue our journey back to Glasgow, and swiftly. There are interesting places to see in this pleasant corner of Scotland, but few that would halt the traveller except through the force of personal association—Langholm, Annan, Lochmaben, Lockerbie, all clean, tidy Lowland towns, and the village of Ecclefechan, birth-place and burial-place of Thomas Carlyle. One place to be visited with devotion is the village of Ruthwell on the Dumfries-Annan road. Here, now under the roof of the parish church, is Ruthwell Cross, an early and remarkably evocative relic of Christian culture. In Ruthwell, incidentally, was born the savings bank movement. At Lockerbie we are back on the main Carlisle-Glasgow road, always very busy, but it is a good thing to branch off at Beattock to look at Moffat, with its villas for the retired genteel, its hotels, and the effigy of a ram in the middle of the High Street, symbol of the main farming interest of this hilly country. It is also well to halt a mile or two northwards and look into the strange, huge and rather fearsome Devil's Beeftub, scooped out of the hillside.

Beattock, a typical small capital of British Railways, is at the summit of the pass from the valley of the Annan into that of the Clyde; and the Tweed, due to run eastwards, rises not far away. Railway and highway run close together, necessarily so, the valley between the high, gaunt hills being narrow. But these hills, their sides scored by the long lines of drystone dykes, have their own nobility. The route passes through Elvanfoot and Crawford, where Allan Ramsay the poet had his schooling, and then the valley begins to open out about Abington, whence the Clyde flows through a very pleasant stretch of pastoral country, the cattle of the fine white farms grazing to the edges of a stream that meanders happily and carries its meed of trout and grayling. Again the hills run really high hereabouts. Culter Fell, above the interesting village of Biggar, rises to 2,454 feet, and its neighbour across the river, Tinto, to 2,335.

That, however, is the end of the high country. At Lanark, a good town with its own sturdy character and lively customs, the river tumbles over a geological fault in the Falls of Clyde. The volume of these waters has been reduced visibly by their impoundment to produce electrical power, and there is no longer a large annual output of oil paintings recording their grandeur, but they still dramatically mark the

Lamington Church has a fine Norman doorway and charming bell tower. Behind it rise the gentle slopes of Tinto Hill, from which there are fine views over the upper reaches of the Clyde.

The three great Falls of Clyde lie within a four-mile stretch of the river near Lanark. Cora Linn is the middle one, and cascades for 90 feet. The falls are used for hydro-electric power, which affects their force at certain seasons of the year.

point at which the Clyde changes course westwards along with the general character of the valley through which it flows.

There is one brief but agreeable stretch of the river, however, before it runs into the region of pit bings and steelworks. This runs for some miles from just below the Falls to about the townlet of Braidwood, and it is given over almost entirely to market gardening on the larger scale. One may not particularly admire the strike of the sun on the glass of acres of tomato houses, but about here, in the spring, the foam of blossoming pear and plum trees is a glory. Then the first of the slagheaps thrusts a dirty snout in the air, and at night the traveller can be affrighted, in spirit at least, by the leap of flames from the rolling mills.

Because it used to yield ample supplies of coal and iron, this countryside was despoiled during the careless expansion of the nineteenth century. It still has its very ugly features—the ruins of old red-brick buildings, like bad teeth, along the railway line and stagnant, useless ponds. But—and this is important and inspiring—the inheritors of those grey domains,

BOTHWELL CASTLE

Set in beautiful grounds stretching down to the Clyde are the picturesque ruins of Bothwell Castle, perhaps the finest thirteenth century castle in Scotland. At the east end of the court on the first floor is all that is left of the banqueting hall and in the south-corner are the slight remains of the chapel.

KILLEARN: THE KNOWE HEAD

The old house of Knowe Head in Killearn, Stirlingshire, is the property of the Killearn Welfare Trust. It has the date 1803 on the door lintel, and was one time occupied by a stone carver or mason. Every effort has been made to restore its original features.

KILLEARN: THE GLEBE

The Glebe also belongs to Killearn Welfare Trust, who aim to preserve this view towards Ben Lomond (on the skyline to the right) and the Conic Hill at Balmaha (low down on the left). From here there are also good views of the Perthshire Hills.

Ravenscraig, near Motherwell, is the biggest steelworks in Scotland. A huge extension was opened in 1957. The new slabbing and hot strip mills are behind the melting shop on the right.

encouraged by the new feeling for amenity, are rapidly clearing up the old messes. Even if the tendency is towards the subtopian, the creation of tidy industrial estates, the studied rearrangement of the road systems and the removal of the old, sad miners' rows are making such a general improvement that the larger towns of the region—Hamilton, Motherwell with Wishaw, Airdrie and Coatbridge—are enjoying new leases of life as dormitories for the monstrous conurbation of Glasgow.

It was never naturally a spectacular countryside, this Clyde basin. Much of the original farmland was of a clayey consistency, and clay, stretching from the Clyde over towards the Forth about Falkirk, seems to bind its own landscape into a pattern of mere decency at the best. Those who generalise with civilised horror about the ugly features of an industrial area should remember, however, that each small place in the complex has its own beauty spot, even if it is only a Lover's Walk down a glen or a pleasant golf course. This Clyde Valley of the factories, mines and steelworks has jewels to show, such as the castle-keep of the Belhaven and Stenton family above a gorge of the Clyde near Wishaw, and the great ruins of Bothwell Castle, "rose-red and half as old as time."

So back to that great city along busy roads, the buses whirling its slaves hither and thither; Glasgow, the problem child of our south-western region; also its governess within the strange dichotomy that is its fate as between Highlands and Lowlands. Glasgow the slattern, Glasgow also the dignified old lady. Coming back into this fascinating city you see the lift of the cathedral towers on the northern skyline and the frieze of the Campsie Fells behind. Thus we have travelled in a region of incredible variety and observed the strange fusion of cultures in the most complex of all the distinct regions of Scotland.

THE WEST

W. H. Murray

THE West Highland scene is of world-wide renown and of the kind commonly called romantic : that is, anything but orderly, wildly chaotic, rather, and ruggedly grand. One glance at the coastline will show us what to expect. The great sea-lochs wind far in among the hills, which on all sides heave skyward, seen thus to full height and in all majesty. They lack those leagues of heather that grace the hills of central Scotland and the Cairngorms, and which have been wrongly identified by Sir Leslie Stephen as the Scottish mountains' one point of superiority. The heather's brief bloom comes in August. But the long arms of the Atlantic cradle the western hills at all seasons—a union of rock and water portrayed to perfection down the seaboard from Kintail to Kintyre.

The area of "The West" is set in this book as the county of Argyll and the western half of Inverness-shire, excluding the Western Isles and Cowal, but including the south-west corner of Ross-shire (Kintail). The western boundary is thus the Atlantic; the southern, the Firth of Clyde; the eastern, the line of the West Highland railway across the Moor of Rannoch to the river Spean, then north to Strath Glass; the northern, Glen Affric, with an upsweep to include Kyle of Lochalsh. For the most part the eastern boundary runs high, across Rannoch and Lochaber at a height of 1000 feet. The west boundary is Scotland's most jagged coastline, indented heavily by a score of big sea-lochs, most of them famous names: Lochs Fyne, Linnhe, Sunart, Nevis, Hourn, Duich—the despair of transport authorities but the greatest scenic asset. Between the two boundaries sprawls a maze of mountains and fresh-water lochs.

Since the waters of the "Atlantic drift" penetrate so far inland, it follows that the valleys of the western seaboard enjoy a relatively mild climate. Even in mid-winter the mean temperatures are several degrees higher than those of the east coast. But this warmth is largely confined to the valleys close to the sea-lochs, as temperature is less determined by nearness to sea than by height above it. Since the hills rise from the sea abruptly, it follows that the mean temperatures for the West are low, while at the same time it may be said that the coast is milder than anywhere in Britain save the south of England and the west fringe of Wales. In a few sheltered places no more than a degree or two of frost are normally recorded. The area as a whole gets less snow than the Pennines of England or the Southern Uplands of Scotland, but this general truth must again be balanced by excepting the high tops, where snow comes earlier and stays later, and comes, too, in greater quantity on the mountain groups of Ben Nevis and Glencoe.

The West is notoriously wet. The very high rainfall comes not on the coastal fringe but several miles inland, extending in a broad belt from the Affric hills to the Arrochar Alps. The Inner Isles are blamed for this heavy precipitation to their east (80-120 inches and more), but on the coastal fringe the rainfall drops markedly to 60-80 inches. The best, driest, and sunniest times of year are from mid-May to mid-June and from mid-September to mid-October. During the last twelve years (and perhaps longer) a drought of six to eight weeks has occurred in the West annually, but this may come at any time between February and November. From all of which we may distil a precept for the visitor : "Put your faith in Providence but prepare for the worst."

Granted sun, the West Highlands are the most colourful country on earth.

Access from the south goes up Loch Lomondside by road from Glasgow, or else up Loch Long either by road or by the line of the West Highland railway. If by road, our first entry is made by striking west from Arrochar, where we round the head of Loch Long under the comb of the Cobbler, then climb through the forested defile of Glen Croe to a pass at 860 feet. At the top of the final hairpin of the old road, which lies below the new, there used to be a rough stone bench inscribed with the words "Rest and be Thankful," from which the pass received its well-known name. The old road is still used in summer for motor-car trials.

The long, narrow crest of the pass, flanked by Beinn an Lochain to the south and Ben Ime to the north, with Loch Restil lying between, is in winter the windiest pass in West Scotland to be crossed by road. In north-westerly gales the wind is funnelled to a blast of enormous velocity, which has been known to overturn heavy lorries and to force buses off the road. The official boundary of Argyll comes farther back at the head of Loch Long, but geographically this pass

THE CRINAN CANAL

The Crinan canal, which was opened in 1801, is nine miles long and contains fifteen locks. It lets small boats pass from Loch Gilp to the sea, and avoids the long and often stormy sail round the Mull of Kintyre. Left: A puffer goes through at Bellanoch. Right: Ardrishaig, with the breakwater and lighthouse at the eastern end of the canal.

INVERARAY

The bridge in the foreground crosses the River Aray and leads to Inveraray Castle, ancestral seat of the Dukes of Argyll. Beyond lies the village and the waters of Loch Fyne, one of the largest sea-lochs in Scotland.

A view of Inveraray from the south, showing the church built in 1794 by Robert Mylne. Beyond is the conical hill of Duniquoich, capped by a watch tower.

is the threshold. Beyond we enter the true land of the Scots, for Argyll was the original Kingdom of Dalriada, set up by the invading Scots around A.D. 500.

The westgoing road zig-zags down Glen Kinglass to Loch Fyne, fairest of the great sea-lochs in the sense of having an open, sunny aspect, for the hills keep low throughout its forty-mile length to the Sound of Bute, and rise to 3000 feet only around its head at Beinn Buie and Beinn an Lochain, which are both set well back. A chameleon may rival its range of colour, but never the luminous intensity.

The upper half of the loch is narrow down to the Otter Spit, thereafter the breadth doubles. On the west shore of this upper stretch stands the royal burgh and county town of Inveraray. In reality it is no more than a village, beautifully set at the mouth of a wooded inlet called Loch Shira. Half a mile to its north is Inveraray Castle, the seat of the Duke of Argyll, chief of Clan Campbell, who is known as *MacCailean Mor*. The castle dates from 1780. The town formerly stood beside it on the river Aray, but was moved farther away to its present site when the ancient castle was replaced by the new one. Behind the castle, the hill of Duniquoich rises to 850 feet and carries a tower on top, which is described in Scott's *Legend of Montrose*. In the main street of the town stands a great cross brought from Iona. The avenue of beeches in the street was planted about 1660. Running north from the town, a road strikes through the woods of Glen Aray beside waterfalls, then climbs steadily up to bare moorland, whence it descends to the shores of Loch Awe.

The village of Tarbert, on East Loch Tarbert, is the principal base for the Loch Fyne fishing industry.

On the east side of Loch Fyne an excellent road goes to Strachur and forks, the main branch striking eastward through the Cowal hills to Dunoon, the other running south by the loch past Lachlan Castle to Otter Ferry, and steadily deteriorating as it goes into one of the worst roads in Argyll. The motorist who persists will eventually arrive at Tighnabruaich on the Kyles of Bute, which is sufficient reward. On the other, westerly, side of Loch Fyne, the road continues down the long peninsula of Kintyre to the Mull.

The Kintyre peninsula has in itself none of the rugged majesty of the West Highland scene. It projects southward out of that scene, a land apart. The hills are low, the coastline unspectacular. But the coasts carry quietly charming bays, like those at Skipness, Crossaig, Cour, Carradale, Saddell, Campbeltown, Southend, and Machrihanish, all of them commanding seaward views that are spacious but never dull, for they are everywhere broken by the heave of islands.

All down the east coast, along the Kilbrennan Sound, the seaward view is to the high mountain ridges of the island of Arran, and that is one of the three most splendid islands around the United Kingdom (Skye and Rhum are the two others). Although these Arran hills stand forever across the Kilbrennan Sound, they never become a mere backdrop, for the scene is not static. The haze thickens and fades, clouds lift and drop, colours change and deepen; one day the hills stand up clear and sparkling, the next they crouch and dwindle. Always they enchant. The most delightful village of this long coast is Skipness. Its sandy bay and old castle command a panorama of the hills to the north of Arran, whose splendid curves suggest the name of "The Sleeping Warrior."

The south coast view is to Sanda, and to Ailsa Craig on a clear day, eighteen miles out on the Firth—farther away than Ireland, which lies just across the North Channel.

From the west coast we look out to the islands of Gigha, Islay, and Jura, to which steamers ply from West Loch Tarbert at the top end of the peninsula.

The most important town of Kintyre is the fishing port of Campbeltown on the south-east coast. It has a good harbour, guarded at the entrance by Davaar Island. About five miles south-east, close by Achinhoan Head, there is a cave just above high-water mark on the shore. It is called St. Kieran's, and is said to be the earliest Christian chapel in Scotland. Due west of Campbeltown, on the other side of the peninsula, is the golfers' West Highland Mecca—Machrihanish. An airport lies midway between the two towns with a service to Glasgow. Machrihanish has fine sands fringing a bay that looks to the Atlantic. The golf course extends over wide dunes to the north. Four miles to the south, a hill called Cnoc Moy (1,400 feet) has seaward slopes honeycombed with caves, in which stalactites are found. These caves are more readily approached from Southend, which, although farther away on the south coast, has a road going north up the Conie glen, then west to Glen Breakerie, from whose head a track leads to the sea under Cnoc Moy.

Southend is a smaller resort than Machrihanish, but it too has a fine golf course, and even better seaward views. St. Columba is said to have first set foot on Scotland here. From Southend a rough road goes to the Mull of Kintyre, descending on the last lap a thousand feet in a mile and a half. The lighthouse at the Mull is the point in Scotland nearest to Ireland. The position is exhilarating on a wild, clear day. On the one hand is the Atlantic, unobstructed to Canada, on the other, the low line of Rathlin Island and the blue hills of Antrim only twelve miles distant.

Once known as Kinlochkerran after the sixth century Irish saint, Kieran, Campbeltown (after the Campbells of Argyll) now has distilleries and a fishing industry.

Knapdale is divided from Kintyre by the long, narrow sea-loch of West Loch Tarbert, which is separated from East Loch Tarbert on Loch Fyne by an isthmus little more than a mile wide. Magnus Barefoot, King of Norway, who conquered the Hebrides and Orkneys, had a galley dragged across the isthmus in 1093. In the eighteenth century a proposal to drive a canal through it was defeated in favour of constructing between Lochs Gilp and Crinan the canal that now marks the northern boundary of Knapdale. The town of Tarbert stands on East Loch Tarbert, the loch being in fact a bay that forms a perfect harbour for the Loch Fyne herring fleet. Little islands decorate the water, and a ruined castle the shore. The castle dates from the fourteenth century and was used both by Robert the Bruce and James II.

Low, undistinguished hills form the bulk of Knapdale. Coast roads encircle it, but only one strikes inland, that from Ardrishaig to Loch Killisport, a sea-loch running in from the Sound of Jura. A second sea-loch runs in to the flat ground immediately to its north. This is Loch Sween, whose low, well-wooded shores might be anywhere but the West Highlands. At the forked head of the loch is the charming village of Tayvallich, where refuge may be sought from the Highland's interminable hills. The southward-running road ends on the Sound of Jura at Keils, known for its ancient Celtic cross in the ruined chapel.

At Loch Gilp, a big bay of Loch Fyne at the north end of Knapdale, stand the twin towns of Ardrishaig and Lochgilphead. A lock opens to the first basin of the Crinan canal behind the breakwater at Ardrishaig.

LOCH ETIVE

One of the many lochs branching off Loch Linnhe is Loch Etive, which reaches north-east into wild countryside. The mountain to the right of this picture is Ben Cruachan, above the Pass of Brander and Loch Awe. Bonawe ferry lies behind the headland in the middle distance.

GANAVAN SANDS

About a mile and a half to the north of Oban lies Ganavan Bay with firm, clean sand, safe bathing, and glorious views across the Firth of Lorne towards Mull, Lismore and the Morvern hills. This picture was taken from high ground near the ruins of Dunollie Castle, which belonged to the MacDougalls, Lords of Lorne.

The canal, which has fifteen locks, runs nine miles to Crinan, thus connecting Loch Fyne to the Sound of Jura, and saving ships a voyage of eighty miles round the Mull of Kintyre. It is used only by small ships—fishing boats, red-funnelled puffers, and yachts. To the yachtsman from the Clyde, it is the Atlantic gate, opening to the sea of the Hebrides. Low, jagged islands lie to northward. The air has a clean tang, the very skies seem more spacious and the water a wild waste. All the mainland of Britain drops out of sight and mind. The Hebrides beckon.

Midway along the canal near its highest point (80 feet), the road turns north to run up the Firth of Lorne coast to Oban. Seven miles along it, a branch road goes east to Loch Awe, but the main road continues by the coast to Loch Melfort, which is screened from the open sea by the islands of Luing, Shuna, and many other smaller ones. At the head of Loch Melfort is the angling resort of Kilmelford, which has numerous fresh-water lochs on the moorland hills above. The Oban road now goes north by the river Oude over the Pass of Melfort, descending to Kilninver on Loch Feochan. This sea-loch opens on to the Firth of Lorne, granting a good view of the island of

Mull and its mountains. A branch road runs south-west to Clachan Bridge, which in one arch "spans the Atlantic," for it links the mainland to the island of Seil. From Seil, a ferry crosses the Cuan Sound to Luing, which is separated from Scarba to its west by the Sound of Luing. Here a notorious tide-race sets through at eight knots, and all small ships have to time their passage for slack water.

Oban is only seven miles from Kilninver. The more usual approach by road from the south closely follows the line of the West Highland railway from the head of Loch Lomond by way of Crianlarich to Tyndrum, then westward to Dalmally on Loch Awe, through the Pass of Brander to Loch Etive, and finally south to Oban. On leaving Loch Lomond behind, we enter briefly into Perthshire at Inverarnan. The old Highland hotel there, white-washed in the best tradition and set among natural woods on the banks of the river Falloch, is a famous resort for climbers, especially in winter, when it becomes the unofficial headquarters of the Scottish Mountaineering Club. The hills close around, Bens Vorlich, Dubhcraig, Oss and Lui, provide no rock-climbing, but an hour's run in a car brings the rocks of Glencoe, and the ski-ing on Lawers and the Blackmount, within reach.

From Inverarnan, the road north climbs steeply up Glen Falloch, rising from near sea-level to desolate moorland at 600 feet. The Falls of Falloch lie a third of the way up this hill, on the right-hand side of the road as we climb. They are not sited as marked on the maps, but lie considerably higher and cannot be seen from the road. They are well worth inspection if the river is in spate. On coming over the wide, bare pass, we see to the east a cluster of old Scots pines, one of the last remnants of the ancient Caledonian Forest. The crossing of the pass often brings one into a weather system different from that operating southward; the rapidity of change can be startling.

The northward descent falls to Strath Fillan at the village of Crianlarich, a good centre for walking the hills to the south-east : Cruach Ardrain, Stobinian, and Ben More (3,843 feet). Ben More is the highest mountain in Britain south of Ben Nevis. Between Crianlarich and Tyndrum, Glen Coninish gives easy access westward to Ben Lui (3,708 feet), the most shapely mountain in Perthshire. Excellent snow-climbing may be had in the north-east corrie at 3000 feet. In this high corrie is the source of a tiny stream. As it flows eastward its successive names are Lund, Coninish, Fillan, Dochart, and finally Tay, the biggest river in Scotland.

At Tyndrum, the road to Oban strikes westward down Glen Lochy to Strath Orchy. The village of Dalmally lies here, on the banks of the river Orchy, where it issues from Glen Orchy to the north-east. Two miles farther west the river flows into Loch Awe, one of the most celebrated lochs of the West Highland area. It is twenty-three miles long and for the most part only half a mile wide. It is "open water," which means that fishing is free. Trout, sea-trout and salmon may be caught without purchase of a ticket. Scenically, the top end of the loch is far more splendid than the head of Loch Fyne. The water here is a mile wide and dotted with islands. Eastward stand the great peaks of Ben Lui and Ben Buie, but these are set back and exclude no sun. On a promontory at the head of the loch is the picturesque ruin of Kilchurn Castle. It dates from 1432 and became the seat of the Breadalbane Campbells. From whatever angle it may be seen, its high walls and turret, not yet broken down, seem to rise straight out of the water, and always it is backed by mountains—Cruachan on the one hand, Ben Lui on the other. Kilchurn Castle is the subject of Wordsworth's well-known poem :

> Child of loud-throated war! the mountain stream
> Roars in thy hearing; but thy hour of rest
> Is come, and thou art silent in thy age;
> Save when the winds sweep by. . . .

The River Falloch breaks into falls as it rushes down the Glen from Beinn a Chroin. Unsuccessful attempts have been made to blast the falls to allow fish to the higher reaches.

The small village of Tyndrum, three quarters of a mile inside the Perth border from Argyllshire, is a fishing and mountaineering centre. Ahead are Beinn Doireann, 3,524 feet high and snow-capped, and Beinn Odhar—both good climbs.

A mile or two down the loch is the island of Inishail, which is an old burial ground. In the sixteenth century wolves were a serious menace to travellers, and numerous enough to force Highlanders to bury their dead on islands. The last wolf was killed in Scotland as recently as the middle of the eighteenth century.

The old name of "Lochow" will always be associated with the Clan Campbell. It was not until Campbell of Lochow decided to support Wallace and Bruce that the family fortunes took that upward trend that brought high honour. The Dukes of Argyll and the Marquesses of Breadalbane are descended from that family—a good fortune now turned sour by savage death-duties.

The upper end of Loch Awe stretches a long arm westward into the Pass of Brander, whence the river Awe cuts a narrow passage through to Loch Etive. Towering above this low pass is the monarch of Lorne, Ben Cruachan (3,689 feet). In a battle fought in the depths of the pass in 1308, Robert the Bruce routed

Kilchurn Castle on Loch Awe has a square keep flanked by bartizans built in 1440. The remainder was built in 1693, and until 1740 it was occupied by the Breadalbane family.

The Pass of Brander, the grand defile through which the River Awe reaches the sea, looking eastward towards Loch Awe. Here Bruce almost annihilated the MacDougall clan in 1308.

the men of Lorne led by John MacDougall, son of the Lord of Lorne. The name Lorne is given to the stretch of wild mountain country lying between Loch Awe and the Firth of Lorne, and extending north to Glencoe, thus including the districts of Benderloch and Appin. The whole of Lorne can be seen in one splendid panorama from the summit of Ben Cruachan. The simplest route of ascent goes up by the Falls of Cruachan near the east end of the Pass of Brander, about three miles west of Loch Awe railway station. But Cruachan has no less than eight tops, and the walker who aspires to traverse the whole ridge will find his better routes at the east or west ends of the massif.

A new hydro-electric scheme has been planned for Cruachan. The project involves a dam across the river Awe in the Pass of Brander, and a second dam across the Allt Cruachan above the falls. Work on the first dam began in 1959 and may well affect the fishing on the loch, where the main catch has been sea-trout. The Falls of Cruachan may eventually disappear.

Road and rail emerge from the pass by Loch Etive-side at the twin village-resorts of Taynuilt and Bonawe. Magnificent views are had from here not only to Cruachan but more particularly northeastward up Loch Etive to the peaks of the Blackmount and Benderloch. The majority of Scottish sea-lochs, however varied in general shape and size, conform to a pattern in having two distinct parts—a relatively wide outer loch divided by narrows from a long but narrow inner loch. Loch Etive repeats the pattern twice, having two narrows, one at Connel Ferry and the second at Bonawe. The river Awe flows into Loch Etive exactly opposite the second narrows, which have long stretches of water to either

GLEN ETIVE

Stob Dubh, the black peak on the left, and Stob na Broige form beautifully symmetrical cones near the head of Loch Etive. The whole of this rugged but beautiful country around lower Glen Etive belongs to the National Trust for Scotland.

At Connel Ferry, Loch Etive is crossed by a large cantilever railway and road bridge. Near the bridge are the Falls of Lora, caused by a ridge of rock across the channel. The water from Loch Etive pours over this ledge at ebb tide with a roar that can be heard for many miles. On the far side of the bridge in this picture is Connel village and the road to Oban.

side in dog-leg formation. At Bonawe a ferry crosses to the Benderloch shore, but farther west at Connel the narrows are bridged both for road and rail. The railway going north up this coast of Lorne ends at Ballachulish on Loch Leven; the main line swings southward to Oban.

The Oban road holds close to the shores of Loch Etive as far as Dunstaffnage bay on the outer loch. On the seaward promontory of the bay stands the old Campbell stronghold of Dunstaffnage Castle, dating from the thirteenth century. The tall, square walls are buttressed by three round towers. In 1308 it was wrested from the MacDougalls by Bruce. During the Jacobite risings it was held for the crown, and Flora Macdonald was imprisoned here in 1746. The site, however, has still greater claims to fame. It was the seat of the first Scottish kings of Dalriada before the union with the Picts. The Stone of Destiny was held here until its transfer to Scone in the ninth century. More than forty Scottish kings are said to have been crowned on it before its seizure by Edward I in 1297, when he removed it to Westminster Abbey.

Three miles farther south is Oban. Its fine harbour is protected from the open Firth by the island of Kerrera. Regular steamer services go to the Hebrides and holiday excursions can be made by steamer to the islands of Mull, Lismore, Iona, and to Staffa for Fingal's Cave. Oban is thus the best possible centre for the exploration of Lorne and its multitude of neighbouring islands, which offer an ever-changing seascape and mountain scene. It is also a yachting centre, and dinghy sailing has become a popular sport among the townspeople. The principal Oban regatta is held at the beginning of August. Highland Games, known here as the Argyll Gathering, take place annually in the second week of September.

Outside the town to the north there is a fine sandy beach and golf course at Ganavan bay, and to the south an outstanding viewpoint at Pulpit Hill, which has an indicator. Eastward in Glen Lonan near Loch Nell is the grave of Diarmid, ancestor of the Clan Campbell; his bones must be well over a thousand years old.

The long, flat island of Lismore, which lies far out in Loch Linnhe, is recommended to all who care for peace and quiet, or who feel an urgent need to get away from the herd. It is served by steamer from Oban to Achnacroish, and by ferry from Port Appin to the north tip of the island. Set all around its broad waters are the mountains of Morven, Mull, and Appin.

The hills of Appin and Benderloch are easily reached from Oban by the road over Connel Bridge to Loch Creran. Glen Creran divides Appin from Benderloch and allows quick access to the high peaks on its Benderloch side—Beinn Sgulaird (3,059 feet), Beinn Fhionnlaidh (pronounced "Ula": 3,139 feet), and Sgurr na h-Ulaidh (3,258 feet). The last, whose name means "the peak of the hid treasure," is reached still more easily from Clachaig in Glencoe. In winter it offers good snow-climbing on the north face.

The road to Glencoe continues north up the Appin shore past a number of charming clachans : Port Appin on the Lynn of Lorne, Portnacroish on the inlet called Loch Laich, where a tiny off-shore island carries the ancient seat of the Stewarts of Appin, Castle Stalker, then to Ballachulish at the narrows of Loch Leven. A car ferry crosses here to the Lochaber shore. Directly behind, to the south, rises that most lovely mountain of Appin, Ben Vair. It has twin peaks in a horse-shoe form, the summit ridge sweeping round with a grace unsurpassed in all Scotland. Like all the Scottish hills, it is seen at its best in winter, snow-clad and glinting icily under the low sun. The best viewpoint from below is across Loch Leven, or even Loch Linnhe.

The Ballachulish ferry commands a most wonderful view across Loch Linnhe to the hills of Ardgour, where the peak of Garbh Bheinn (2,903 feet) is always pre-eminent, for its summit is given a noble lift by a great buttress of rock. When the sun is setting behind the Ardgour hills the beauty of the scene is typical of the best in the West Highlands, to be equalled several times as we go north, but not to be surpassed till we reach Kintail. Looking in the opposite direction, up Loch Leven, we see the shapely Pap of Glencoe dominating the entrance to the glen. The true village of Ballachulish lies a mile east of the ferry and straggles

The northern part of Oban Bay, with the ruins of Dunollie Castle overlooking the Firth of Lorne.

Oban's busy harbour, with the town centre beyond and McCaig's Folly on the skyline.

CASTLE STALKER

Castle Stalker, perched on an islet on the sound between Appin and Lismore at the mouth of Loch Laich, was built by Duncan Stewart of Appin as a hunting lodge for James IV. For some time it was the home of the Stewarts, the unconquered enemies of the Campbells.

LOCH LAICH

Loch Laich is one of many tiny lochs around the shores of Loch Linnhe, and lies between it and the Strath of Appin. During the last war it was used by commandos as a training area. The hills are those on the west of Loch Linnhe, in the district of Kingairloch.

out for another mile or more. It is an unprepossessing place, marred by a huge slate-quarry that has now closed down.

Glencoe is rarely approached through Appin unless by someone centred on Oban. The direct route from south Scotland goes through Tyndrum over the Moor of Rannoch. At the top of the steep pass above Tyndrum, road and rail leave Perthshire and re-enter Argyll. They fall at a long, gentle incline to Bridge of Orchy. The main feature of this passage is the magnificent sweep of Beinn Doireann to the east of the road; from summit to foot the slope falls in one smooth curve like the leech of a sail.

The mountain is one of a group of high peaks strung in a chain north-eastward, giving delightful ridge-walking and known to climbers as the eastern Blackmount. The true Blackmount rises straight to the north, and is the high swell of ground between the Moor of Rannoch and the huge Corrie Ba of the Stob Ghabhar-Clachlet massif over to the west. The old Glencoe road from Bridge of Orchy traversed the very centre of the Blackmount, reaching 1,450 feet on the shoulder of Meall a Bhuiridh before the final drop to Glencoe. It was a most exposed situation and the road was blocked by snow in winter, sometimes for long periods. The new road (1935) is scarcely less exposed but it holds to lower ground, skirting round the eastern slopes of the Blackmount at a maximum height of 1,143 feet. Even so, it too is often blocked, but rarely for more than a few hours, in blizzard conditions: Argyll County Council give a most efficient snow-plough service.

Bridge of Orchy is an excellent centre for fishing, stalking, skiing and mountaineering. From Loch Tulla, which lies only a mile to the north, the river Orchy, a famous salmon river, flows down Glen Orchy south-west to Loch Awe, and Loch Tulla is in turn fed by Loch Dochard and a score of burns that pour off the great cirque of peaks to the west. It remains to be seen, however, to what extent the new dam across the river Awe will affect the fishing on the Orchy.

The range west of Loch Tulla is known to climbers as the "Blackmount group." It comprises all the hills between Bridge of Orchy and lower Glen Etive,

Barcaldine Castle, built in the fifteenth century, is a Campbell property on the large Barcaldine estate which covers the whole of the south shore of Loch Creran.

Ballachulish Ferry connects Appin with the road to Fort William and saves a nineteen-mile journey round Loch Leven.

which form a great ring round Loch Dochard. This loch is reached by following the old Glencoe road as far as the Forest Lodge at the head of Loch Tulla, whence a good track strikes west to Loch Dochard. It continues over a pass to Glen Kinglass, thence to upper Loch Etive. The track is worth walking for its own sake. It leads right through the heart of one of the best deer forests in West Scotland, and the mountain scene is exceptionally good.

The more westerly peaks of the group, the wedge-shaped Ben Starav (3,541 feet), and Stob Coire an Albannaich (3,425 feet), are best reached by the aspiring climber from Glen Etive, but for him the best climbing on the range is to be found on the nearer mountain of Stob Ghabhar (pronounced "Gowr": 3,565 feet), whose eastern ridge gives an exhilarating walk, and eastern corrie some fine snow-climbs in winter. The Upper Couloir of the corrie offers a short but testing ice-climb of 300 feet between January and March. The best high-level ridge-walk of this area is the traverse of Stob Ghabhar to Clachlet, descending over Meall a Bhuiridh to Kingshouse.

Around the head of Loch Tulla, and again at Crannach Wood to the north-east in Glen Tulla, are further splendid remnants of the old Caledonian pine forest. At the road near the head of the loch, the old Inveroran Inn has long been a resort for anglers. The new Bridge of Orchy Hotel on the new road is in winter a popular centre for skiers northbound for Meall a Bhuiridh.

Thus far road and rail have run side by side. After Bridge of Orchy they part, for while the road zig-zags north up the Blackmount, the railway swings far eastward to the other side of Rannoch Moor, bound for Fort William and Mallaig. Between Gorton and Rannoch station the ground is so boggy that the railway line is carried on floating brushwood.

Rannoch Moor is a vast triangle, its points on Loch Tulla, Loch Rannoch, and Kingshouse Inn, and its sides enclosing an area of fifty-six square miles. In foul weather there is no place quite so desolate in all Scotland. Much of it is so level that one can find places where it is possible to walk in a straight line for ten miles between the 950- and 1000-foot contours. It undulates, none the less : the lowest point is at 550 feet at Loch Tulla, and small hills rise to 1,795 feet near Loch Laidon. The moor sends its rivers both to the Atlantic and the North Sea : to the former by way of the rivers Etive and Orchy, to the latter by way of its main drainage line of the river Ba, which falls from the gigantic Corrie Ba between Clachlet and Stob Ghabhar. This river enters on the moor at Loch Ba, then flows into Loch Laidon, from which it empties into Loch Rannoch at the river Gaur, thence into the Tummel and finally the Tay. Stretching right across the moor there is thus a continuous line of river and loch, flowing sluggishly, for the level drops only fifty-seven feet in eleven miles between Loch Ba and the railway bridge over the Gaur near Rannoch station. On a hot June day it is possible to swim most of the way over the moor.

Were its countless tarns all tiny, the moor might resemble a cratered battlefield, but a few of its waters are broad enough to add beauty to desolation, both of their kind unique. There is no road from west to east, but a track does leave Rannoch station heading westward towards Kingshouse (thirteen miles). It stays good as far as Loch Laidonside, but disappears when it turns to the higher ground near the ruined

Bridge of Orchy. The Orchy stream, which has its head waters in Loch Tulla on Rannoch Moor and flows into the north-eastern end of Loch Awe, is good trout-fishing water.

cottage of Tigh na Cruaiche. When at last Black Corries Lodge is reached a motor-road eases the last four miles to Kingshouse.

In good clear weather the Moor of Rannoch gives excellent if rough walking. Its legendary reputation for bog probably derives from the West Highland railway tale about "floating" the permanent way. True, the bog is there, in the shape of countless tarns, but the ground between is wide and dry, for the tarns drain it. In fine weather one gets across with dry feet. An excursion far out into the middle is strongly recommended. From nowhere else can the mountains of the Blackmount and Glencoe be seen to such advantage, free of all foreshortening, not too close for a full appreciation of shapes, which are seen at last in proper perspective, full in stature, clean-carved by glen and corrie, yet far enough off for atmosphere to clothe their hollows in deep and dusky blues, and in subtle colours that cannot be seen nearer.

The best route in goes along the south sides of Loch Ba and Loch Laidon, where wild swans fly in and duck come down among the heather. In the breeding season, the lochs are visited by black- and red-throated divers, which behave like submarines when alarmed, slowly submerging until only the head and neck remain above water. In the wide mosses farther away from the lochs, greenshanks take cover. There are few peat-hags, but where they are seen they still expose the bare bones of the Old Wood of Caledon. Were it not for the hungry deer there is every reason to believe that the natural forest might grow back again, for the small islands out on the lochs are well-wooded with birch, rowan, and pine.

Loch Laidon is indented with innumerable tiny bays filled with a clean and gravelly sand, most tempting on a hot day; the northern shore, by which one returns to Kingshouse from Rannoch, is pleasanter than the southern. There one will find wild flowers by the path, a little bay full of water-lilies, and about a mile down the loch the best of all its sandy beaches, backed by short granite crags.

Returning to the Glencoe road over the Blackmount, we find our eyes drawn by the huge corries of Clachlet, which appear to great advantage behind a foreground of sparkling lochans. The road sweeps round the east side of Meall a Bhuiridh, and there at last springs the dark tower of Buachaille, at the strait gate to Glencoe. The Buachaille Etive Mor (3,345 feet) stands in the angle between Glencoe and Glen Etive. The name means the "Great Herdsman of Etive," for its main ridge flanks that glen for four miles to Dalness, and there has always been good cattle-grazing in lower Glen Etive. The name Buachaille, however, is applied more particularly to the summit peak at the north end, which presents to the Moor of Rannoch a clean pointed wall of rock. The mountain is the most popular rock-climbing centre in Scotland—just two hours' car-run from Glasgow. The rock is a rough rhyolite, one of the best climbing rocks in Scotland.

The mountain is seen to greatest effect from the first big bend of the road beyond the Glen Etive road-fork. From there, the famous Crowberry

GLENCOE

A view from Rannoch Moor towards the eastern entrance to Glencoe, guarded by Buachaille Etive Mor — The Great Herdsman of Etive. This impressive mountain of 3,345 feet is the most popular rock-climbing centre in Scotland.

RANNOCH MOOR

One of the many small lochs on Rannoch Moor, a desolate area of fifty-six square miles. The West Highland Railway line crosses the moor and in places is laid on floating brushwood. Remains of the ancient Caledonian Forest are found in some of the peat-hags.

Tower can be sighted projecting close under the summit. The ridge plunging 700 feet down from the tower is the best-known rock-climb in Scotland, and the big gully to its immediate right is one of the finest ice-climbs in Britain. In the early morning, the most tremendous view of all is to be had from Kingshouse Inn, situated on the river Etive just off the new road. The sun's rays stretch level across the moor and floodlight the great cone of rock, suffusing it with fiery pink in winter when snow-clad.

Facing Buachaille across Glen Etive is Clachlet. Its nearer top, Sron na Creise, presents to Kingshouse a formidable-looking wall, a mile to the left of which (south-east) rises the summit of the massif, Meall a Bhuiridh (3,636 feet). The upper north slopes of Meall a Bhuiridh are the principal skiing grounds of west and central Scotland. The Scottish Ski Club has in recent years provided a ski-tow on the final thousand feet, and this has proved so popular that the venture has now been taken over for development by a commercial company.

By long custom, the whole valley running from Rannoch Moor to the sea at Loch Leven is called Glencoe, but in fact the headwaters of the Coe lie

Sron na Creise overshadows Kingshouse Inn, a favourite base for climbers in Glencoe, and a frequent rendezvous of the Scottish Mountaineering Club. The Inn stands on the old Glencoe road, and was called King's House after George III, whose soldiers used it as a barracks while the road was being built.

about four miles west of Kingshouse near the Devil's Staircase—an old military road that climbs the hills above Altnafeadh and drops to Kinlochleven. The mountains on both sides of the glen belong to the National Trust for Scotland, whose property (about thirteen thousand acres) forms a rough triangle with its points at Kingshouse Inn, Dalness Lodge in Glen Etive, and Clachaig Hotel. The Buachaille itself is almost entirely surrounded by a tributary of the Etive. As we travel west from Buachaille, the next great peak to appear on the left is the Buachaille Etive Beag, separated from its big brother by the deep glen of the Lairig Gartain, and separated again from its still bigger neighbour, Bidean nam Bian, by the Lairig Eilde, through which a path runs from Dalness in Glen Etive to the Study in Glencoe. By the roadside under the Lairig Eilde is Lochan na Fola, "the loch of blood," where several men of the glen were slain after a fight. On passing the smaller Buachaille we cross the watershed at 1000 feet and at last travel by the waters of the Coe itself. A mile and a quarter farther on we come to the Study—and the true head of the glen.

The accepted name "Study" is in fact a misnomer for the old Scots "stiddie," which means "anvil." It is a point on the old road above the head of the gorge, through which the Coe plunges in a big waterfall to carve a series of clear green pools. The Study gives

This little croft on the main Glencoe Road is known to thousands of impecunious mountaineers as "Downie's Barn," and many of them have slept in the straw of its outhouses. The bulbous peaks are Gearr Aonach and Aonach Dubh, two of the Three Sisters which brood over this part of Glencoe, and give it majesty if not beauty.

that impressive view of the Three Sisters of Glencoe, which figure in MacCulloch's famous painting in the Glasgow Art Gallery.

As Scottish glens go, Glencoe is no great beauty. We cannot begin to compare it with Glen Affric, or Glen Lyon, or Glen Feshie. It is bare and bleak, adorned by no tree or heather. It is in truth a deep trough. But, viewed from the Study, it cannot be denied a wild and ugly majesty. When we lift our eyes away from the glen itself to the mountains towering above, we see an array of rock peaks packed close, trenched by ravines—of its kind unrivalled. All other glens become a little tame by comparison; they are certainly not so uncompromisingly precipitous. On both flanks cliffs rise to above 3000 feet from the green fields around Loch Achtriochtan. The whole south side of the glen is walled by the highest mountain in Argyll, Bidean nam Bian, "the peak of the bens." It has nine tops and three great corries. The summit, 3,766 feet, is not seen from the Study, but three of its mountain buttresses, Beinn Fhada, Gearr Aonach, and Aonach Dubh (the Three Sisters) hang over the glen in bulges of black rock that finally lift the eye up and back to the peak of Stob Coire nan Lochan (3,657 feet), which stands close to and screens the peak of Bidean. The north side of the glen is walled by the unbroken flank of the Aonach Eagach. The name means "the notched ridge," and the crest gives

a long scramble along one of the two most narrow and shattered ridges on the Scottish mainland (the other being An Teallach in Ross-shire). The crest is broken up into a series of rocky pinnacles, divided one from another by steep stone chutes. The traverse of this ridge in winter conditions is very similar to that of an Alpine ridge.

Bidean nam Bian is one of the most interesting mountains in Britain. Its structure is complex, and one can walk twelve miles on its high ridges. The flanks are rocky, and route-finding is unusually difficult in cloud. No one, however experienced, should set foot on the mountain without map and compass. It ranks second to Nevis as the most dangerous mountain in Scotland, and a great many fatal accidents have occurred on it during the last fifteen years, especially in winter.

The summit is hard to see from Glencoe, being hidden by its outliers. The best position from which to see it is from the road-fork half a mile above Clachaig. From there one looks into Coire nam Beith and Bidean appears above the upper lip of the corrie. Twin buttresses form the summit. The left-hand one is the Diamond Buttress, the right-hand one

BEN NEVIS IN WINTER

Although, at 4,406 feet, Ben Nevis is Britain's highest mountain, the lack of a definite peak tends to detract from its height. It is an impressive mass, however, becoming even more so when snow-covered and seen from the western shore of Loch Linnhe.

LOCH LOCHY

Loch Lochy, which is ten miles long and never more than one mile broad, is one of the four lochs in the Great Glen which Thomas Telford joined to form the Caledonian Canal. The canal allows small vessels to travel between the east and west coasts without having to round Cape Wrath, but is too shallow for most cargo boats.

MacBrayne's steamers are almost as much a feature of the West Highland scene as the natural landmarks. Here the "Lochfyne" sails up Loch Linnhe past Corran Light.

the Church Door. They appear to be dwarfed by the nearer, cone-shaped cliffs of Stob Coire nam Beith to their right. Low down on the left, the corrie is walled by a row of triple-tiered buttresses on the west face of Aonach Dubh. It can be seen at a glance that there is much sport here for rock-climbers.

For the hill-walker, the best and most interesting route to the summit lies up this corrie, then on the saddle to right or left of the main peak. For the less ambitious walker, the most rewarding excursion on Bidean is the penetration of Coire Gabhail (pronounced "Gyle"), known to climbers as the Lost Valley of Bidean. It lies between the two upper Sisters, and is invisible from Glencoe. Access is had below the gorge, near the Meeting of Three Waters, where a footbridge crosses the Coe. It is unique among Scottish corries. The route goes up the true left bank of the Allt Coire Gabhail, which plummets through a ravine. The path at first keeps high up on the flank among birch trees, which make a lovely sight in spring or autumn. Higher up, the path disappears among a mass of huge rocks, where the stream also vanishes. There are several caves here. Beyond this barrier we break out on to the flat floor of the upper corrie. It is carpeted in grass and stretches half a mile. Great cliffs on either flank, and the jagged encircling ridge of Bidean, give the place a remarkable air of seclusion. It is a true mountain sanctuary. In the days of clan warfare the Macdonalds of Glencoe are said to have herded their plundered cattle in this corrie. This may well be so : they were notoriously a thorn in the flesh of near and distant neighbours.

On the face of Aonach Dubh, the lowest of the Three Sisters, is the well-known Ossian's Cave. A moderately difficult rock-climb of two hundred feet is required to gain entry. It was certainly never occupied by Ossian. The floor of the cave is set at forty-five degrees, and one can hardly stand without handhold. A metal box on a ledge at the back contains the names of visitors. The first entry to the cave was made by Neil Marquis, a Glencoe shepherd, in 1868—the first recorded rock-climb in Glencoe.

Below Clachaig Hotel at the west end of Aonach Eagach the character of the glen greatly changes. It widens to a strath, through which the Coe flows gently to Loch Leven. The village of Carnoch stands at the mouth of the river in a fine sunny situation with a splendid outlook to the rugged hills of Ardgour. Near Clachaig, beside the lochan of Torren, is a knoll crowned by a rock. This is called the Signal Rock, from which the signal is alleged to have been given for the massacre of the Clan Macdonald on 13th February, 1692. But this is almost certainly untrue. The Macdonalds inhabited the glen from Invercoe to Achtriochtan and beyond, a stretch of five miles, and the government troops were billeted over the whole area. The chief's house was at Invercoe. No signal would be seen or heard there from Torren, unless it were a beacon, and the essence of the massacre was surprise attack under cover of darkness.

The massacre was ordered by the Secretary of State, Sir John Dalrymple, Master of Stair. In 1691 the rebellious Highland chiefs were ordered to take the oath of allegiance to William III before 1st January 1692. Macdonald of Glencoe presented himself to Colonel Hill, the governor of Fort William, on 31st December. Hill would not accept his oath, which he said could be administered only by a civil magistrate, and sent Macdonald off to Inveraray. Macdonald was an old man, and his journey south was delayed by a snow-storm; when he reached Inveraray on 2nd January the sheriff-depute was absent, failed to return till the 5th, and administered the oath on the 6th.

On 7th January the Master of Stair, writing from London, ordered Livingstone, the officer commanding troops in Scotland, to ravage Glencoe, adding : "I hope the soldiers will not trouble the government with prisoners." By the 9th he had learned of Glencoe's submission, which he acknowledged in a letter to Livingstone. But Macdonald's hereditary foes, the Campbell earls of Argyll and Breadalbane, were in London with the Master of Stair that very month. It is probable, although not certain, that through their influence his original orders to Livingstone were never countermanded. He wrote again to Livingstone on 30th January : "I am glad that

Glencoe did not come within the time prescribed. . . . I think to herry their cattle or burn their houses is but to render them desperate. . . . I believe you will be satisfied it were a great advantage to the nation that thieving tribe were rooted out and cut off. It must be quietly done, otherwise they will make shift for both the men and their cattle." In a letter to Hill at Fort William that same day, he wrote : "Pray, when anything concerning Glencoe is resolved, let it be secret and sudden . . . better not meddle with them than not do it to purpose, to cut off that nest of robbers who have fallen in the mercy of the law now when there is force and opportunity."

On 1st February, a hundred and twenty men of Argyll's regiment arrived in Glencoe under the command of Campbell of Glenlyon, whose property had once been raided by the Macdonalds. He informed Macdonald's son that the garrison at Fort William was overcrowded, and that they must be billeted in the glen. Young Macdonald suspected no ill. The soldiers were given quarters up and down the glen and for two weeks were hospitably entertained. Campbell of Glenlyon visited the chief's younger son every day, and on the night of the 12th played cards with both sons.

In the early hours of the morning, while it was dark, the soldiers fell on their hosts. Men, women and children were butchered. The old chief at Invercoe was shot in the back as he rose from bed, his wife stripped and despoiled of her rings. Up and down the glen the work of burning and butchery went on, apparently indiscriminately, for men of eighty were killed or burned alive in their thatched shielings. A heavy blizzard broke during the night and delayed the arrival of eight hundred troops from Fort William, who were to have blocked the upper reaches of the glen. Thus, under cover of the snow-storm, many survivors of both sexes and all ages escaped to the hills. But the burning of the houses left them without shelter, and the driving away of all livestock left them without food, so they died from exposure in numbers no less than those murdered.

Ben Nevis from the Carn Mor Dearg arête. A famous ascent is that of the north-east buttress, which is shown on the right of the picture, and which leads directly to the summit.

"This business of Glencoe makes a scurvy noise," wrote a Secretary of State a month later. Indeed, the tale seems destined to live forever, so shameful was the underlying treachery. The breach of hospitality was soon to be denounced by Parliament as "Murder under Trust," which Scots law considered a crime so heinous that it carried the penalties of treason. (A traitor was hanged, disembowelled, beheaded, and quartered). A Commission of Inquiry was appointed. Breadalbane was declared by a Commissioner to have been the Master of Stair's adviser, but was never brought to account. Although all three Campbells (Argyll, Breadalbane, Glenlyon) escaped justice, their name in the Highlands has ever since been execrated. The Master of Stair was deprived of his secretaryship but given a pension. As for Livingstone, he ended up with a peerage and a monument in Westminster Abbey.

Immediately to the north of Glencoe, across Loch Leven, stretch the famed lands of Lochaber. The name is said to have come from a loch of that name, which has long since dried up. The western boundary is upper Loch Linnhe and the Great Glen; the northern, the upper reaches of Glen Roy and the river Spey; the eastern, down the line of Lochs Laggan, Treig, and Eilde Mor to Kinlochleven. Nether Lochaber is the Cameron country of the Mamore Forest, and Upper Lochaber is the MacDonnell of Keppoch country beyond Ben Nevis.

The Mamore Forest is deer forest, not tree. It almost wholly consists of one long range of sixteen mountains stretching seven miles from west to east. These are neatly sandwiched between the Leven and Glen Nevis; they can be reached from either with equal ease, but whereas Kinlochleven has become one of the ugliest townships in Scotland through the activities of the British aluminium industry, Glen Nevis is, so far, unspoiled.

The Mamores offer delightful ridge-walking. A strong walker in good training can traverse the whole ridge in a day, which involves ten thousand feet of ascent. The peaks are bold and the ridges well-defined. Although mica-schist mountains, their sharp and shapely tops have been preserved from weathering by quartzite caps. Quartzite is white. In consequence, the upper slopes often look snow-clad even in summer, and this is especially true of Sgurr a Mahaim (3,601 feet), and Stob Ban (3,274 feet). The beautifully cone-shaped summit of the last-named is a feature of the view up Glen Nevis.

Lochaber is entered from the south by crossing the Ballachulish ferry to Inverness-shire. The ferry saves a sixteen-mile detour round the head of Loch Leven, but if time is no object the journey is worth making for the sake of the loch scenery. A mile beyond North Ballachulish we enter the village of Onich, a sun-trap, open to the south with views down Loch Linnhe and along the shores of Ardgour and Appin. By the roadside one mile to the north, a car-ferry crosses to Ardgour by the Corran Narrows of Loch Linnhe. Proceeding up the shores of the inner Loch Linnhe, we arrive in eight miles at Fort William. The town is named from a fort built in 1655 by General Monk.

Fort William ranks with Oban as one of the two most important towns and touring centres in the West Highlands. Whereas Oban's importance derives from its harbour and sea-links, Fort William's comes of its triply strategic situation : at the west end of the Great Glen, which links it by the Caledonian Canal to Inverness and the north-east coast; at the east end of Loch Eil, which allows the railway to Mallaig and the road to the Isles ("By Ailort and by Morar to the sea") ; at the head of Loch Linnhe, which gives it a seaport.

In the town itself is a West Highland museum. One of its rooms contains many relics of Prince Charles Edward, who first raised his standard at the head of Loch Shiel, just twelve miles to the west, and after the rout at Culloden wandered widely in Lochaber and the country to the west of the Great Glen. About one mile north-east of the town, by the banks of the river Lochy, is the ruin of the fifteenth-century Inverlochy Castle. A famous battle was fought near

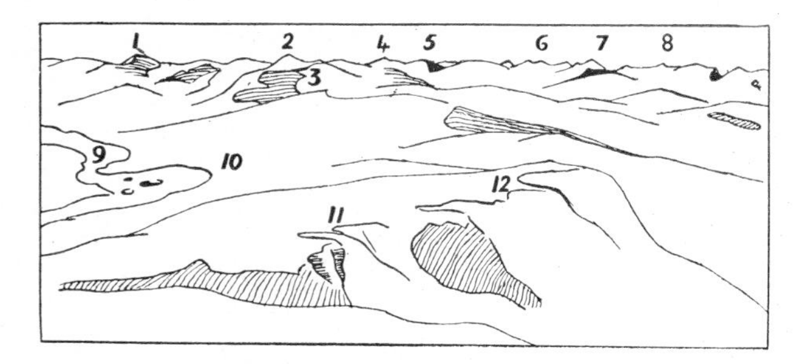

1 Sgurr Nan Coireachan; 2 Ladhar Bheinn and Sgurr Na Ciche, Knoydart; 3 Gulvain; 4 Ben Sgriol, Loch Hourn; 5 Sgurr Mor; 6 The Saddle; 7 Sgurr A' Mhaoraich; 8 Five Sisters, Kintail; 9 Loch Eil; 10 Corpach; 11 Head of No. 4 Gully; 12 Summit of Carn Dearg.

SUMMIT OF BEN NEVIS

This picture, taken near the summit of Ben Nevis, shows the view to the north-west; but there are fine views in all directions, from the Hebrides to the Ochil Hills. Beyond the plateau in the centre of the picture stands a mile of cliffs.

Fort William from the air. This thriving township on the shores of Loch Linnhe was established by General Monk in 1655, and now has almost 3000 inhabitants. It is popular with holiday-makers for its sailing excursions and motor tours through some of Scotland's finest scenery. It also has important distilling and aluminium industries.

it in 1645, when the famous Marquis of Montrose led his army through the Lochaber mountains in forced marches to defeat the Covenanters. The castle should not be confused with the modern Inverlochy Castle, which stands two miles farther out.

Although sited at the foot of Britain's highest mountain, Fort William grants no view of it. Ben Nevis (4,406 feet) can be well seen from Corpach across the river Lochy. From this angle its true shape can at once be grasped—a huge, whale-backed mountain, like Moby Dick when the snow lies on its back, which it does from October to June. Ben Nevis is very nearly that rare thing, an isolated mountain. It is bounded on the north by the Great Glen, on the south and west by the deep trench of Glen Nevis, to the north-east by cliffs two miles long plunging two thousand feet to the corrie of the Allt a Mhuilinn. At the east shoulder alone does a thin ridge sweep around the head of the Allt a Mhuilinn to join the peak of Carn Mor Dearg at 4000 feet. This great corrie and its cliffs can be seen in part from the road near the modern Inverlochy Castle.

Many hundreds of people climb Ben Nevis annually, for the ascent is easy by the path up its back, starting from Achintee Farm in lower Glen Nevis. Yet thirty-three people have been killed on this mountain in the last eight years. Three important things to remember about Nevis are its height, its isolation, and its site on the west coast. Its summit lies close to the level of perpetual snow and right in the storm track of the North Atlantic hurricanes, so that weather conditions vary with extreme speed. The summit has an average of two hundred and sixty-one gales each year, and no other mountain breaks the blow when a storm strikes. Hurricanes exceeding one hundred miles an hour blow not only annually but in winter often, laden with snow, and they gust up to a hundred and fifty miles an hour. For these reasons the mountain is dangerous, quite apart from its having the biggest and most complicated cliff in Britain.

The great cliffs cannot be properly seen from the summit, but are well seen from the Allt a Mhuilinn glen at 2000 feet. Entry to this glen is best gained from half-way up the Achintee path at Lochan Meall an-t-Suidhe (pronounced "Mell an Tee"), from which a descent into the glen can be made eastward. The snowfields seen at the base of the cliffs normally remain all the year round. The finest viewpoint of all is from the summit region of Carn Mor Dearg.

The summit of Ben Nevis is a flat desert of boulders. An observatory stood there, close to the cliff's edge, for twenty years until 1911, but is now a ruin since the government declined to supply funds. On a fine day the view ranges from Ben Lomond to Torridon, and from the Cairngorms to the Outer Hebrides. On exceptional days, Ireland can be dimly discerned one hundred and twenty miles away. As seen from Nevis, the Scottish Highlands are unmistakably a level plateau, from which mountains have been carved by water-erosion. The winter effect is much like that of a storm-sea frozen. The most dramatic scene is that across Glen Nevis, where the Mamore Forest range bites into the sky with quartzite teeth.

From Loch Treig a fifteen-mile pipe-line has been driven through Ben Nevis to feed the British Aluminium Company's power-house near the mouth of Glen Nevis. The power-house vicinity is the eyesore of Lochaber, rivalled only by Kinlochleven. Glen Nevis, on the other hand, is the fairest glen of Lochaber, in its upper part one of the most beautiful of all Scottish gorges. The river Nevis rises on the eastern flank of Binnein Mor of the Mamore Forest and flows fourteen miles round the south and west sides of Ben Nevis into the head of Loch Linnhe. The highest reaches of the glen are desolate moorland, but the middle is pinched by a southern buttress of the Ben, where that meets a north buttress of Sgurr a Mhaim. Between these two the river has carved a gorge through the rock rampart. It plunges wildly from cauldron to cauldron, bursting in one mile from bleak moors to the wooded beauty of the lower glen. The Nevis gorge is a truly Alpine gorge without equal in Scotland. Its whole course may be followed by means of a rocky path high up on the right flank. Cars may be taken to the lower end. Thus far the gradients are slight, for the top end of the road is only 450 feet above sea-level. The slope from here to the summit of Nevis is four thousand feet at an an angle of more than thirty-five degrees—the longest and steepest slope in Britain.

The Glen Nevis road provides good access to the mountains of Mamore, and to Aonach Beag (4,060 feet) east of Nevis. It offers, too, a through route from Fort William to Loch Treig and Corrour station on the West Highland railway, a distance of twenty-two miles. A six-mile section in the middle of this course is trackless : the walker should choose good weather, for the going is heavy.

The Hydro-Electric Board has recently made plans for damming the upper reaches of the river Nevis. If this plan is carried through (against much opposition) the beauty of the gorge will be destroyed. It is the water that gives it life, and the wildness of its beauty will go when a motor-road is driven through. This country has no similar gorge to be left unmarred.

Ten miles to the east of Nevis lies Loch Treig, and between the two is a group of twelve mountains called the Grey Corries. These are best seen and reached either by following the main road north to Glen Spean or else by using the West Highland railway station at Corrour, south-east of Loch Treig. Both these approaches then make use of a deep depression that splits the Grey Corries right through from Spean Bridge to Lochtreighead. The summits of these twelve mountains, which are all above 3,100 feet and

The stone archways of this bridge over the River Lochy combine dignity and strength. The bridge leads to Inverlochy village, where Montrose won a most extraordinary victory.

rise to 3,858 feet, give splendid ridge-walking with magnificent views to Ben Nevis and the Mamores.

Glen Spean and the neighbouring Glens Roy and Gloy are remarkable for the geological phenomena known as Parallel Roads, which puzzled our forebears for centuries. These are parallel shelves high on the mountain flanks, seen most clearly in Glen Roy, which opens north off Glen Spean. The Roads in Glen Roy are in three tiers, at 850 feet, 1,067 feet, and 1,148 feet. In Glens Gloy and Spean they appear at only one level, 1,165 feet and 855 feet respectively. The problem has been solved by demonstrating that a great glacier flowing northward from the Nevis massif had dammed the entrances to the glens. The mountain waters flowing in behind the ice-dams formed lakes a thousand feet deep, and the Parallel Roads are the beaches.

A geological phenomenon still more extraordinary is the Great Glen, a fault extending right across Scotland from the Moray Firth to the Firth of Lorne. This valley includes Loch Linnhe and the fresh-water lochs of Lochy, Oich, and Ness. The fault was originally caused by a great land movement, when the northern part of Scotland slid sixty-five miles south-

ARDNAMURCHAN POINT

At the seaward end of the Sound of Mull stands Ardnamurchan light, flashing over the waters between Muck and Coll. The Ardnamurchan peninsula is one of the loneliest and loveliest areas in Scotland, and can be approached only by sea or by the rough Loch Sunart road.

LOCH SUNART AT STRONTIAN

Loch Sunart is a narrow sea-loch which winds for some 20 miles between the wooded shores of mountainous Morvern and the "Rough Bounds" of Ardnamurchan and then opens out to the Sound of Mull, opposite Tobermory. Its name is a reminder of Norse domination and means "The Fiord of Sweyn". Sweyn was Canute's father.

At Spean Bridge stands a monument to the commandos who trained in the area during the Second World War. It was designed by Scott Sutherland and was erected in 1952.

westward in relation to the main southern part. The series of lochs in the glen is now linked by the Caledonian Canal, on which work was begun in 1803 and took forty-four years to complete. The actual canal is twenty-two miles long (the glen itself being over sixty) and has twenty-nine locks. The highest point comes at Loch Oich. The south gate to the canal at Corpach has eight locks, called Neptune's Staircase. By means of the canal small ships from the North Sea can sail through to the Atlantic without having to make the stormy passage round the north coast by Cape Wrath. An excellent road connects Fort William to Inverness.

West of the Great Glen lie the true West Highlands. Their straight eastern boundary, eighty-five miles from Morvern to Inverness, makes a striking contrast to the length of the west coast, which from Morvern to Strome Ferry on Loch Carron is three hundred and twenty-four miles. This highly indented coast was caused by still another geological phenomenon. We have seen from the summit of Nevis how the Scottish mountains are in reality an eroded plateau. After the raising of this plateau, and its erosion, it took a downward and westward tilt. The Atlantic then flooded into its westward-running valleys, giving the splintered coastline that is one of the main geographical features of Scotland—to which the Great Glen makes a contrasting counterpart, a boundary equally fantastic in origin.

The true West Highland area is best described as a mountainous maze. No fewer than sixty of its mountains exceed 3000 feet. Starting at the south, in Morvern, the hills are low (barely 2000 feet), gradually increasing in height northward to reach their maximum above Glen Affric, where they are little less than 4000 feet. The whole of this mountain fastness is deeply moated by zig-zag lochs, both sea-water and fresh. The scenery of the long twisting glens is of a high order, so many rivalling one another in claim to the greatest beauty that hardly two men can be found to agree which is supreme—with this qualification, that prior to the activities of the Hydro-Electric Board almost all granted the highest award to Glen Affric. But the building of the dam there, and the flooding of the former shores of Loch Beneveian, have deprived that glen of its pre-eminence.

A great part of this district was the scene of Prince Charles Edward's wanderings after Culloden. It has thus been given a romantic appeal in addition to its scenic, and strongly attracts the walker as well as the mountaineer. There is one drawback to their activities : great mountain areas are given over to deer-stalking, and are thus out-of-bounds in late summer. There are two compensations. First, the roads and right-of-way paths are free at all times, and although the roads are few the paths abound, radiating in all directions. Secondly, one is free to wander anywhere in spring and early summer, which are the best and driest times of year.

The sea-lochs along this coast are the greatest glory of the Scottish mainland. At Lochs Sunart, Moidart, Ailort, Nevis, Hourn, Duich, and Carron, all running into the very heart of the mountains, we meet that wedding of rock and water in a colourful perfection hard to find elsewhere in the world.

From Fort William or Glencoe, access to Morvern is gained by ferrying across the Corran Narrows or else by rounding Loch Eil and running down the shores of Loch Linnhe. The quick route is by Corran to Inversanda at the east end of Glen Tarbert. For Morvern is a peninsula in the fullest sense. Loch Linnhe, the Sound of Mull, and Loch Sunart to its north, encircle it save for the six-mile neck of Glen Tarbert. Its western half is again cut deeply in two by a low glen (summit 94 feet) that runs from Loch Teacuis on the Sunart coast to Loch Aline on the Sound of Mull. The Morvern hills are better to look from than to look at. They are quite undistinguished, yet good to tread underfoot. The highest hill is Creach Bheinn (2,800 feet) on the south side of Glen Tarbert. The best centres from which to explore Morvern are the hotel at Lochaline, where a steamer calls from Oban, or the Strontian Hotel at the head of Loch Sunart, or the Ardgour Hotel at Corran.

Ardgour is the most northerly district of Argyll, extending north from Glen Tarbert to the south

Loch Aline is a narrow sea-loch eating into the rugged lands of Morvern from the Sound of Mull. Its west shore has remarkable banks of silica sand, which is mined and used in the manufacture of optical glass.

shores of Lochs Shiel and Eil. Entry from the south is made at Corran to save a twenty-five-mile detour round Loch Eil. The latter road is the only public road in the district. It comes south past Corran to Inversanda Bay, then east through Glen Tarbert to Strontian and Salen on Loch Sunart, and finally north to Acharacle at the foot of Loch Shiel. There are numerous paths to entrance the walker : for example, that from Strontian across to Glen Shiel and up to Glen Finnan. The whole district is moor or mountain with the exception of the Strontian and Corran vicinities and a coastal strip facing Fort William.

None of the mountains rise to 3000 feet, but eight exceed 2,500. Garbh Bheinn (2,903 feet) is acknowledged by all to be one of the finest rock mountains on the Scottish mainland. It stands on the north side of Glen Tarbert, whence it is approached by a charming glen called Coire an Iubhair, "the corrie of the yew tree." The outstanding feature of Garbh Bheinn is the great range of cliffs on its east face. The rock is a mixed quartzite and gneiss of superb rough quality, ranked by rock-climbers among the best in the country. The summit is buttressed by a great rock ridge dropping twelve hundred feet to the glen, and this gives to the mountain's head that proud lift by which, from a distance, it can always be distinguished from the other peaks of Ardgour.

The second most distinguished mountain is not Sgurr Dhomhnuill, the highest in the district (2,915 feet), although its height and sharp top at the centre of the group make it conspicuous, but rather Sgurr Giubhsachain (2,784 feet) on the south-east shore of Loch Shiel, three and a half miles down from Prince Charles's monument. It is the mountain that lends so much grace to the view down Loch Shiel from Glenfinnan.

Ardgour is best explored from hotels at Strontian, near the head of Loch Sunart, or Salen bay, half-way down the loch at its great bend, or Acharacle at the foot of Loch Shiel. Loch Sunart is a long sea-loch of great beauty, well-wooded on its western reaches, dividing Ardgour from Morvern. Both Strontian and Salen are small fishing resorts situated on little bays on its north shore. Between them, on the hills behind, rises Ben Resipol (2,774 feet), which is easily climbed and gives an unusually fine view of the area, commanding as it does the seaward view down Loch Sunart, the northward view up Loch Shiel, and the southward across Morvern to Mull. There are good camping spots up and down the loch, but especially around Acharacle at Loch Shiel, a beauty spot of renown. The road to it from Salen crosses the isthmus of Ardnamurchan.

The Ardnamurchan peninsula is eighteen miles long by six wide. Its hills are low, nowhere reaching 2000

feet, but what they lack in height they make up in character, more especially the western third where the rocks are igneous and the hills extremely rugged. They are in fact the wreck of a great volcano. The rocks now exposed are largely gabbro—the best of all for the climber—although it is often wrongly said that Scotland has no gabbro hills outside the islands of Rhum and Skye. Only one hill, however, presents gabbro cliffs large enough to attract a cragsman. This is Beinn na Seilg (1,123 feet), two miles west of Kilchoan, opposite the north tip of Mull. The hill is a mountain in miniature but with nothing small in its view, for it is the most westerly hill on the mainland of Great Britain. The islands of Rhum, Eigg, Muck, Coll, Tiree, and Mull all lie close around. Beyond rolls the Atlantic, a wrinkled grey like the hide of an elephant, or a blue of intenser flash than can be seen in the soft airs of the Mediterranean, but always, beyond the isles, an empty desolation.

The main road west from Salen ends at Kilchoan, to which there is also a steamer service from Tobermory in Mull. Facing the pier across the bay is Mingarry Castle. James IV held court there in 1495. A rough gated road, practicable for cars, runs from

GLENFINNAN GAMES

The annual Highland Games at Glenfinnan have a long tradition. The setting is a particularly delightful one and lies at the head of Loch Shiel within sight of the Prince Charles Monument. The smaller picture shows the tug-of-war, one of the most popular events at Highland Games.

Loch Eilt, with its steep shores and wooded islets, is one of the most beautiful lochs in Scotland. It lies in the deep glen between Moidart and South Morar, and is linked to the sea by Loch Ailort. Its sheltered position makes it a good sea-trout loch.

Kilchoan to Ardnamurchan Point and its tall grey lighthouse. The point is the most westerly of the British mainland; it lies twenty miles farther west than Land's End. Two miles north-east is Sanna Point, and between the two points is Sanna bay with a sweep of white sands. The most interesting of all routes to Ardnamurchan Point is to walk or drive along the track from Kilchoan to Plocaig near Sanna bay, and then to follow the delightful bays of this remote coast southward, pausing en route to remark the very primitive houses at Portuairk.

Acharacle at the east end of Ardnamurchan is well situated for the exploration of Moidart, and also of the complex series of bays to either side of the Kentra peninsula, which lies within the bounds of Ardnamurchan. A narrow road runs to Ardtoe on Kentra bay, a lovely place looking to the Inner Hebrides. Moidart is the country west of Loch Shiel and bounded on the north by Loch Eilt. This is Clan Ranald country, closely associated with Prince Charles Edward and the '45. Only two short roads serve the district and these skirt its north and south frontiers : the road from Glenfinnan to Loch Ailort in the north, and the road from Acharacle to the head of Loch Moidart in the south-west.

Moidart is largely given over to fishing and shooting; in consequence, there are few houses other than the gamekeepers' and the big lodges. The hotel centres from which to explore Moidart are round the fringes, at Acharacle, Glenfinnan, and Lochailort, the last two standing on the road and rail from Fort William to Mallaig.

An excursion excelling all others is the walk from Acharacle to Loch Ailort—perhaps the most rewarding coast-walk in Scotland. Before starting, take note of the state of the tide, and from Acharacle cross the Shiel Bridge into Moidart proper. If the tide is known to be low, follow the east side of the river Shiel to Loch Moidart, from whose wooded shores you may get a man to row you over the south channel near Castle Tioram and Riskay Island to the island of Shona Beag. The passage is one of remarkable beauty, especially in the early morning if the sun is shining, and the water glowing like a stained glass window. On the far side of Shona Beag a ford crosses the north channel to Kylesbeg, from which a path crosses the hill to Glen Uig and the Sound of Arisaig. A good track with wonderful seaward views then leads to Kinlochailort. At the mouth of Loch Ailort is the little Eilean nan Gobhar, where the French ship bringing Prince Charles Edward anchored in July, 1745. His great adventure was to end here just one year later. If, when you leave Acharacle, the tide is unsuitable or you know that the boatman is not available, it becomes necessary to strike east from

Looking down from Beinn Ghuer over the east end of Loch Moidart, Dorlin House is in the centre of the picture, and behind stands Castle Tioram and the small island of Riskay.

Shiel Bridge to Kinlochmoidart, and thereafter follow the north shore to the Glen Uig path.

Flowing south from the farthest hills, the river Moidart joins the loch at Kinlochmoidart. Prince Charles stayed here with the Macdonalds in 1745 before raising his standard at Glenfinnan, and a line of beeches in a nearby meadow honours the "Seven Men of Moidart," those faithful companions who came with him from France. Farther down the loch, offshore in the south channel, stands the fourteenth-century Castle Tioram of the Macdonalds of Clan Ranald. Except at high spring tides it has a link to the mainland.

To the north, encircling the head of Glen Moidart, are the highest hills, which fall into the two groups of Rois-bheinn (2,876 feet) and Beinn Odhar Bheag (2,895 feet). In the former group the finest individual peak is Druim Fiaclach (2,852 feet), which is best reached from Lochailort. The mountain has a cliff-like north face and three well-defined ridges. If the weather is clear, the best way to climb all these hills is from east to west (this is true of most West Highland mountains). The most exhilarating views are then always in front, which eases the ascent, and when the climber steps to the summit all is brought to sudden culmination with the great lochs rushing out below into seascapes of unimagined splendour.

Beinn Odhar Bheag is seen and climbed most conveniently from Glenfinnan. It rises from the west shore of Loch Shiel three and a half miles down from the head of the loch and, together with Sgurr Ghiubhsachain on the Ardgour shore, makes a noble frame for that renowned view from Glenfinnan. On a meadow at the head of the loch Prince Charles Edward raised his standard for the Jacobite rising on 19th August, 1745. A monument now stands at the site, set up in 1815. On a sunny day, Loch Shiel as seen from the monument is of rare beauty. The wide, nearer waters are broken by a curved island, where well-grown trees at the margin throw green reflections. The mountains beyond thrust their spurs into the loch with just enough irregularity to give the distant waters a double twist. Thus the eye seems to be led farther, and the loch to penetrate deeper into the heart of these mysterious hills, receding ridge behind ridge, than could ever seem possible were the shores straight.

A motor launch plies up and down the eighteen miles of loch between Glenfinnan and Acharacle. Full advantage should be taken of this service to enjoy the real wealth of Ardgour and Moidart. Between Glen Finnan and Loch Ailort the westward-running road and rail traverse four miles down either side of Loch Eilt. At Lochailort we turn north-west into the district of Morar.

The lands of Locheil and Morar are bounded on the south by the line of Lochs Eil, Eilt, and Ailort, and on the north by Loch Arkaig, Glen Dessary, and Loch Nevis. Locheil in turn is divided from Morar by the trough through Glen Finnan north to the head of Loch Arkaig. Only two roads serve this large area, and once again they hold to the fringes. The first is, as before, the road to the Isles ending at Mallaig; the second is from Corpach to Glendessary, which lies one and a half miles west of Loch Arkaig.

The mountains are again higher than those to the south, several exceeding 3000 feet, notably Gulvain (3,224 feet). These high peaks are concentrated at

On the shores of Loch Shiel, near Glenfinnan, stands Greenshields' famous monument to Prince Charles Edward Stewart. It was here that the Jacobite standard was raised in 1745.

the centre of the district, to the west of Locheil, and the farther west we go into Morar the more they dwindle, until we come to the broad green belt of the Arisaig coast, where men play golf and keep cows instead of deer. The hotel centres for exploration are at Corpach, Glenfinnan, Lochailort, Arisaig, Morar, and Mallaig—all on the West Highland railway. At the west end of Loch Arkaig a bed may sometimes be obtained in one of the houses.

Locheil and Morar are disappointing districts for the mountaineer. His mountains are certainly a little higher than those of Ardgour and Moidart, but not one half so interesting, shapely, or rugged. East of Gulvain, the hills are so many mounds. The central group is better, notably Gulvain, Streap, Sgurr Thuilm (3,164 feet) and Sgurr nan Coireachan (3,133 feet), which can all be reached from Glenfinnan. The Morar district is relatively low. The highest hill is Sithean Mor (1,970 feet) in south Morar. But Morar is of extraordinary beauty and the walker there will have no disappointments if only the weather holds, for in foul weather the greatest beauty spot is no less miserable than anywhere else. Quite apart from the open hills, he has a wide variety of paths from which to choose for his explorations.

From the shores of Loch Lochy in the Great Glen, access is had to Loch Arkaig along the famous tree-lined avenue called "The Dark Mile." It joins the loch at the north side of the river Arkaig, while to its south among woods stands Achnacarry House, the home of Cameron of Locheil. A rough, narrow road runs the length of the loch, and is practicable for cars as far as Glendessary. The setting at first is splendidly wooded, but the scene becomes wild and bare as we travel west.

From the head of the loch, two footpaths cross passes to the Atlantic coast. One goes up Glen Dessary to the long-used pass of Mam na Cloich' Airde at 1000 feet, under the highest peak of Knoydart (Sgor na Ciche, 3,410 feet), then drops to the head of Loch Nevis. This descent is exceedingly rough and rocky, but the path is well marked. The other goes through Glen Pean to Loch Morar. The mountain scene is much inferior to that of the Mam na Cloich' Airde, but the pass is lower—only 400 feet.

Among numerous interesting routes for the walker, one of the most useful is that up Glen Finnan, through the *bealach* between Streap and Thuilm, and down to Loch Arkaig. There is no path beyond the head of Glen Finnan. Once over the pass, the route should be chosen down the right bank of the stream. Another useful route is from Lochailort to Loch Morar, and on to Loch Nevis if so desired, by the direct path north over the hills. The hill-path starts near the west end of Loch Eilt and follows the right bank of the Allt na

Loch Morar from the north-western shore. Although it is only thirty feet above sea level, the loch is more than 170 fathoms deep, the deepest water in Britain.

Criche to the *bealach* at 1000 feet. We look down from there over the far side on to the little-known Loch Beoraid, stretching east as thin as a wire rope. On the steep descent the path comes under some rock overhangs to the right. Among the big boulders strewn round the foot of the cliff are several caves, one of which the maps mark as Prince Charles's. One grows sceptical—perhaps unnecessarily, for he did occupy many. From the foot of Loch Beoraid a good road leads to Loch Morar. If a boat can be hired across the loch, one can follow the short easy track which goes north to Loch Nevis.

Lochs Nevis and Morar have no roads along their shores, save for a three-mile stretch at the foot of the latter. They are long lochs of varied scene, Loch Nevis having only two peers (Hourn and Alsh) among the sea-lochs of a coast where great beauty is found at every turn. This magnificent scenery is open only to long-distance walkers, unless a motor-boat is hired from Mallaig for the passage up Loch Nevis.

Unlike Loch Nevis, Loch Morar is not a sea-loch. A narrow land-barrier separates it from the Sound of Sleat, and through this barrier bursts the river Morar, its falls being harnessed by the ubiquitous hydro-electric scheme. The bay at the river's estuary is famed for its white sands, and for the westward view to Rhum and Eigg. Loch Morar is yet another of Scotland's geological freaks. Its depth is 1,077 feet although it is only one mile from the sea, which is shallow along the coast and does not reach an equivalent depth until the dip of the Continental Shelf beyond Rockall. How was this chasm gouged? It is the deepest water in Britain. The problem is not yet finally solved.

Travelling west from Lochailort by road or rail, we come in three miles to Loch nan Uamh, which is really a great bay of the Sound of Arisaig. From Sithean Mor above, the Beasdale and Borrodale burns flow south into the loch. At Borrodale, the French brig with Prince Charles on board anchored on 25th July, 1745, and at Borrodale House he had the fateful meeting with Locheil and the Highland chiefs to decide on the rising. They came to dissuade him, and they left to raise the clans. A year later he was a fugitive in the Beasdale woods. He escaped to the Outer Hebrides, where he was saved by Flora Macdonald's resource, but had to return again via Mallaig, hiding this time in a cave on the shore below Borrodale House, then at Macleod's Cave "upon a high precipice in the woods of Borrodale." For another two months he wandered over the West Highlands between Moidart, Kintail, and Badenoch, until 19th September, 1746, when he embarked on a French ship at Borrodale, and with a large party of his clansmen sailed for the last time out of Loch nan Uamh.

Road and rail end at the fishing port of Mallaig, on the north-west shore of North Morar. It has an

EIGG AND RHUM FROM SOUTH MORAR

From their vantage point in South Morar the children are looking across the Sound of Sleat to the islands of Eigg and Rhum. Eigg, easily identified by the oddly shaped Sgurr, contains the cave where the MacLeods of Skye murdered two hundred Macdonalds. Rhum, whose hills can be seen at the right of the picture, is now a bird sanctuary.

LOCH HOURN

This loch, enclosed by the hills of Knoydart, is in some of the most inaccessible country in Scotland. Although the road to the head of the loch has been improved, many of the hill tracks were obscured when the level of Loch Quoich was raised by a hydro-electric scheme. As a result, the western part of Loch Hourn is hard to reach, but the journey is rewarded by views like this.

excellent harbour. Steamers sail to the Inner and Outer Hebrides, and a motor-launch carries mail and passengers to Inverie on Loch Nevis. The visitor to Mallaig with four hours to spare should make a point of climbing Carn a' Ghobhair (1,794 feet), three miles east of the town. The view is the finest in Morar. It commands the entire lengths of Lochs Morar and Nevis. The vast seaward panorama ranges south to north from the distant point of Ardnamurchan westward over the Small Isles to the great black teeth of the Cuillin of Skye, then far up the Sound of Sleat to Kintail.

Immediately to the north of Loch Nevis is the country of Knoydart, bounded to its north by Loch Hourn. East of Knoydart stretches the land of Glen Garry, whose southern boundary is Loch Arkaig, and northern the line through Glen Garry to Loch Hourn, including the hills immediately flanking this line to its north.

Mallaig lies at the terminus of the West Highland Railway and is a busy fishing port with a fine harbour. It has quiet corners, attractive scenery, and excellent sailing.

Although this district is much the biggest so far considered, it has only one road, that from Invergarry on Loch Oich to Kinlochhourn. The reason is partly that the area is very much more mountainous, a dozen peaks exceeding 3000 feet and a dozen more coming close to that magic figure. The highest is Sgor na Ciche (3,410 feet), at the head of Loch Nevis. Seen from seaward it is one of the sharpest peaks in Scotland. The main geographical feature of this country is Glen Garry, stretching twenty-six miles from the Great Glen to Knoydart. It carries two big sheets of water, Loch Garry and Loch Quoich (pronounced "Kooich"). Loch Quoich and its tributaries are incorporated in a big hydro-electric scheme comprising several dams, and this scheme should thrive in what is notoriously the wettest district in Scotland. The rain-maps indicate over 120 inches.

At the western end of the glen there are two passes over the watershed, one to Loch Nevis, the other to Loch Hourn : so into Knoydart, the wildest district in Scotland. Its appropriate name is the Rough Bounds of Knoydart. But one has to walk in this land fully to appreciate what "rough" means. Lochs Nevis and Hourn are the grandest sea-lochs of their particular kind. Loch Hourn is the more impressive in its upper part when seen from high ground to the east; Loch Nevis better than Hourn when seen from seaward. Upper Loch Hourn has the steeper flanks; it is narrow and bare and it twists. Hence it brings to mind the Norwegian fjord. There are several other lochs of equal beauty—Alsh, for example—but none with the savage majesty that distinguishes these two.

The centres for exploring the district are Invergarry Hotel at Loch Oich, Tomdoun Hotel, eleven miles west along Glen Garry, Mallaig, using a motor-launch to reach Loch Nevis, Inverie on Loch Nevis (camping), Arnisdale on the north shore of Loch Hourn (camping), reached by a rough hill-road from Kintail, and Kinlochhourn (camping), reached by road from Glen Garry. The last two roads are both open to cars.

At Invergarry on the Great Glen, the river Garry flows into Loch Oich. To the river's south, on the right-hand side of the road, stands the ruin of Macdonell's Castle, where Prince Charles Edward slept before and after Culloden. It was burnt down by the Duke of Cumberland. At the river's north bank the road through Glen Garry strikes sharp left, soon traversing the north shore of the loch. At Tomdoun a branch road leads north over the hills to Cluanie and Kyle of Lochalsh. Tomdoun is a famous angling resort.

The westward road by Loch Quoich is largely new,

The country around Mallaig is as beautiful in winter as in summer. This picture was taken on the south shore of Loch Nevis, only two miles from the town, looking across the loch to Sandaig Bay and the peak of Drum na Cluain-Airidhe.

the old road having been flooded by the new dam at the east end of the loch. The former and singular beauty of this loch's shores have been entirely ruined. From the economic viewpoint, it seems proper that the district's principal product, rain, should be put to use and transformed into a national asset. The difficulty is to know where the limits should be set to these developments.

On both sides of Loch Quoich and around its head are a dozen fine mountains, which are most easily climbed from this glen, except those that border Glen Dessary, including Sgurr na Ciche. If the ascent of this mountain is made from Inverie on Loch Nevis it means a long expedition—seven thousand feet of ascent and twenty miles' walking. It is possible, however, to hire the launch from the Marine Hotel at Mallaig and go right to the head of the loch, and this makes the ascent quite short.

From Loch Quoich, Knoydart can be reached over the pass to Loch Nevis, but if the intention is to carry heavy packs and stay several days the route is not recommended. The proper course is then by sea from Mallaig. The motor-road to Loch Hourn is a tempting alternative, with the disadvantage that the road ends at Kinlochhourn, leaving one at the narrow upper end of this sunless loch, with very long walks either to reach the outer loch, where the greater interest lies, or to strike south-west into the true Knoydart country.

The most rewarding excursion to be made from Kinlochhourn, or from Arnisdale on the outer loch, or from Inverie on Loch Nevis, is the ascent of Ladhar Bheinn (pronounced "Larven": 3,343 feet). It is a mountain of most distinctive character, superbly sited. From either Kinlochhourn or Arnisdale the first move is to get to Barrisdale bay under the mountain. From Arnisdale a boat may be hired. The ascent is then made from the east by Coire Dhorrcail. The mountain has a high summit ridge, two miles long. The south-eastern half carries fine crags on the flank of Coire Dhorrcail. If the climb is to be made from Inverie, the direct route goes up Mam Uidhe to the south-west slopes of the mountain. But the more interesting route is from Barrisdale bay. Ladhar Bheinn is the most westerly "Munro" (3000-foot mountain) on the mainland.

Northward of the Hourn-Garry axis, and parallel to it, is that of Kintail and Cluanie. Their south boundary is a thin mountain-chain running thirty miles unbroken from Kyle Rhea to the head of Glen Moriston, the crest of which range is also the frontier of Ross-shire.

The central feature of Kintail and Cluanie is the enormous trough cutting over the watershed of Scotland from Loch Alsh to the North Sea by way of Loch Duich, Glen Shiel, Glen Cluanie, Glen Moriston, thus to the Great Glen at Loch Ness and thence to Inverness. The district of Kintail is strictly the stretch of mountainous country between Lochs Hourn and

Long, the latter being the north branch of Loch Alsh. In other words, Kintail is the land on all three sides of Loch Duich, which is the south branch of Loch Alsh. The eastern boundary in Glen Shiel is most conveniently taken as Bridge of Shiel, the site of the battle in 1719, which is six miles up the glen and not to be confused with Shiel Bridge at the foot.

The Cluanie country goes from there eastward to the dam at the foot of Loch Cluanie, and embraces the hills to either flank. The north boundary is the southern range of Glen Affric. Entry to Cluanie from Glen Garry is made by the road from Tomdoun, climbing steeply over the hills to Loch Loyne, thence to Loch Cluanie. An alternative route goes up the Great Glen to Invermoriston, thence west up Glen Moriston to Loch Cluanie, where both roads join as the second Road to the Isles.

Great ranges flank both sides of Cluanie. On the south side seven tops exceed 3000 feet; on the north side, ten tops. The ideal centre for exploring these hills is Cluanie Hotel at the west end of the loch.

The Cluanie hills are grassy and offer no rock-climbing, but they yield magnificent ridge-walking. The seven linked summits on the south flank never drop below 2,500 feet at the *bealachs*. Their height and distance from the coast give them a heavy cover of snow into late spring, when the traverse of the crest from end to end on old firm snow becomes one of the best ridge-walks in West Scotland. All Cluanie is under deer, hence climbing may be restricted in the stalking season.

On the north side of the glen, the mountains standing directly above Loch Cluanie are the end peaks of a range extending north to Glen Affric and forming one of the greater mountain masses of the Highlands. It contains thirteen tops between 3000 and 3,700 feet. Like its neighbouring range to the south, it carries much snow and gives good walking. On the west flank of the group a deep glen cuts through to Glen Affric at Alltbeath. The path, which holds to the east side of the burn, is a right-of-way.

Between Glens Cluanie and Shiel is the watershed at 889 feet. Close to its north stand a group of four peaks, all over 3000 feet. Four easier mountains could not be found. Smooth and grassy, the slopes stretching unobstructed to the summits, their traverse can well be combined with that of the Five Sisters of Kintail.

A large part of Kintail belongs to the National Trust for Scotland. The property consists of two main parts : first, the whole western part of the Balmacara promontory between Lochs Carron and Alsh, including Kyle of Lochalsh and Plockton, but excluding Strome at the Carron Narrows; second, the Five Sisters of Kintail, which lie between Glen Shiel and the narrow Glen Lichd to the north, both glens send-

KINTAIL

The National Trust for Scotland owns fine stretches of Wester Ross, among them the country between Glen Shiel and Glen Lichd in which stand the Five Sisters of Kintail, one of the most striking groups of mountains in Scotland. This picture looks across Loch Duich towards the Five Sisters, with the hamlet of Letterewe in the foreground.

The crofting village of Plockton lies in a sheltered curve at the mouth of Loch Carron. Across the loch stands the modern Duncraig Castle which is now in use as a school.

ing parallel rivers into the head of Loch Duich at opposite corners. It extends north across Glen Lichd to include Ben Attow at the head of Glen Affric, and the famous Falls of Glomach, which Ben Attow feeds. The property does not extend south of Glen Shiel, nor does it include the great promontory between Lochs Hourn and Duich.

As one first enters into Kintail from Cluanie, the most imposing sight of all from upper Glen Shiel is the lance-like peak of the Saddle (3,317 feet) It appears to block the exit from the glen, its graceful shape compelling admiration. On reaching Shiel Bridge the road forks to go round both sides of Loch Duich. The westward branch again forks, offering to the right a dead-end road down the south side of the loch to Totaig at the head of Loch Alsh, and to the left a steep climb over Mam Rattachan to Glenelg on the Sound of Sleat, where a ferry crosses the narrows to Skye.

The climb up to Mam Rattachan is 1 in 6 with hairpin bends but a new surface. The pass at 1,116 feet is the county boundary between Ross and Inverness. From this point the Five Sisters are seen at their best, standing in file over the long pool of Loch Duich, and holding their heads rather stiffly upright. Scour Ouran (3,505 feet) dominates the group, its face lifted back, averted from the dark defile of Glen Shiel. The grand views from Mam Rattachan are now partly screened by the growth of new forestry plantations.

Glenelg is a car-ferry point for the crossing to Skye at Kylerhea. On both sides of the water the approaches to the ferry are hilly, but in mid-summer it pays to cross here rather than join a queue for the main ferry at Kyle of Lochalsh, which often involves a considerable delay. From Glenelg a rough and hilly road goes south round the coast to Arnisdale. Where it crosses high ground at outer Loch Hourn the views over the loch to Ladhar Bheinn, and Skye and Rhum across the Sound of Sleat, are exquisite. One mile south of Glenelg is the beautifully wooded Glen Beg, which has the two best examples of Pictish brochs on the mainland. (A broch is a prehistoric castle shaped as a round tower).

Back at Shiel Bridge, the northward-going road rounds Loch Duich, crosses the Dornie bridge at the narrows of Loch Long, and forks, one branch going to Strome, the other to Kyle of Lochalsh on the strait of Kyle Akin. Kyle is the main gateway to Skye and a fishing port, with steamer services up the coast to Applecross, down the coast to Mallaig, and outwards to the Hebrides. A few miles short of Kyle, a side road goes north to Plockton, perhaps the most beautiful little village in the Highlands. It has been long frequented by artists, for its setting on a small bay of outer Loch Carron has unique charm : sheltered, yet with views to the enchanting mountains of Applecross and the wild scenery of Torridon. Up and down the coast are many other little bays and islands. Last century (before the railway was built through Strath Carron from Inverness) Plockton was a port for schooners trading with the Baltic and used by tough local fishermen, who made light of rowing seventy miles across the Minch to Stornoway. Now the liveliness of its waters comes of its yachts and sailing dinghies, and many of the houses are holiday homes.

Returning over the Dornie bridge, we find Eilean Donan Castle on the farther shore. It projects out of the water at the meeting place of all three lochs, Alsh, Duich, Long. The site is ideal. It can be criticised as a "picture postcard" castle, and so indeed it looks in its photographs. But he who sees this castle with his own eyes, set in its living scene, will be deeply moved, unless he be impervious to beauty. It is the scene down Loch Alsh that bewitches, when a low sun flushes the clouds over the Cuillin of Skye. Against that unearthly light the water burns like a river of fire twisting in and out among sharp capes and bays, thinning at last to a distant trickle and vanishing into the black jaws of the Cuillin, for these gape like caves against the sky. There is nothing in all this land to equal the scene. The opposite view up Loch Duich to the Five Sisters, with the castle in the foreground, is splendid enough in all conscience, but it can be matched in several of the great lochs down the Scottish seaboard. The view from Eilean Donan down Loch Alsh is an experience altogether different.

The present castle is a restoration built to the original plan. The ancient building was completely surrounded by water, but the new is linked to land by

Looking down Loch Affric from Glen Affric Lodge, which is situated on a promontory on the north shore of the loch. Spring comes slowly in the Highlands, and there is still snow in the corries as the trees begin to bud.

a causeway. The origins of the castle are prehistoric : it was once a vitrified fort. The first "modern" castle was built in the early thirteenth century by order of Alexander II as a defence against Norse invaders. Thereafter it belonged to the Mackenzie Lords of Kintail, for whom the clan MacRae provided Constables. It had a lively history in the days of clan feuds, but this came to an end in 1719. In that year a Jacobite rising was attempted, based on Spain. The ships were scattered by storm, but two made Kintail on 5th April. The Earl of Seaforth, Lord of Kintail, landed with some three hundred Spanish troops, and, hoping for reinforcements, occupied Eilean Donan. Rob Roy and his MacGregors joined the party. Three British warships sailed up the loch, bombarded the castle till the Spanish garrison surrendered, and then blew it up. On 10th June the rising was finally broken in a battle at Bridge of Shiel, when government troops dispersed the Highlanders and captured the Spanish. The ruined castle was finally restored in the period 1912-1932 by a descendant of the MacRaes, and is still occupied.

The best centre from which to explore Kintail, either as a traveller, climber, skier, walker, angler, or pony-trekker is Kintail Lodge Hotel at the head of Loch Duich. The hotel has the lease of salmon and sea-trout rights on the south bank of the river Croe, which flows down Glen Lichd, and can give information about brown trout fishing on hill lochs and burns, including Loch Cluanie, provide ponies for the angler and trekker, boats for either sea-fishing or sailing, and detailed information for mountaineers. On the river Shiel, salmon fishing may be adversely affected by netting at the mouth.

In the whole mountain area west of the Great Glen, Kintail is the most rewarding district for climbers. The head of Loch Duich is the strategic centre from which to get on to these hills : up Glen Choinneachan for the seven-mile ridge-walk along the crest of Beinn Attow; up Glen Lichd for the peaks of Glen Affric; up Glen Shiel for the Five Sisters, which in good weather must be traversed from east to west facing the Hebrides. Ascent is made from the site of the battle at Bridge of Shiel on to Sgurr na Spainteach, named after the unfortunate Spaniards. But the finest mountain in Kintail, both in distant shape and on close acquaintance, is the Saddle. Its summit ridges are narrow and notched, its corries have ice-worn rock, its flanks are precipitous. The actual summit is truly a saddle slung between two peaks of equal height.

In short, it is no impostor, but a true mountain. The most sporting route to the summit goes up the Sgurr na Forcan ridge, which is reached by way of the stalker's path south-east of Achnangart in Glen Shiel.

No visit to Kintail is complete without a visit to the Falls of Glomach, the highest in Britain. They lie to the south of upper Glen Elchaig on the Allt a Glomach, which flows into the river Elchaig at Loch na Leitreach. The easiest way of access is by car round Loch Duich and up to the head of Loch Long. If permission is gained to take the car up Glen Elchaig by the private road, one may drive straight to Loch na Leitreach, cross to the south bank of the Elchaig on stepping stones, and up the Glomach to the falls. The ravine is seven hundred and fifty feet high and the falls are three hundred and fifty feet. The first drop is three hundred feet sheer, then the water hits a rock and goes fifty feet more into the cauldron at the bottom. Unless one is a climber, prepared to accept some exposure in traversing a flank, it is impossible to see the falls in their entirety.

If the approach is made on foot from Loch Duich, the best route is from Croe Bridge north-eastward up the glen to the keeper's house at Dorusdain, where two

EILEAN DONAN CASTLE

Eilean Donan Castle, on Loch Duich, is an old Mackenzie stronghold which was badly damaged by an English warship in 1719, but was restored in 1932. The island is connected to the mainland by a bridge, but can be reached by the shore at low tide.

GLEN GARRY

Snow often causes severe hardship in the Highlands, but here it enhances the beauty of Loch Garry in Inverness-shire. The road leaves the Great Glen at Invergarry, climbs over the hills to Tomdoun and Cluanie Bridge, and finally reaches Kyle of Lochalsh and Kyle Akin.

Kyle of Lochalsh, a pretty little town, is the railway terminus and the centre of a district famous for its sea-lochs. The car ferry from Kyle of Lochalsh to Kyleakin is a popular way of going to Skye and it is a pleasant sail in summer, with fine views of Kyleakin and the Red Hills.

alternatives offer. One path climbs east under Ben Attow to the loch that feeds the Glomach. The subsequent line of descent is then clear and gives a dramatic view of the burn's abrupt plunge. The second path goes north through a forest of spruce and larch, then north-east over the Bealach na Sroine at 1,700 feet. The final drop to the falls is sharp. The most rewarding time to see, and hear, the falls is immediately after prolonged or heavy rain, when the burn roars down in spate. But in that event the approach by Glen Elchaig will grant no comfort of stepping stones over the river.

In our long journey through the West Highlands from Kintyre to Kintail, the variety and majesty of scene has steadily mounted even as the low hills of the south have grown in height stage by stage. In Kintail everything culminates. Nothing lacks. It is the epitome of the West Highland scene. And yet, down south around Cowal and Knapdale, by the little bays of Loch Fyne, or the Sound of Jura, or Lorne, the low hills and moors have the faded colours of a tapestry worn with age, though ageless in its delicate beauty. The scene is not inferior to that of the tumultuous north, it is simply very different. And these differences appear in every district, each appealing to men of different mind, even to the same mind in different mood. The conclusion is plain. We must learn to know and love them all, at all seasons if we can, in every kind of weather. The principal merit of this ideal is that our journeyings will have no end.

THE HEBRIDES

J. S. Grant

There are five hundred islands and islets off the west coast of Scotland, about eighty of them inhabited, some by only a single family or a changing population of lighthouse keepers. The land area of the Hebrides is 2,182 square miles, but that takes no account of the scatter : some of the islands are so small in relation to the sea distances between them that they ride out the winter storms like the little specks of dust we call the stars, rolling through empty space, light years apart.

From the Mull of Oa at the south-west tip of Islay to the Butt of Lewis covers nearly three degrees of latitude; and Barra Head is more than two degrees longitude from Shuna, a little island snugly land-locked in Loch Linnhe.

Beyond the Butt are the outliers of Rona and Sulisgeir which properly belong to the group, and forty miles west of Uist St. Kilda can be seen on a clear day heaving out of the ocean like a huge whale come up to blow on the far rim of the Atlantic. One might make a claim for the inclusion of Rockall, now that it has been formally seized by Britain—it certainly has its place in Hebridean story—but, even without Rockall, if we square off the limits of the Hebrides on a map, we enclose an area which would blanket most of England stretching from Dungeness almost to Robin Hood Bay, and from Morecambe back to the Needles.

In this vast area there are only 80,000 people, yet when the government first set up an authority to deal with the social and economic problems it was called, quite appropriately to its task, the Congested Districts Board. That is one of many paradoxes which confront us in the isles.

Because of the mountainous nature of so much of the area, the importance in days gone by of harbourage for fishing, and the comparative richness of the machairs for agriculture, the population is crowded into little pockets almost all on the coast, creating the contrasting, but still related, problems of congestion (in relation to natural resources) and isolation.

One might say that the islands are like a trayful of dishes which have crashed to the floor : the pieces are of all sizes and shapes, scattered at random over a wide area, and their essential characteristic is their fragmentation.

Few Hebrideans know the Hebrides. Each knows his own island and loves it with an intensity, almost a ferocity, which is not diminished by time or distance : but few know anything about the neighbouring islands. Each island is self-contained, self-sufficient, unique, and in so far as it cannot live to itself, the ties are with the mainland, not with the other islands.

Yet when islanders meet, be it in Glasgow or London, New York or Yokohama, they are conscious of a community of interest, resting mainly on the Gaelic language or, now that the tie of language is loosened somewhat, on Gaelic song.

The sense of belonging is naturally strong in an islander. The little patch of heather, hill and beach which claims him, or which he claims, is so well defined : there is no shading off. To leave an island is to lift one's roots, and the natural beauty of all the islands, the neighbourliness, the peace, the freedom for growing children to roam at will in pleasant surroundings, all intensify the nostalgia which the islander feels when he leaves home, as so many must, in search of work.

Each island has its own personality. It does not necessarily follow that to love one is to love all. There

The long, narrow island of Jura lies between Islay and Kintyre, and is separated from Scarba on the north by the tide race of Corrievreckan. The picture shows a characteristic scene in the chief village, Craighouse, looking north-west towards the Paps of Jura—Beinn Siantaidh ("hallowed mountain"), Beinn-a-Chaolais ("mountain of the strait") and the highest, Beinn-an-Oir ("mountain of gold") which is over 2,500 feet. The island, much of which is deer forest, is almost bisected by Loch Tarbert: to the north is the Ardlussa forest, to the south Jura forest. In spite of its beauty, Jura is rarely visited, for the population is declining and accommodation is scarce.

is no parallel in the outer islands, for instance, to the fantastic grandeur of the Cuillins of Skye and Rhum. Their beauty is in the beaches. The northern half of Lewis is a flat, rather featureless moor, and even the hills of Harris are quite different from those which beckon blue across the Minch in clear weather. The Cuillins are, geologically speaking, young—brash, up-thrusting volcanic peaks, still showing in the strangely contorted shapes which challenge the climber something of the exuberance of the forces which thrust them molten from the ocean bed. The hills elsewhere in the Western Isles are ancient, grey and weathered, rounded and tamed, but furrowed deeply by the moving ice, like a careworn face.

It is exhilarating to climb in summer sunshine or through winter snow "the dark wind-swept pinnacle" of Sgurr Alasdair in the Black Cuillin, and look like a conqueror on the myriad peaks and islands and lochans spread below. It is an experience of quite another quality to sail from North Uist to Benbecula on a quiet evening with a full tide, and lift one's eyes to the hills; or to cross the same brimming bowl of water into a November sunset when the sea, catching the colours of the sky, is like a crazy pavement made

IONA CATHEDRAL

In 1899 the Duke of Argyll presented the remains of Iona Cathedral to the Church of Scotland. Restoration was begun soon after, and under Dr. George MacLeod, the Iona Community undertook the work. The abbey was completed in 1959.

DUART CASTLE

Duart Castle on Mull, handsomely restored in 1912 after being confiscated following Culloden, is again the home of the Chief of Clan Maclean. It stands high on a headland on the easternmost tip of the island, facing Loch Linnhe and the Sound of Mull.

Another view of the Paps of Jura, this time looking east from Cable Bay on the island of Colonsay. Colonsay is named after St. Columba, and is noted for its rich pasture land; but like most of the Hebrides its population is declining. The picture shows a stretch of fine sand characteristic of Hebridean beaches, whose whiteness enhances the colours of the water and rocks.

Some fifteen miles south-west of Iona stands Dubh Artach lighthouse, on St. John's Rock. Construction of this lighthouse was made difficult by treacherous reefs.

from fragments of a rainbow. Even close neighbours like Islay and Jura are quite different. Islay is rich, flat farm land with a Lothian look about it, Jura is mountainous, lovely—and almost emptied of its folk.

Iona, in many ways, is the jewel of them all. Scotland's ancient Christian shrine and the burial place of kings, it is also a favourite haunt of artists trying to capture on a flat piece of canvas for a static moment the blue-green colour of the water, which is neither blue nor green but alive and in motion like the sea itself; a subtle ever-changing harmony played out by sunshine and shadow on the spectroscope. Since the war the "Friends of Iona" have raised more than £100,000, and most of the standing ruins of the medieval abbey precinct have been restored; but although the name of Iona is cherished in Hebridean song and story, and the Hebridean is a great traditionalist, those at home in the islands have little part, and even little interest, in the work of restoration, for Hebridean history is almost as fragmented as the landscape; the continuity of cultural life from indigenous roots has been broken by violent change or is languishing for lack of nourishment, although thin strands of memory still reach tenaciously into the past.

In the summer of 1953 an International Conference on Celtic Folklore was held in Stornoway. It was organised jointly by Glasgow University and the British Council and was attended by delegates from seventeen European universities ranging from Abo in the north to Pisa in the south.

At one of the sessions an elderly crofter from the village of Peninerine in South Uist recited for the delegates the well-known folk tale *Fear Na H-Eabaid* ("The Man with the Habit"). He told the story simply but dramatically, just as he must have told it many times in his home in Uist. When the recital was over, the delegates acclaimed him with enthusiasm as a master of the story-teller's art. One of the delegates described the story as belonging to the oldest literary tradition surviving in Western Europe, while another said, a little sadly, that he felt as if he had been present at the death-bed of a culture.

At the time of the conference Mr. Calum I. Maclean of the School of Scottish Studies estimated that there were still half a dozen in Scotland who could recite the old heroic tales, although none so well as Duncan Macdonald, the crofter from Uist. Macdonald has since died, but his genealogy was given at the conference as "Duncan, son of Donald, son of Duncan, son of John, son of Donald, son of Norman," and Norman was described as the son, or possibly the grandson, of the last who held the office of professional bard to the Macdonalds of Sleat when they held court in Duntulm Castle.

The musical tradition has survived the onslaught of compulsory English education much better than the oral but even there one can see the evidence of decay. At the same conference the complaint was made that the Mod—the national music festival of the Gael—while popularising Gaelic songs, is changing the essential quality of Gaelic singing.

"The intonation (*i.e.* of genuine Gaelic folk-singing) is something that always takes the unaccustomed ear by surprise," says Mr. Francis Collinson. "One's first impression is that it is merely singing out of tune; but it is an out-of-tuneness that is consistent, and is in fact a characteristic and constant modification of the intervals of the scale. When one gets used to it after hearing it continuously for several weeks in the Hebrides, and then returns to the mainland and the music of the concert room, it is the tempered scale of the pianoforte that takes getting used to, for it sounds quite insipid after the other."

The essential quality of Gaelic folksong has been missed in the Kennedy Fraser collection of *Songs of the Hebrides*. Mrs. Kennedy Fraser did a great work in making Hebridean music known and accessible, but her aim was not the scientifically accurate recording of the songs as sung; she assimilated them to the taste of non-Gaelic-speaking audiences. More accurate work has since been done by the School of Scottish Studies and private collectors like Margaret

Tobermory is an attractive little town near the north end of Mull. The Dukes of Argyll have frequently but unsuccessfully tried to salvage a Spanish galleon sunk in the bay.

St. Martin's Cross is one of two tenth-century Celtic crosses which stand intact on Iona. It is made of granite deeply carved with runic inscriptions and decorations.

Fay Shaw, whose recent book of songs and folk traditions of South Uist is worthy of a place with Carmichael's *Carmina Gadelica*.

In the Catholic islands, notably South Uist and Barra, the songs and the oral tradition have been better preserved than in the Protestant islands, but there are still many good singers in the traditional manner to be heard in all the islands, and the singing in the churches has a strange, undisciplined, elemental quality, mournful but exciting, with a rhythm that seems to owe more to the sea than to conscious art; and, although the Gaelic of everyday speech is becoming thin and debased with many English and even American intrusions, it remains the language of the people: in the Outer Hebrides, at least, the majority of children speak no English until they go to school. Most islanders are genuinely and fluently bi-lingual. Gaelic is the language of the nursery, the playground, courtship and the church; English is spoken in the class-room, and is used for official business and almost exclusively for correspondence. The balance between Gaelic and English varies from district to district; in some English predominates. Generally speaking, as the result of an educational

FINGAL'S CAVE, STAFFA

The island of Staffa is uninhabited but its unusual columnar rock formation evokes keen interest among tourists. Each summer many make the trip by steamer to view Fingal's Cave, which has a strange grandeur that is echoed in Mendelssohn's "Hebridean Overture".

SCARINISH HARBOUR, TIREE

Scarinish is a sheltered harbour on the east side of the low and windswept island of Tiree, which is separated from Coll by the Sound of Gunna. Tied up at the quay is a "puffer", that universal load-carrier of the islands made famous by writer Neil Munro. Tiree is the most fertile of the Islands: in addition to the traditional farming, there is a bulb-growing industry.

Looking north-west from Ardtoe, in the north of Ardnamurchan, towards Eigg, Rhum, and the Point of Sleat. Fine sandy bays and secluded bathing spots make Ardnamurchan an ideal holiday area when one wants to forget the world and be forgotten by it.

Sheep graze above Canna harbour: a peaceful scene typical of the Western Isles. In the background are Sanday and Rhum.

system which set out originally to "extirpate" Gaelic and has come only tardily and grudgingly to recognise its value, Gaelic has become the oral and English the written language. Many islanders still leave the schools practically illiterate in their mother tongue.

Gaelic is living but languishing. Fortunately, Scotland is at last awakening to the importance of recovering what remains of a great oral and musical folk-culture, although it is doubtful whether the language will regain the lost ground, or indeed resist the process of disintegration from within, which is all too evident in the impoverished vocabulary of every-day speech.

The outlying islands no longer have an indigenous population. St. Kilda was abandoned in 1930, but is now temporarily re-occupied by the services in connection with the Uist rocket range. Rona lost its population in 1844 and has not since been occupied except by two rather eccentric Lewismen who lived there as hermits because of a religious dispute at home, and finally died of exposure and exhaustion. Sulisgeir has never been permanently inhabited so far as is known—in winter the great Atlantic breakers sweep across it in parts from side to side—but it is visited annually in the autumn by fishermen from Ness who kill and salt the young of the solan goose, or "guga", a local delicacy, and each night, before they bed down in the cave-like stone shelters which have existed there for unknown centuries, the sound of the Gaelic psalms sung in traditional fashion with a precentor "throwing out the line" mingles with the cry of the seabirds. There is one rough bothy on the island spoken of as a "temple", although it seems inconceivable that even the Celtic church could ever have had an outpost in so desolate a spot.

All of these islands are now nature reserves and have their few but faithful visitors, their devotees. The grey Atlantic seal, the majestic solan, the puffin, the fulmar, Leach's fork-tailed petrel (the tiny bird which comes to land from its ocean journeys only in the darkness), the primitive Soay sheep, the St. Kilda variants of the wren and the mouse, all have their interest for the naturalist, and for the historian and archaeologist each island (with the doubtful exception of Sulisgeir) can provide evidence of the work of the missionaries of the Celtic church, spreading outwards in their frail coracles from Iona to the last inhabitable limits of the land.

In contrast with these small, remote and now almost completely desolate outposts, Lewis, Skye and Mull are all greater in extent than the Isle of Man and carry quite large populations by Highland standards. Lewis with Harris—"which two although they ioyne be a necke of land ar accounted dyvers Ylands"—is the largest of the islands round the British coast, with an area of nearly 800 square miles, and a population of 27,000 in nearly 150 crofting villages and in the town of Stornoway, which, with its 5000 inhabitants, is the only burgh in the Hebrides.

Stornoway was granted a royal charter by Charles I, but it was withdrawn without ever being effective, on the representations of Inverness and other mainland burghs whose people feared that the little island seaport, close by the rich fishings of the Minch, would put them out of business if granted the privilege of foreign trade. Stornoway has since had to be content with the status of a burgh of barony. Nevertheless, until the end of the Second World War it ranked third among Scotland's herring ports in the annual value of the catch. Stornoway's fish trade is now sadly diminished, although efforts are being made to revive it, but in the period of decline the townspeople and the crofters have built up a valuable trade in Harris Tweed, of which they produce about six million yards a year, much of it for export.

Although it is much the largest centre of population, Stornoway is in no sense the capital of the Hebrides. It is not even the capital of Harris, or properly speaking of Lewis itself. Lewis forms part of Ross-shire and the county town is Dingwall, from which it is separated by the full width of Scotland and the Minch. Harris, the Uists, Barra, Skye and the smaller islands of Rhum, Muck, Eigg and Canna are administered from Inverness. The other islands form part of Argyllshire, of which the county headquarters are in Lochgilphead, but which is so scattered and irregular in its topography that the most convenient geographi-

Portree, where Prince Charles bade farewell to Flora Macdonald in 1746, is the port for Skye's steamer traffic and fishing fleet.

Dunvegan Castle, ancient home of the MacLeod of MacLeod, displays styles of architecture ranging from the fifteenth to the nineteenth century.

We look from Elgol north-west across Loch Scavaig towards the great arc of the Cuillins round Loch Coruisk. Gars Bheinn is the pointed peak, then Sgurr nan Eag and Sgurr Alasdair, with Sgurr nan Gillean on the east and Sgurr na Stri in front.

THE CUILLINS FROM ELGOL

cal centre lies outside the county altogether in the city of Glasgow.

Islanders generally feel that the development of their social services has been hampered by the fact that they are appendages—often inconvenient and inaccessible appendages—of mainland counties, but it would be impossible to treat them as a unit, or even two or three units, to make counties of their own. The difficulties of administration are inevitable, they inhere in the facts of geography. In recent years relations between the mainland majorities and the island minorities have improved, and much of the leeway in roads and other services has been made good, but the period of what has sometimes been described as "colonial" administration of the islands has left is mark—most notably, perhaps, on the islanders' temperament.

The islands did form a coherent political unit in the days of the *birlinn* and the galley. Indeed it wasn't until the coming of the railway that they really fell apart. With a well-found boat and a few stout oarsmen it was easier, until comparatively recent times, to go from island to island of the Hebrides than from township to township through the interior of the Highlands. In the days of the Lordship of the Isles, the Hebrides had sufficient political power to rock the Scottish throne. Prior to the battle of Largs in 1263, the Hebrides belonged to Norway, and the long Viking occupation is still attested by many of the place-names, and in some areas by the physical characteristics of the people.

During the Lordship of the Isles, the dominant chiefs were the Macdonalds of Islay, the southernmost island of the group and one of the richest agriculturally, but it is in Skye that the clan tradition now survives most effectively. Dame Flora Macleod of Macleod has made Dunvegan Castle, with its fairy flag and its celebrated drinking horn, a place of pilgrimage for Macleods from all over the world. Sir Charles Maclean, in the same way, entertains Macleans from overseas at the family seat at Duart in Mull, and Macneil of Barra, an American by birth and an architect by profession, has restored part of Kismul Castle in Barra as a similar rallying point for the Macneils.

The ambivalence of the old clan system under which the chief might be a ruthless tyrant but was still a kinsman of his followers is reflected in the crofting system. The croft has been described as a small piece of land surrounded by regulations, a witticism which has this to justify it: the croft is an artificial creation of the lawyers to approximate as near as may be to the loose, ill-defined tenure which existed when a feudal hierarchy of individuals

St. Kilda lies forty-five miles west of North Uist. In 1930 the thirty-five inhabitants were evacuated, mostly to Lochaline in Morven, and the island was abandoned to half-wild Soay sheep. The picture shows Village Bay and the eastern coastal strip, with ruined cottages, a sandy beach, and a storm beach. Behind are the slopes of Conachair and Oisewal, dotted with "cleits"—dry stone cells once used as stores.

holding land by charter from superiors was superimposed on the native tradition that the land belonged to the clan, not to the chief.

The crofter is generally the tenant of his land, but the owner of his house. If he gives up the tenancy of his croft he can call on the landlord to compensate him for any permanent improvements which he has carried out, of which the house is generally the most important. In the event of disagreement the compensation is assessed by the Scottish Land Court.

If a crofter pays his rent and keeps his land in cultivation, he cannot be removed by his landlord, however long the notice given him. His rent cannot be arbitrarily raised, none of his privileges can be taken away and, within wide limits, he has the right to nominate his successor, irrespective of the landlord's wishes.

The rigidity of the crofting system, however, led to anomalies, the most serious being that many crofts fell into the hands of absentees who had no continuing interest in them or at best wished merely to keep the croft house as a summer home, or a place to retire to at some indefinite date in the future. The misuse and neglect of land which this entailed was more serious in a crofting township than in ordinary farming, because the crofter conducts many of his agricultural operations communally and, when land is held by absentees, an undue burden falls on the active men remaining in the township.

In 1955 Parliament set up a Commission for the reorganisation, development and regulation of crofting, armed with power to dispossess absentees where that is in the interests of the township.

The Scottish Land Court still has jurisdiction in many matters of dispute arising between landlord and crofter, or between individual crofters or groups of crofters. The questions which arise most frequently in the Land Court concern the boundaries between crofts, rights of way, applications by landlords for the resumption (i.e. the removal from crofting tenure) of land for public purposes, and disputes about peat banks.

In the old days boundaries were marked by making a fire, placing a large stone on the ashes to prevent them being dispersed, and whipping the youngest boys from the villages concerned beside the stone. The theory was that the thrashing would help the lads to remember the spot and the ashes would confirm their recollection. That picturesque custom is long since dead, but even today, when township boundaries are disputed the crofters sometimes maintain that, if one digs in the correct spot, the ancient fire marks can be found.

The crofter generally has a small piece of arable

land near his dwelling which he cultivates as an individual, although there are still many "open" townships where the gates are taken off in winter and the stock have the free range of everything. Besides his individual holding he generally has a share in the common grazings of the township, and possibly a share in hill grazings held by a group of townships. The extent of his share in these pastures is regulated by the "souming", that is the number of cattle, sheep and horses which they can carry. Each croft has a stipulated share in the "souming" related to the rental. The crofter also has the right to cut peats.

Most townships have a grazings committee elected every three years, which has the power, among other things, to fix the date on which the sheep must be moved from the in-bye land to the hills, the allocation of peat banks, the requisitioning of labour, or the fixing of levies for communal tasks like fencing or building a sheep fank.

There is a tendency towards the amalgamation of crofts to make larger units and also towards the apportioning of grazings and common *machairs* in individual shares so that the crofter becomes in effect a small farmer, but most crofting villages still function communally for many purposes, and many crofters are still only part-time agriculturalists.

At Daliburgh in South Uist, for example, ten townships still share a common *machair* of which a portion is cultivated each year while the remainder is rested and grazed. The unfenced fields to be cultivated each year are chosen by the grazings committee, but strips are balloted for and change hands annually. As some of the crofters sub-let their *machair* shares to others it may happen that one crofter holds half a dozen long narrow strips in different parts of the *machair*. This system ensures fair shares for all, but the obstacles it raises in the way of efficient agriculture are obvious.

The Crofters' Commission operates a scheme of cropping grants and improvement grants, both designed to raise the standard of agriculture and in particular to encourage the growing of good grass pasture, for which the climate is ideally suited. One of the most hopeful features of the crofting scene at the moment is the enthusiasm with which individual crofters and township committees in some of the islands have taken up the new technique of surface seeding to create pasture on peat bogs or skinned land (*i.e.* land from which the peat has been removed down to the underlying clay).

Another promising development in crofting agriculture is the creation of a bulb-growing industry, pioneered in Tiree by the West of Scotland College of Agriculture. The bulbs are sold to commercial growers, mainly in Lanarkshire, and forced for the

A woman spins fine yarn at Port-nan-Long, in Skye. Behind is an old "black house", once used as a dwelling-house.

Almost all the spinning is now done in mills, but the weaving is still hired out to crofters, who return their work for checking and "darning".

spring flower market. The Hebridean *machairs* are deservedly famous for the profusion of wild flowers, but the bulb industry is introducing a new and welcome splash of colour into quite a number of the crofting villages.

Tiree, once the granary of Iona, has long been celebrated in the Hebrides for its fertility and its sunshine, but when the meteorologists discovered Tiree "officially", within the last thirty years or so, they were most reluctant to accept the fact that in May the sunniest part of the British Isles is not the south-east coast of England, as they had always supposed, but Tiree and some of the neighbouring islands in the Inner and Outer Hebrides. Over many years the sunshine recorded at Tiree has exceeded eight hours per day throughout May, and has been just under eight in June.

The Hebrides have the reputation of being cold, wet, and windy, mainly because visitors come at the wrong season. The wind is indubitable—at the Butt of Lewis gales are recorded on average for twelve hours a day throughout January—but from November to March the Hebrides are warmer than London,

BLAVEN HILLS, SKYE

Between the Cuillins and Loch Slapin, at the head of the Strathaird peninsula, rise the famous Blaven Hills. Blaven itself is over 3000 feet, Garbh-Bheinn, to the north, is a little less. The snow shows up the peculiar serrations in the grey-green hypersthene rock.

An island steamer calls at Castlebay, in Barra, the most southerly port in the Outer Isles. Behind stands Kismul Castle, the twelfth-century seat of the Macneil of Barra, which was restored in 1956-57. Barra is famous for its fine beach, which is used as an airfield.

prolonged snow is unusual and fog is almost unknown. On some of the outlying Atlantic islands, like Heisker off the coast of North Uist, cattle can be outwintered without artificial shelter or hand feeding.

The central problem of the Hebrides is the provision of wage-earning employment alternative or ancillary to agriculture. In the past, crofting and fishing supplemented each other. In some islands agriculture predominated, in others fishing, but generally the two were dovetailed on a seasonal basis. The Hebrides have now almost completely lost their foothold in the fishing industry, except to a small extent in lobster fishing. Attempts are being made to establish a local fleet of modern boats—an uphill task, because it requires the re-establishment in a new form of a broken tradition, in an area short of capital and distant from the markets. Even if the attempt succeeds, as it seems likely to in a modest way, the industry must be concentrated on one or two of the better ports, working into mainland markets, and dissociated completely from agriculture.

Forestry is a useful ancillary in Skye, Mull, and some of the other islands in the inner group, but it will not help the Outer Hebrides, or any of the smaller islands.

The weaving of Harris Tweed has proved an ideal partner for crofting, and provides much employment in Lewis, Harris and South Uist, and a smaller amount in some of the other islands of the Outer Hebrides. While the spinning and marketing side of the industry has been concentrated, the weaving is still carried out at the homes of the people.

In Skye the tourist industry has become more important than agriculture, but it is more difficult to establish in the islands beyond ferry reach of the mainland where there is no stream of passing traffic to encourage the crofter to put up his "bed and breakfast" sign. The opportunities are unlimited, for the islands have so much to offer with their beaches and

On the left is the puffin, the clown of the island birds; on the right the fulmar, particularly common on North Rona.

Stornoway, on the east coast of Lewis, is the largest town in Ross. The harbour used to be crowded with fishing boats, but now only a few can be seen, huddled against the quay. Even the tweed industry has been badly hit by a government tax. But the castle on the left of the picture is now a fine, modern technical college.

machairs, their hills, their brown trout fishing and sea fishing, their interest for the naturalist and the photographer, and indeed for anyone who places a value on peace and pure fresh air, but capital and business skill are lacking.

Access to some of the islands remains difficult, but the aeroplane has brought others into closer touch with Glasgow, Inverness, and London than many places much nearer these centres in terms of distance. Lewis, Benbecula, Tiree and Islay all have modern airports, and at Barra planes land safely and regularly on the cockle strand. Barra must have one of the few airports in the world where the movement of traffic is dependent on the tide. It is a lovely island, hospitable and interesting, less than two hours journey from Glasgow, and offering the visitor almost everything in the way of peace, beauty and purity of air which the city lacks.

The problems of the islands have been increased in many ways by recent social legislation. The lot of the old and the needy has been eased, but the young must have steady wages to meet their weekly "stamp", with the result that many are compelled to leave home in search of work, and there are many townships with few young men at home between the ages of eighteen and forty. Some of the smaller islands have been evacuated in recent years, others may be unless they are taken over by people seeking solitude for its own sake, and the maintenance of the population at a viable level will be difficult even in some of the larger islands. In theory a reduction in population should help to restore a balance between the natural resources and the families dependent on them, but it does not work that way. Migration is selective; it takes the young and leaves the old and, in any event, the smaller the population becomes the more difficult it is to maintain the essential services without which there may be a complete collapse.

But even the problems are part of the interest: life in the islands offers a perpetual challenge, and there are many compensations for the inevitable isolation.

THE NORTH

Seton Gordon

MY task in writing on "The North" is not an easy one. Inverness, on my southern boundary, is often called the Capital of the Highlands, while Shetland has historic associations with Norway rather than with Scotland. Many people, even in Scotland, are unaware that a native of Shetland (or of Orkney too, for that matter) would be as little pleased to be called a Highlander as a citizen of Edinburgh would be to be called an Englishman. Neither Shetland nor Orkney, nor the county of Caithness, except for its borders, are Highland. This is clearly seen in the place-names, which are almost all of Norse origin. I may almost be said to be writing of two countries. For centuries, Norsemen and Celts contended here in relentless strife, and in the Norse sagas, which are still in existence, the bravery, and sometimes the treachery, of those who fought can be read by all.

We will suppose that the traveller to the north begins his journey at Inverness, which is considered to be the capital of the Highlands. It occupies an attractive position on the banks of the Ness, a river which has never been known to freeze.

The castle of Inverness has associations with the Lords of the Isles and, at a later date, with the great Montrose. It was for a time the headquarters of the Government troops under the Earl of Loudon in the Jacobite rising of 1745, and it was from Inverness in February of the year 1746 that these troops set out for Moy Hall to attempt to capture Prince Charles Edward. Just a hundred years earlier, Montrose had been led captive, a prisoner on horseback, through the streets of Inverness. He had been betrayed while in hiding in the wilds of Sutherland and had aroused the admiration of the inhabitants of Inverness by his dignity and nobility of bearing, although he was seriously ill. When Cromwell's troops occupied Inverness, a few years later, a frigate with four pieces of cannon was built in the town and was dragged overland to Loch Ness, which she patrolled to overawe the inhabitants of the district. Shipbuilding, indeed, must have been an old-established trade in Inverness long before Cromwell's time, for it is said that a vessel built there in 1087, called *Wonderful Ship* became the flagship of the Viennese navy.

The county families of the north-west Highlands at one time had their town houses in Inverness, where they were accustomed to spend the winter. The Northern Meeting at Inverness, which consists sometimes of two balls and two days of piping, has for long been a leading event of the social year in the northern Highlands.

The traveller's way would take him along the shore of the Beauly Firth and he would pass near, but scarcely in sight of, Beaufort Castle, the seat of Lord Lovat. One might be surprised to find this medieval French name in the Highlands. It is Beau Lieu, Beautiful Place, and was named by the Vallis Caulium monks as long ago as 1232. In that year the monks founded a priory here. The patronymic of the Frasers of Lovat is MacShimi, that is, the Son of Simon. The barony of Lovat dates from the early fifteenth century; the second Lord Lovat married a sister of David Wemyss of Wemyss. When Prince Charles Edward Stuart landed to claim the throne of his fathers, the Lord Lovat of the day made his cause with him. After the failure of the rising he was a fugitive on an island of Loch Morar in the west. He was beheaded in 1747, and it is believed that he was the last man to

GLEN STRATHFARRAR

The River Farrar rises in the West Monar Forest above Loch Carron on the west coast; with the River Glass it becomes the Beauly, and flows into the Beauly Firth on the east coast. It forms three lochs on the way, and the mountains on either side rise over 3000 feet. It also provides some of the best salmon fishing in Scotland: here we see a fine stretch in Glen Strathfarrar.

GLEN AFFRIC

Loch Affric lies to the south-west of Loch Beneveian, and the waters from both lochs flow towards the Beauly Firth by the River Affric, Strathglass, and the Beauly itself. The name "Affric" is said to be derived from the Gaelic for "greyish water": in spite of the effects of a hydro-electric scheme, its variety of colours and shades make it one of Scotland's most beautiful lochs.

die by the axe in the Tower of London. The present holder of the title had a most distinguished record in the Second World War, and is one of the best known figures in the Highlands.

The river Beauly, which enters the firth near Beaufort Castle, passes on its tortuous course from the high hills far to the west. The rivers Farrar and Glass feed it. Despite great hydro-electric works this remains a lonely and unspoilt country.

Still keeping to the main north road along the coast, the traveller reaches the town of Dingwall. This name is almost pure Norse, and is the same as Thingvallir in Iceland, where the open-air parliament is, or was until recently, held. It means "field of assembly", and was therefore the seat of Norse administration in the county of Ross. It is not without interest that Dingwall is almost the most southerly Norse name in this part of Scotland, the most southerly being Eskadale near the River Beauly which, according to that great Celtic scholar Professor W. J. Watson, is from old Norse *eskidalr*, the "ash dale."

As one travels north from Inverness to Dingwall the great bulk of Ben Wyvis (3,429 feet) rises on the

There are few towns where one can catch salmon while standing in a main street, but it can be done in Inverness, as the River Ness flows through the centre of the town. This picture shows some of the many spires and fine modern buildings; on the right is Inverness Castle, built on the site of an old stronghold and now accommodating the county offices and law courts.

horizon ahead. The name Ben Wyvis is the anglicised form of Beinn Uais, from an old Celtic word, *uas*, meaning "noble." The great ancestor of the Macdonalds was Colla Uas, or Noble Coll. The ancient owners of the hill, the Munros of Foulis, have for centuries held their lands on condition that they are able to supply a bucket of snow to the King or Queen of Scotland at the Palace of Holyroodhouse on Midsummer Day, if called upon to do so. This they are able to do with ease, since there is always a certain amount of old snow on Ben Wyvis in June. One might imagine that the golden eagle and ptarmigan are to be seen high on Ben Wyvis, but the great assembly of swifts I found here one Midsummer Day was unexpected. In fine weather insects rise high, and the swifts follow them. As I crossed the broad summit ridge of Ben Wyvis, swifts in scores, and perhaps in hundreds, were my companions. Some of them were flying so low that I looked down at them as they passed at the speed of an express train; they wheeled, banked, and glided—and then were gone—perhaps to Dingwall far beneath, where they nest.

From Dingwall a road leads west to Achnasheen, where its branch to the right takes the traveller to Loch Maree, Torridon and the north-west seaboard. Loch Maree, a majestic loch, is named after Saint Maelruba; he died in the year 721 and his grave is at Applecross, looking out on to Raasay and the hills of Skye. The old name of the loch was Loch Ewe and the hamlet of Kinlochewe stands at the head of the loch. Eilean Maruighe, Isle of Maree, a small island on the loch, has sacred associations with the saint. This isle was, even in the days of the Druids, a sacred place, and ancient oaks, symbols of Druidic worship, grew here. It is said that Saint Maelruba introduced the Christian holly as a rival to the pagan oak on this small island. The Wishing Tree on the island was a sacred tree which grew near the holy well. It was customary to wish one's wish at the well and then place an offering, usually a coin, in the bark of the tree. Queen Victoria visited the island and the tree in September, 1877. She read a short sermon (the day being Sunday) to those who had rowed her out, and fixed her coin to the Wishing Tree, no doubt at the same time wishing her wish. The Wishing Tree, an oak, was still alive in Queen

Victoria's day, but has long been lifeless. Its death may have been hastened by the treatment it received from human hands. Hundreds of nails were driven into it by those who had bathed themselves with water from the holy well. These nails originally had attached to them a fragment of clothing belonging to the sufferer. The coins, driven edgeways into the bark of the tree with strong blows, are also witnesses of offerings, some dating from the distant past.

If, as seems probable, Isle Maree has associations with the pre-Christian past in its Druidic rites, it occupies a distinctive place in Highland history. A relic of those rites seems to have been practised on the isle long after Saint Maelruba's time. Before telling of these rites, may I quote from *A Voyage to the Hebrides*, by the distinguished traveller and naturalist, Thomas Pennant? Pennant landed on Isle Maree, or Inch Maree as he calls it, on August 2nd, 1772, just 105 years before the visit of Queen Victoria.

> "Land on Inch-Maree, the favored isle of the saint, the patron of all the coast from Applecross to Lochbroom. The shores are neat and gravelly; the whole surface covered thickly with a beautiful grove of oak, ash, willow, wicken, birch, fir, hazel, and enormous hollies. In the midst is a circular dike of stones, with a regular narrow entrance; the inner part has been used for ages as a burial place, and is still in use. I suspect the dike to have been originally Druidical, and that the ancient superstition of Paganism had been taken up by the saint, as the readiest method of making a conquest over the minds of the inhabitants. A stump of a tree is shown as an altar, probably the memorial of one of stone; but the curiosity of the place is the well of the saint; of power unspeakable in cases of lunacy. The patient is brought into the sacred island, is made to kneel before the altar, where his attendants leave an offering in money : he is then brought to the well, and sips some of the holy water : a second offering is made; that done, he is thrice dipped in the lake. The same operation is repeated every day for some weeks : and it often happens, by natural causes, the patient receives relief, of which the saint receives the credit.
>
> I must add, that the visitants draw from the state of the well an omen of the disposition of St. Maree. If his well is full, they suppose he will be propitious; if not, they proceed in their operations with fears and doubts : but let the event be what it will, he is held in high esteem. The common oath of the country is, by his name : if a traveller passes by any of his resting-places, they never neglect to leave an offering, but the saint is so moderate as not to put him to any expense.
>
> A stone, a stick, a bit of rag contents him."

Gairloch, at the head of a sea-loch with the same name, is a scattered hamlet in Ross-shire. Its fine sands are backed by the hills of Flowerdale Forest.

A remarkable relic of the pagan rites practised on Isle Maree long before the time of Saint Maelruba is related in the Minutes of the Presbytery of Dingwall in the year 1656. One of the last records of the Presbytery is as follows;

> "At Dingwall, 6 August 1678.
> That day Mr. Roderick Mackenzie, minister at Gerloch by his letter to the prebrie, declared that he had summoned by his officer to this prebrie day Hector Mackenzie in Mellan in the parish of Gerloch, as also Johne Murdoch, and Duncan Mackenzies, sons to the said Hector—as also Kenneth McKenzie his grandson, for sacrificing a bull in ane heathenish manner in the iland of St. Ruffus, commonly called Eilan Moury in Lochew, for the recovering of the health of Cirstane Mackenzie, spouse to the said Hector Mackenzie, who was formerlie sicke and valetudinairie."

This record, in comparatively recent times, of a pagan rite in the Scottish Highlands is unexpected. The names of some of the delinquents summoned two years before to appear before the Presbytery at Dingwall are worth quoting, as showing the Gaelic patronymics of those days—*Donald McConill chile* (Donald, son of Donald of the Church), *Murdo McFerqure vic Conill Eire* (Murdo MacFarquhar, son of Donald from Ireland), *Duncan McConill uayne vic Conill biy* (Duncan, son of green Donald son of yellow Donald), *Murdo Mceaine voire vic Eaine ghlaiss* (Murdo, son of great John, son of grey John). These names bring vividly

before the mind the old Highland way of life, where the modern surname as we understand it was unknown. This old custom is still adhered to in some of the more remote districts of the West Highlands and the Hebrides.

The river Ewe empties the overflow waters of Loch Maree into salt-water Loch Ewe. Gairloch (Gaelic *Gearr Loch,* the Short Loch) is the ancestral home of the MacKenzies of Gairloch, whose hereditary pipers, the Mackays, in the seventeenth and eighteenth century were almost as celebrated as the MacCrimmons of Skye. The Mackay pipers came from Sutherland. The first of the family, Ruairidh, came to Gairloch in a curious manner. The chief of the Sutherland Mackays was on his way south to visit the laird of Gairloch. At the ferry at the Kyle of Sutherland a dispute arose between Mackay and his followers and another party as to who had priority of crossing. Ruairidh Mackay, a lad of seventeen, cut off the hand of a groom who endeavoured to impede his chief. Because of this deed, Ruairidh had to flee from Sutherland, and MacKenzie of Gairloch asked him to be his piper. He continued to be piper to the

LOCH CARRON

This quiet bay is near Plockton at the mouth of Loch Carron. Plockton is a favoured retreat of those who like a peaceful holiday, and Loch Carron, a sea-loch opening on the Sound of Skye between Loch Alsh and the Forest of Applecross, stretches far inland among the mountains.

LOCH COULIN

Loch Coulin is lovely but inaccessible. It lies to the north of Glen Carron, and is joined by Loch Clair to Glen Torridon. The picture looks south-west across the loch towards Coulin Lodge and the slopes of Ben Eiath Mhor, which is over 3000 feet. As often happens in the Highlands, the snow contrasts with greens and browns, and the beauty of the scene is enhanced by reflection in the loch.

Across Loch Clair the bulk of Liathach's 3,456 feet is easily recognisable. Its sandstone strata are typical of the geological formations of the area, but it is oddly capped with quartzite.

The road between Kinlochewe and Torridon provides this vista of Beinn Eighe, which lies in the 10,450 acres of the Nature Reserve now well established in Wester Ross.

lairds of Gairloch for eighty years. He was over sixty when his only son, Iain, was born, he who become known as Iain Dall ("Blind John") or Am Piobair Dall ("The Blind Piper") because when he was only seven years old he lost his sight through smallpox. He became a piper of renown. He was early sent to the MacCrimmon College of Piping at Dunvegan in Skye. The pupils of the college, jealous of the Blind Piper's skill, planned to kill him.

They chased him over a rock, where he fell between twenty and thirty feet, but he escaped serious injury. The marks in the ground said to have been made by his feet I have been shown near the College of Piping, or rather its ruins. Iain Dall was piper to the first baronet of Gairloch, Sir Kenneth MacKenzie. He was a gifted personality, and had the rare distinction of combining the office of bard with that of piper; his fame as a poet was almost as great as his renown as a piper. He died at the age of ninety and his only son Angus succeeded him as MacKenzie's hereditary piper. A great competition was arranged in Edinburgh, and it was expected that Angus would win. There was always jealousy among pipers, as among other musicians, and just before the competition one or more of his rivals pierced the bag of his pipe with their knives. A friend named Mary came to his assistance and found him an undressed sheepskin which, working against time through the night, he fashioned into a bag for his pipes. Next day he won the big competition, and later composed the well-known pibroch *Moladh Mairi* or "Mary's Praise for her Gift". The last of these great Gairloch pipers was John, son of Angus. He had a numerous family, and decided that there would be a better future for them if he and his wife emigrated to America, thus ending a long and honoured association.

The coast road from Loch Maree to the north-west passes Gairloch and soon reaches the celebrated gardens of Inverewe, now in the care of the National Trust for Scotland. These gardens are a memorial to a remarkable Highlander, Osgood MacKenzie of Inverewe, whose daughter Mairi Sawyer carried on his good work. Osgood MacKenzie, who spoke the Gaelic and wore always the Highland dress, was a courtly figure, and is still known to the public because of his classic *A Hundred Years in the Highlands*. In his garden at Inverewe are to be seen tropical trees and shrubs and, in the early summer, a magnificent show of azaleas and rhododendrons. The coast road winds, by broad bay and narrow sea loch, northward along the seaboard. The crofters here still live the hard way; their fields are small, their fuel is peat, their language the Gaelic.

Far across the Minch is the long outline of the island of Lewis. South are the Torridon giants, and from the higher ground the Cuillins of Skye are to be seen. I remember one June day sailing up the coast here, some distance off-shore. It had been an exceptionally cold spring, and the Cuillins even in June had great snow-fields in their corries. As the twilight of evening approached, and we steamed northwards at twelve knots, the high Cuillins on the far horizon became almost nebulous. The greatest snow-field was in the corrie of Bruach na Frithe : only a few days earlier I had walked across it and had seen its depth and extent, and had heard the loud hill stream of snow water which emerged from it. I was thus able to take an intimate interest in that distant view. As grey clouds of night formed above the hill the snow took on the greyness of mist, and I found myself

Inverewe House is surrounded by the two thousand acres of the famous sub-tropical gardens, which now belong to the National Trust. The gardens were designed by Osgood MacKenzie in 1862, and are remarkable for the wide variety of strange and lovely plants which flourish in the open and attract gardening experts and enthusiasts from all over the world.

recalling a similar view years before on the coast of Norway, this time of the snow-splashed hills of the Lofoten Isles, where the white-tailed eagle, now extinct in the Scottish Highlands, nests to this day and takes its toll of the fish of the ocean. I remember that I told the skipper of the *Virginia* that perhaps only once in a lifetime would he see the Cuillin so deep in snow in the month of June.

Travelling north by sea along the north-west coast is so much more direct than by land that the slowest steamer or yacht could make a faster passage than the highest-powered car. The road, after leaving Poolewe and the gardens of Inverewe, skirts Aultbea and, on the shore of Gruinard Bay, passes townships with strange names, like Laide, First Coast, and Second Coast. The word Gruinard is Norse, and in its original form is *Grunna Fjord*, ("Shallow Fjord"). Beyond Gruinard Bay the road, after passing over higher ground, keeps close to Little Loch Broom. Here the great hill, An Teallach, dominates the view. The name An Teallach is an unusual one : it means "The Forge." It may be that the grey mists which so often form and eddy here gave it the name, from their fancied resemblance to the smoke rising from a forge. It is a splendid hill of 3,483 feet, with several peaks, one of which bears the name Spidean a' Ghlas Tuill ("Pinnacle of the Green Hollow"). Beyond the lochs which lie north-west of the hill is Carn na Beiste ("Cairn of the Monster"). At the foot of An Teallach, to the south, is a long and narrow loch, four miles in length. This is Loch na Sealg ("Loch of the Hunts") into which Strath na Sealg leads. The name shows that the district in old times was celebrated for its hunting; perhaps the red deer was the quarry.

The north promontory at the entrance to Little Loch Broom is Sron na Caillich; near it is Bodach a' Chleirich ("The Cleric's Carl"). Here, at Scoraig, is one of the most isolated communities of the north-west coast. The road now for a time leaves the coast and takes an easterly course, reaching an elevation of 1,100 feet. Here it passes near a hill loch named Lochaidh Bhraoin. This loch evidently gives the name to Loch Broom (and Little Loch Broom also), because we find in the year 1275 Loch Broom spelled "Lochbraon". Near the hill loch is the supposed site of a fifteenth-century clan fight, in which the Munros participated. In tradition its name is the

Battle of Bealach nam Brog, and the pibroch or classical pipe tune associated with it is considered to be one of the oldest in existence. Bending towards the north once more, the road, at Braemore, descends to Loch Broom by way of Strath Mor. Near Braemore the river Broom flows at the bottom of a deep chasm named Corryhalloch. The waterfall here is magnificent in times of flood. A range of splendid hills rise to the east. The highest, Beinn Dearg ("The Red Hill") is 3,547 feet high, and in its east-facing corrie is a snow-field which sometimes remains throughout the year. A neighbouring peak bears the romantic name Sgurr Eididh nan Clach Geala ("Peak of the Garment of White Stones"). The name arose because of the stones of white quartz on the hill. It used to be said, I think truly, that a likely place for Cairngorm stones (amber-coloured quartz crystals) is where a vein of white quartz disappears beneath the surface of the ground, and one sometimes finds signs of early digging here.

I recall that while I was fishing on the river Broom for elusive salmon one early summer day I saw a stoat run along the opposite bank and plunge into the cold water to save itself a short overland journey. Only a short time before these lines were written, a friend, fishing a loch of the north-west at seven o'clock one morning, saw an object moving through the water. Thinking it was a young otter, he rowed after it, and found it was a stoat. He put his landing net under the animal and lifted it out of the water, but it climbed out of the net, dropped back into the water, and was later heard crawling along the underside of the boat. The stoat was half way across the loch, which is a mile broad.

The sparsely inhabited country between Loch Ewe and Loch Broom is in winter the haunt of many sea and shore birds. Purple sandpipers from Greenland and Spitsbergen cluster on the skerries at low tide, prising open the small barnacles with their strong bills : they are almost unique among shore birds in their choice of food. Great northern divers, also from the Arctic, swim deep in the water a little way off-shore. Their favourite food is the flounder and they are adept at swallowing a flounder whole. I am often asked how it is possible to distinguish, at a distance, between a great northern diver and a cormorant. There is one certain distinction. The diver submerges with scarcely a ripple : the cormorant's dive is clumsy by comparison, and a splash is never avoided.

The south shoals of Gruinard Bay are specially favoured by long-tailed ducks. These small ducks, also expert divers, nest in Iceland, on islands of the great fresh-water lakes, and after the young can fly live a seafaring life until the next nesting season. The drake is a handsome black and white bird, with long tail streamers which curl into the air. The food of the

BADACHRO AND THE GAIRLOCH

Badachro, on the south shore of the Gairloch, is an artist's paradise and a snug anchorage for yachtsmen. This picture gives some impression of the clear light and subtle variations of colour. The mountain in the far distance is Slioch, about fourteen miles away on the south-east shore of Loch Maree.

The fishing village of Ullapool, on the north shore of Loch Broom, was originally established by the British Fishery Society in 1788. Commercial fishing still thrives, and the neat, white houses reflect prosperity. There is also good sea-trout fishing in Loch Broom, a safe anchorage for yachts, good bathing and fine scenery for holidaymakers. The peak in the distance is An Teallach.

long-tailed duck is chiefly small shellfish, which it takes from the ocean floor, sometimes at considerable depths. Flocks of dunlin feed on the sandy shores throughout the autumn and winter; their more brightly coloured confreres, the sanderlings, are seen here chiefly during the autumn migration, from August until November. White-fronted geese in winter haunt the boggy land and small tarns a little way inland.

The fishing port of Ullapool, on the north side of Loch Broom, has increased in importance during recent years, since the transport of fish by road, as opposed to rail, has become popular, and from Ullapool, and from Gairloch also, a considerable fleet operates in the Minch. Ullapool (the name is Norse and means "Ulli's Steading") is a small and attractive town, with a Norse flavour. To the north-west of Ullapool rises a prominent hill, Ben Mor Coigeach, just under 2,500 feet in height. Like An Teallach, Ben Mor is a hill range rather than a single hill, for it has several summits. Ben Mor Coigeach takes its name from the district of Coigeach which it overlooks. Coigeach means "Place of Fifths". The division of land into fifths was an ancient Celtic practice. The five-fifths of Coigeach are still known in the tradition of the district.

I had on one occasion the interesting experience of playing the bagpipe on the top of Ben Mor Coigeach. A friend of mine, well known in the film world, had in mind a master film of the Lordship of the Isles. We were staying at the time at the foot of Ben Mor, when he suddenly said, "Will you play your pipes for me on the hilltop?" It was a sunny April day and we had it in our minds to climb the hill. I said that I should be delighted to play, if someone carried up the pipes. Greatly to my surprise, two other friends in the expedition agreed to do this. I am sure it was the first occasion on which the music of the Highland pipe was heard on this lonely hilltop. The summit is broad and grassy, and as I played, in clear air and bright sunshine, the view extended from Skye and the Outer Hebrides to the great hills of the Central Highlands. I wondered what the golden eagle thought of this, and the ptarmigan and the red deer, which had the peace of their home thus disturbed. At this height one realised the number and size of the fresh-water lochs in the district. All of those lochs contain brown trout, and many of them salmon and sea trout, so the district of Achiltibuie, although remote, is an angler's paradise.

Fifteen miles north of Ben Mor, as the golden eagle flies, but much more by road, is the port of Lochinver.

Now that road transport in the north-west Highlands has largely replaced shipping, Lochinver has less importance than formerly. MacBrayne's steamers used to call in here regularly with goods from the Clyde. They also carried passengers, but now this voyage along much of the most beautiful part of the north-west coast is no longer available. No one who visits the country of Lochinver should omit to visit a very wild promontory named Rhu Stoer, spelled more correctly Rudha Storr. Beinn Storr in Skye and Rudha Storr in Sutherland both take their name from the Norse word *storr* (meaning a "stake" or "pillar"). In Skye the "Storr" is a magnificent rocky pinnacle; at Rhu Stoer the "Stake" is an almost equally imposing one, but rises not from a hill but from the Atlantic coast. On this high and rocky headland is a lighthouse with a powerful beam. A great colony of fulmars breed here. They return sometimes to the nesting colony before the New Year, for brief visits to lay claim to breeding territory. In January and February the visits become more frequent, and by March the full colony is in firm residence.

Beyond Rhu Stoer the coast road passes the island of Oldany and, beyond Drumbeg, the narrow and sheltered sea loch, Loch Nedd. This place is a remarkable contrast to the wind- and spray-swept character of Rhu Stoer, and trees grow, untouched by the storms overhead, almost to the tide-mark on the shore. Some miles beyond this point the road reaches Unapool and the ferry at Kylesku. No one knows who Uni was whose Norse farm-steading is commemorated in the place-name, Unapool. The ferry at Kylesku is operated by Sutherland County Council and (a rare thing in the Highlands) motorists are ferried over without charge. The ferry plies across the narrows (Kylesku is more correctly *Caolas Cumhang,* "The Narrow Strait") which separate Loch Carnban to the west from the two sea lochs, Loch Glencoul and Loch Glendhu, to the east.

Typical Sutherland coastline is exemplified by this prospect of Stoer Bay with Rhu Stoer in the distance.

The road from Kylesku to Lochinver provides interesting motoring and views of Suilven, the "sugar loaf" mountain.

I once had a curious experience when walking along the rough track from the head of Loch Glendhu to the road. A friendly pig overtook me and insisted on following me for several miles, greatly to the annoyance of our collie, Dugie, who felt outraged but was at a loss to know what to do. My own feeling was that this large pig would present a problem if, on reaching the car, it attempted to board it and usurp Dugie's place on the back seat. The problem was fortunately solved by a fence which was evidently the pig's boundary. The animal stopped short, did not attempt to follow me through the gate, and metaphorically waved a friendly good-bye before turning and heading for home.

From Kylestrome, on the north shore of the ferry, the narrow road winds through lonely country. Caravans are a problem here, for they are difficult to pass, as indeed they are elsewhere on the narrow roads of the north-west. As one approaches Scourie, the high, bird-haunted island of Handa rises ahead. This island is a bird sanctuary and in early summer, when seen from a boat, the sight here is an unusual one. One of the most numerous species of sea fowl that nest here is the kittiwake. These attractive sea birds raise a shrill clamour when they court on their firmly built nests; the deep boom of Atlantic surf sucking at the basalt walls of the cliff is an accompaniment to their cries. It is long since Handa (which is derived from Sanda, "Sandy Isle") was inhabited. In a manuscript dated 1726 it is stated that Handa is "inhabited by one or two families". The account continues : "It yields corn and pasture, and a great number of sheep". At an even earlier date there was a considerable human population on Handa; most

LOCH MAREE AND SLIOCH

The contours suggest that Loch Maree and Loch Ewe once formed a single great sea-loch, but they are now connected only by the small River Ewe. This south-eastern end of Maree, near the rugged mass of Slioch, is narrow and secluded, and the harmony of trees, rock and water give it a character of its own.

BEN ALLIGIN

At the end of March, the tops of Ben Alligin and its neighbours often retain a covering of snow. The picture looks north across Loch Torridon, and shows Alligin in the centre of an arc of quartzite mountains which provide some of the finest climbs in the country.

of these people emigrated to America in a sailing vessel.

Beyond Handa is the sea-loch, Laxford, and at Laxford Bridge the coast road meets the main road which crosses from Lairg in the east by way of Loch Shin and the Reay Forest to the Atlantic seaboard. As one travels towards the north one sees the great hills, Arkel and Foinne Bheinn (which I can see on a clear day from my home in Skye, rising in distant beauty across the Minch, seventy-five miles away) and the shapely cone of Ben Stack. All the old accounts of the district agree that the red stags of Arkel had forked tails. The Highlander was always a hunter of deer, and it is scarcely likely that he would have permitted this strange fact to be set down unless there were some grounds for it. It is possible that a stag with a forked tail was indeed shot here, and that the unusual incident was repeated and magnified until it was believed that all the stags of the hill had this peculiarity.

Beyond Rhiconich, the road to Kinlochbervie branches to the north-west. Here a comparatively new fishing venture has had much success. The fish caught are chiefly white fish (cod and ling, haddock

The winding road from Kylestrome to Scourie follows the east shore of Eddrachillis Bay, with its deep, jagged indentations and numerous small islands.

and skate) and the boats which fish here are manned mostly by crews from the Moray Firth. Each week day, the boats steer out into the Minch and the Atlantic beyond it. They return to port with catches of excellent quality fish, which fetch a high price in the markets of Scotland, and even England. Sea fish which swim where the tidal streams are strong are always of good quality, and the tides are strong where the Atlantic meets the Minch. Each week, the crews of the vessels cross Scotland by bus to their homes on the Moray Firth, leaving on Saturday and returning on Monday : they thus have the week-end with their wives and families and return to the north-west in time to put to sea on Monday.

Along the coast, some six miles as the osprey (which formerly nested in the district) flies, is a small loch with a strange atmosphere. It is Sandwood Loch and the word Sandwood is from the Norse *sandvatn* or "sandwater." It is aptly named, because there is a sandy shore here. Even at the present day a high tide may enter this fresh-water loch, and there is no doubt that when Loch Maree, then named Loch Ewe, was a fjord, Sandwood Loch was an arm of the Atlantic. The wrecks of a number of ships, deeply embedded in the sand, may be seen where the small stream leaves the loch and flows across the sand. It is strange to see all these wrecks lying so close together. I am inclined to think that the explanation is that the loch, while it remained an arm of the sea, gave good shelter in a storm and that these boats were wrecked when attempting to enter the loch, or, as it was then, the bay, while under sail. The old account says that this loch is "within a bow shot of the sea". Even in these days of improved transport Sandwood Loch is not an easy place to reach, as the main road from Rhiconich to the north keeps at a distance of seven to eight miles from the coast. At Gualann House it reaches its greatest elevation above sea level between Lairg in the east and Durness in the north-west. Gualann, which means "The Shoulder", stands 600 feet above the sea. It was an inn when it was built a century ago by the ducal family of Sutherland : it is now a shooting and fishing lodge, owned by the Fergussons of Baledmund. The late Commander Edmund Fergusson was a man greatly loved in the district. He was a very fine fisherman. One of the gillies paid him a tribute when he said to me, "The Commander is a fair otter!" On his river, the Dionard, he spent many a long and happy day salmon fishing, and it was rare indeed for him to return without result.

Strath Dionard is a glen of austere beauty. One early July morning just before sunrise I was sitting behind the small cairn on the hilltop above the celebrated Quirang in northern Skye. At the moment of sunrise it was extraordinarily clear, and the peaks of the distant Reay Forest stood out dark against the increasing glow of the north-east sky. The orb of the sun at length appeared, and so vast was it that it seemed to fill the whole of Strath Dionard which, from my viewpoint, was just over 80 miles distant. It was inspiring and strange to see so clearly, at so great a distance, a glen with which I have happy associations.

The salmon of the Dionard are not usually noted for their size, but I once had an exciting half hour with a monster fish in one of the best pools of the river. The Dionard was in spate, and when I hooked my big fish I was alone. As ill luck would have it,

In Norse the word "Laxford" means "salmon river", and the River Laxford, which joins Loch Stack to Loch Laxford is famous among anglers everywhere.

Cape Wrath lies at the north-west extremity of Scotland. It can be a wild and stormy place and its precipices afford striking examples of the action of the sea. At the spot where this photograph was taken the cliffs are 900 feet high, and in the distance the lighthouse can just be seen on the point.

John George Mackay, who is a first-class fisherman and was gillieing for one of the party, had just gone out of sight up the river, round a bend. Do what I might, I could not bring the salmon nearer to the bank than four or five feet from me. There he rested "as big as a pig" as gillies will say of an out-sized fish. Twice, once above me and once below me, he did come close in, and had John George been at hand with his gaff I should almost certainly have landed him. At long last, when the monster was tired out, the fly came away. The salmon made no effort to escape but rested, half on his side, for about half an hour, before rousing himself and swimming majestically away. I am aware that the angler often overestimates the size of the fish he has lost, but later on that summer George Ross, an experienced fisherman and the stalker and fisherman at Gualann, on several occasions watched that salmon. He later in the year saw it spawning on the redds, and estimated the weight to be between thirty and forty pounds.

The Dionard river empties into the Kyle of Durness, a long and narrow firth where, at ebb tide, it flows, a narrow, amber-coloured thread, across firm, golden sands. Here one is almost in sight of Cape Wrath but, like Sandwood Bay and its loch, this is not an easy place to reach. There is a ferry across the Kyle of Durness, but it carries only foot passengers. On the far side of the ferry there is a road leading to Cape Wrath eleven miles distant. It is narrow and is kept up by the Northern Lighthouse Commissioners for the conveying of necessary material for the lighthouse and lightkeepers. It is a long and tiring walk, and the hard road surface makes it wearisome. There is little distant view until one approaches the north-west coast where two great rock pillars, black as night, are often drenched in Atlantic surf. Am Bodach ("The Old Man") rises near, and south of it A' Chailleach ("The Old Woman"). The lighthouse is suddenly in sight, standing on the headland, high above the sea.

I often think that this must be one of the most

interesting mainland lighthouse stations in Scotland for a lover of nature. The name Cape Wrath is the anglicised version of a Gaelic name which superseded the old Norse name for the promontory, which was *Hvarf*, a "turning-point". This in course of time became changed to a Gaelic form of the word, *Am Parbh*. The name is an apt one, for the coast here takes an abrupt turn, even more abrupt than a right angle. Because of this, ocean birds on passage from nesting grounds to fishing banks fly close to the land while passing Cape Wrath and there is an excellent view to be had of them from the lighthouse, four hundred feet above the sea. Passing fulmars are seldom absent, but the most spectacular travellers are the gannets or solans. These strong fliers often fish a hundred miles from their nesting rocks or islands. I have watched the gannets of St. Kilda and Sulisgeir returning homeward from their fishing. When they rounded Cape Wrath, the birds swung off into two flight lines, one westward, in the direction of St. Kilda, the other north-west, towards Sulisgeir which, incidentally, is the only British station where the young gannet or "guga" is still taken for food.

King Haco of Norway sailed south with his fleet of

KERRY DAM

The River Kerry, which flows north-west through the narrow pass of Kerrysdale towards the Gairloch, has been dammed for hydro-electric purposes, and the spillway forms the silver curtain in this picture. The peak in the middle distance is Baosbheinn, which rises to 2,689 feet.

STACK POLLY

Stack Polly in Ross is a single peak of Torridon sandstone only just over 2000 feet high but famous and distinctive because it juts up sharply from low ground on all sides. The motor car has brought remote places such as this within reach of week-end climbers and skiers.

Loch Eriboll is a calm sea-loch reaching ten miles inland, but open to the stormy Atlantic on the north. The Vikings sheltered here after their rebuff at Largs in 1263, and a landing party was overwhelmed by the local inhabitants. The soil in this district is poor and stony, and the crofting population is small.

war galleys past Cape Wrath in the year 1263. The contemporary "Haco Saga" tells something of that historic voyage, which ended in the Firth of Clyde with the indecisive sea fight, the Battle of Largs, between the Norsemen and the King of Scotland. The Norse are generally pictured as invaders, as they often were, but it is worth recording that on this particular occasion King Haco brought his fleet across from Norway because of a cry for help from the people of Skye, which in those days had associations and ties with Norway rather than with Scotland. The Saga tells us that Haco anchored his fleet near the north entrance to Loch Inchard, approximately twenty-five miles south of Cape Wrath. The weather was stormy, and it is said traditionally (although this is not mentioned in the Saga) that one of the galleys foundered on the high, inhospitable coast a couple of miles south of Am Parbh, and that her crew, all except two, were lost. These two scaled the cliff. It used to be said, fifty and more years ago, that under certain conditions it was possible to see, half way up the cliff, a deeply rusted and corroded hatchet, and it was surmised that this belonged to one of the climbers and that it was discarded, or fell from his belt, during the perilous ascent.

From Cape Wrath lighthouse on a clear day the long, low coast of the Island of Lewis can be seen, and the lighthouse on the Butt of Lewis. In very clear weather North Rona is visible. In addition to its duty in warning mariners of the vicinity of a dangerous coast, Cape Wrath is a meteorological station. Its climate is often bleak and misty, but there are occasions, with a south-east wind, when remarkably high temperatures are recorded. For example, in the early days of March, 1958, the B.B.C. told us of almost record temperatures in the south during a minor heat wave. It was later discovered that Cape Wrath, in the extreme north-westerly corner of Scotland, had quietly recorded a temperature of sixty-nine degrees in the shade and had beaten all the other records.

After Cape Wrath, the coast of Scotland, while still retaining its Norse character, bends round to the east or even to a little south of east. At Durness are the remains of an old monastery and a remarkable epitaph on an old gravestone to a celebrated character of the past, Donald Mac Mhurchaidh who was "ill to his friend, war to his foe." A mile to the east of Durness, and close to the main road, is the impressive Cave of

Smoo, in its older form "Smoa". This curious name is said by scholars to be derived from the old Norse word *smuga,* meaning a cleft through which it is possible to creep. It was stated in 1726 that "on the floor of the cave there is room enough for 500 men to exercise their arms." It is easy to walk into the mouth of this great cave, where on high ledges fulmar petrels brood on their eggs, or chicks, but it is necessary to be agile to climb the slippery rock and look, from a ridge, into a Stygian lake, from beyond which comes the deep music of an invisible waterfall. The old account says that "in this large and deep pond trouts are catched". It would be interesting to examine some of these trout, which must live throughout the year in darkness. Near the Cave of Smoo, on the shore, is the Pool of the Wild Cat. It may be that some large and ferocious wild cat was slain here long ago.

Smoo is on the north coast, and it does not need an exceptionally clear day for Orkney to be seen across the sea. The coast road now makes a considerable detour inland to round the deep indentation of the sea, Loch Eriboll. While anchored in Loch Eriboll in October, 1263 (the remnants of the fleet had sailed north after the Battle of Largs) the Norsemen witnessed a total eclipse of the sun. Their awe at witnessing this phenomenon, far from home, is recorded in the "Haco Saga", as is also the excursion ashore of a party of Vikings, ostensibly for water. They were attacked by the natives, and only one man returned to tell the tale. The tradition of the country is that the Norsemen came ashore, perhaps on the pretext of obtaining water, but in reality on a raiding expedition. The rude graves where the raiders were buried are, it is said, still to be seen on the shore of the loch.

Lying parallel with Loch Eriboll, and a few miles to the east, is Loch Hope, now a fresh-water loch but, like Sandwood Loch, evidently a sea-loch in the past, for even today the tide comes half way up the river Hope which flows from it into the sea. This short river has a great name for its salmon fishing. The river which flows into Loch Hope from the high hills wanders through Strath Mor, the Big Strath. Here is a remarkable *dun,* or tower, the history of which is quite unknown. The traveller Pennant, who wrote nearly two centuries ago about this ancient ruin, Dun Dornadilla, mentions the belief then held that it was named after a legendary or imaginary prince who lived two hundred and sixty years before the Christian era. A writer in the *Edinburgh Magazine* in Pennant's day thought it was a Druidic building and the greatest antiquity in Scotland. It is in form circular, and in height at least twenty feet : it was evidently considerably higher, and appears to have been conical. It is beautifully built of stones, without cement. The entrance is through a very low and

On the shore just east of Durness is the entrance to the first of the three great chambers of the Cave of Smoo.

narrow doorway, to pass through which much stooping is necessary. Round the sides of the walls are ranged stone shelves "for little men to lie in," and there are to be seen the vestiges of a staircase.

From the river Hope, and Hope Lodge, the view is dominated by Ben Hope, a splendid hill 3,040 feet in height and the most northerly hill in Scotland of that elevation. The road along Loch Hope is narrow and greatly ridged, and may be disastrous and nerve-shattering for the driver of a car with low clearance, as I found to my cost. At Muiseal, a farm at the roadside near the head of Loch Hope, the celebrated Sutherland bard, Rob Donn, lived with John Mackay of the family of Sherray, from early years until his marriage. As one travels along the shore of Loch Hope, one realises how apt is its Norse name, "Loch of the Bay or Harbour." It was almost certainly a sea-loch, even in historic times, for it is even now only twelve feet above the level of the ocean and, as is well-known, the sea is gradually receding round this coast. The beauty of Ben Hope, which takes its name from the loch, was well seen from my bedroom in Hope Lodge. Each morning the rising sun lit up its high slopes and lofty summit, while its western precipice was still in deep shadow. In the mystic light of sunrise Ben Hope reminded me of the Matterhorn. In height it is far less than that Alpine giant, and its summit is more rounded, but at sunrise this resemblance was apparent, although it was less striking in full sunlight.

STOER BAY

Looking south from Stoer Bay towards Suilven, Cul Mor, Cul Beag, Stack Polly, and the curious, individual peaks of Coigeach on the border of Sutherland and Wester Ross. The clouds make a striking and ever-varying backcloth to the mountains and the jagged coastline.

ACHMELVICH

Immediately north of Loch Inver and Loch Roe, in Sutherland, lies Achmelvich Bay. Its shallow waters and fine sand make for safe bathing, and some of the more adventurous caravanners have found it a charming spot for holidays.

On a July morning my wife and I climbed Ben Hope, along with our hostess and Morag, the cairn terrier. Up the steep, heathery slopes we toiled. Morag with her short legs was almost exhausted and had to be assisted where the heather was longest. The sun beat down with intense heat. In fact, even driving up the loch side earlier I had found the steering wheel too warm to grasp in comfort. The gadflies or clegs, late in appearing that summer, flew stealthily and hungrily around us in their search for human blood. Bell heather in flower scented the air, and when we reached the first ridge we saw a burn of clear water flowing strongly down the hill. This stream, Allt na Caillich or the "Carlin's Burn", is of historic interest, for the Reay bard, Rob Donn, was born at its foot in the farmhouse now derelict. On a memorial to the poet at Durness, erected in the year 1829, he is honoured in four languages—Gaelic and English, Latin and Greek. In those days there were more classical scholars in the Highlands than one finds now.

As the climber toils up the broad slopes of Ben Hope he has the impression a hill of unusual grandeur and individuality. Slopes of white quartzite extend

The Kyle of Tongue is an arm of the sea east of Loch Eriboll. It is long and shallow, and lies in what used to be the Lord Reay's country. On the promontory are the ruins of Castle Varrich, whose origins and history are unknown.

as far as the eye can see. These slopes are firm and easy to walk over. That arctic plant, the black bearberry, grows here. It is a plant found here and there in the northern Highlands but I have yet to see it on the Cairngorm Hills. In autumn its deciduous leaves assume a billiant pink and sometimes crimson colour. The tiny alpine azalea was opening its small pink flowers on the ridges, a month later than usual. The most striking plant of the high slopes and plateau was a dwarf form of sea thrift. On sea cliffs the month of May is the flowering season of this plant but here, 2500 to 3000 feet above the sea, it was only now, in mid-July, in full flower. Its red blooms contrasted brilliantly with the quartz slopes, dazzlingly white in the strong sunlight. It shared this high and remote country with a dwarf form of the mountain everlasting (*Antennarea*) and the cyphel (*Cherlerea*). Only an occasional rosette of the cushion pink (*Silene Acaulis*) was seen, whereas at this elevation on the Cairngorms it would have been plentiful.

In intense heat we crossed to the east ridge to receive the cool air-flow from the east. Sea fog was enveloping the hills of Caithness, although Morven remained clear. Over the ocean lay a woolly blanket, hiding Orkney, and Suleskerry and its solan-haunted stack. Far below us, in a deep basin, lay Loch an Deerie : beyond it were the grand corries of Ben Loyal or Laoghal, where, it is said, Diarmid slew the fabulous wild boar. A number of Highland districts claim the site of that historic encounter, among them Glen Shee, some twenty miles south of Braemar. Across the lower slopes of distant Ben Wyvis sea mist flowed, white and diaphanous. On the ridge lay a ptarmigan's feather, but there was no ptarmigan, nor eagle, seen that day. We could see a kilted figure near the hilltop. He paced as if in thought, slowly across the slope, his head bent, his glance directed downwards. Later we spoke to him and found that he was a botanist, and that he was in process of writing a thesis on alpine flora.

The east wind had gone to rest and the top of Ben Hope was bathed in the warm sunshine of early evening. The marten still haunts these northern hills and Morag showed interest in a small burrow which may have been the home of one of these animals. Beyond the great hill of Foinne Bheinn to the west, the outline of Lewis was visible. We had left the clegs below us, but the midges, which are ubiquitous, became active as the sun lost much of its strength. On the descent we found a colony of cow-wheat (*Melampyrum*) at 2000 feet and, beside a clear spring, an exceptionally fine flower-head of butterwort. We drank of the cold, clear waters of Allt na Caillich, left behind us the wide acres of white quartzite, and reached green Strath Mor, where stands Dun Dornadilla. That evening we looked from Hope Lodge, across Loch Hope, on to Ben Hope. Grey sea fog had crept over the lower slopes of the hill. Above this ocean of mist the upper slopes and summit rose in beauty, the sunset glow bathing them and the precipice on the western face. That night there was no darkness. The afterglow merged into sunrise, and Ben Hope was the first of the hills to greet the sun as, glowing and benign, he climbed slowly above the sea horizon to the north-east and another summer day of strong colour and radiance was born.

East of Hope the road crosses high ground to Melness and the Kyle of Tongue. For centuries Tongue House was the home of the Mackay chiefs. One of them, Sir Donald Mackay, the first Lord Reay, was a legendary figure. It is said that he studied the black art and in bright sunlight cast no shadow as he walked. He raised two thousand men of his clan for the service of the king of Bohemia and afterwards entered the service of the king of Denmark. At his death he was governor of Bergen. The Lords of Reay continued to own the great estate of the Reay Country until the year 1829, when the first Duke of Sutherland bought, for the sum of £300,000, the whole of the property. The Sutherland property

Garrons graze on the shores of Loch Loyal, with the peaks of Ben Loyal behind. Once used as pack-horses, these sure-footed beasts are now favourites for pony-trekking.

then extended from Dornoch in the east to Cape Wrath and Tongue in the west. Although close to the sea, the House of Tongue is singularly well sheltered from the wind and the garden is a most attractive one. There is here a sun-dial of unusual design which carries the date 1714.

The great hill, Ben Loyal, dominates the district of Tongue. For its height (2,504 feet) it is perhaps the most imposing hill in the Scottish Highlands. My wife and I climbed it from Loch Loyal, at the shepherd's house at Leitirmhor. There are several summits, the most spectacular of which is An Caisteal ("The Castle"), which is a vast rounded cone of rock. There was a brood of young ptarmigan here, and golden plover were not far away. One could see, across moors and lochs, Ben Klibreck and, to the east of that hill, Beinn an Armuinn ("Hill of the Knight, or Hero"). On the lower slopes of Ben Loyal also the word "Armuinn" is found. Here is Clach an Armuinn ("The Hero's Stone"). I have not heard the tradition associated with it. The road from Tongue to the rail-head at Lairg leads across many miles of bleak, unpopulated country and at The

Loch Inchard stretches from Rhiconich to Kinlochbervie and the open sea, and is the most northerly of the deep indentations in the west coast. The picture looks south-east towards Arkel and Ben Stack, and shows some typical glaciated Sutherland terrain.

LOCH INCHARD

Crask reaches a height of 800 feet above sea level. Scarcely a winter passes without the road being drifted up by powder snow. The daily bus is frequently snowed up. It may be remembered that some winters ago "Operation Snowdrop" was organised here, when supplies were dropped by air to those completely cut off. There was one amusing incident in this air lift. In one of the most remote parts of Sutherland the owner of a house heard the noise of a low-flying plane, hurried outside, and was just in time to see a dark object, dropped from the plane, hurtling towards him. The sack of coals (for such it was) crashed through the roof and landed on the floor beside the fire, together with the plaster and wood it had torn off during its fall. On protesting to the authorities, he was told that he ought to be doubly thankful; that he had been provided, not only with coal for his fire but with kindling material also! One extraordinary incident was reported in the press at that time. An aircraft carrier was sent up from the Clyde to Loch Eriboll, in order that its aircraft might distribute food supplies to homes cut off by the blizzard. Her speed on the voyage mysteriously dropped, and she arrived at Loch Eriboll considerably later than had been expected. It was discovered that a sturgeon had been sucked into her condensers. This was doubly remarkable because the sturgeon is a rare fish, and if one is caught by a fishing vessel the practice is to forward it to the Queen.

The road across the backbone of the north-west Highlands, from Lairg to Scourie and Durness, is less exposed, but even here the local mail bus is often snowed up. After leaving Lairg, the road, mile after mile, is close to Loch Shin, and later passes through the ancient deer forest, in old times called Diri More, which means "The Great Ascent." An old description of the district, probably written in the seventeenth century, tells us that "Macky (that is, the Great Mackay, whose lesser title was Lord Reay) hath a summer dwelling in an Island within Loch Stalk (Stack is the modern spelling) in the Diri More." An English translation of a Latin manuscript of about the same period is as follows:

> "There are three localities among the mountains of Sutherland called by the name of forests. These forests are known by the names of Diri Moir, Diri Chat, and Diri Maenach, and in them . . . there is delightful and abundant hunting. All parts here are replete with stags, does, wolves, foxes, wild cats, martens, badgers, and every class of woodland birds that can be reared in this climate. There is also a kind of bird not everywhere met with, closely resembling a parrot, and called the knag, which annually burrows a nest for itself in the trunks of oaks, and may possibly be classed with the great

Winter in the north is usually severe; snow closes the roads, farms and villages are cut off, and the deer are forced down to low ground in search of food. Here farm workers and men of the Automobile Association's Highland Patrol help the Lochinver snow plough to clear the way to Lairg.

black woodpecker. On the borders that look towards the south west there is a mountainous and wooded track, and in it is Ben Arkel. All the stags found here have forked tails, by which they are easily distinguished from the rest."

The parrot-like bird mentioned under the name "knag" is supposed to be the greater spotted woodpecker. The old Highland race of woodpecker disappeared, and the greater spotted woodpeckers found in the Highlands at the present day are comparatively recent comers to that district. It may be noted in passing that the hill where the fork-tailed stags lived is named Ben Arkel. This is an instance of the Celtic name for a hill being superimposed on the original Norse name : it is now more correctly written Arkel or Arcuil, without the "Ben". A leading scholar in old place-names gave it as his opinion that the word is old Norse, and means "Ark fell, or hill," perhaps from its fancied resemblance to the ark in shape. This indeed I have noticed myself.

The Diri More leads from Lairg, by way of Loch Shin, Loch a' Ghriam, and Loch Merkland, beyond which, at an elevation of 420 feet, it crosses the watershed and descends to Loch More, Loch Stack, and by the Laxford river to the west coast. A former continuation of this great deer forest north-westwards was the Cape Wrath area, then named Am Parbh.

Great deer drives took place here, the animals being forced by a wide-spread line of "beaters" into the sea, where the hunters in boats attacked and killed them as they swam.

If we now return to Tongue and continue our journey by the coast road, we soon reach the boundary between Sutherland and Caithness, but we must first cross Strath Naver near its mouth and pass Bettyhill, a singularly attractive place with excellent bathing on a firm sandy beach. After Strath Naver, one passes through Strathy and Melvich and, two miles after crossing the Halladale River, finds the county boundary at the small Loch Hollistan. We now enter an area which has been entirely transformed in recent years by the great atomic power station at Dounreay. The coast becomes less Highland in character, and there are few Celtic place-names. At the town of Thurso one reaches the port of embarkation for Orkney. Still farther east, beyond Dunnet Head, is the stately Castle of Mey, now a residence of the Queen Mother and, at no great distance from it, a noted tidal race of the Pentland Firth, the Merry Men of Mey. The waves of this tidal stream, flashing white in the sunlight, have given it this name. The whole of the Pentland Firth is indeed a vast ocean river and is treated by seafaring men with respect even in these days of large and fast vessels. I had first-hand information of a warship of the largest size which was turned completely round by a vortex here during stormy weather. A little way off-shore is the island of Stroma, and on the mainland shore opposite is John o' Groat's House, or rather the site of it.

Before continuing on our journey to Orkney and Shetland, we should perhaps return a certain distance south, to Dornoch in the east, and then move northwards once more, this time along the east coast. Dornoch is the principal town in Sutherland. No trace is left of the ancient church of St. Bar which, it is said, was built by "St. Bar, Bishop of Catteynes". The cathedral, "built by St. Gilbert in honour of our Lady", was burnt in the year 1570, but was restored by Sir Robert Gordon, Tutor of Sutherland. North of Dornoch is the castle of Dunrobin, built magnificently high above the sea and perhaps the most prominent of all Highland habitations when seen from the air. Most of the coast is low and, as the old record says, "There are the fairest and largest Links of any part of Scotland, fit for Archery, golfing, riding, and all other exercise." There is a well-known pipe tune "The Dornoch Links", and the Dornoch golf course is renowned. But Dunrobin Castle rises north of these green, low lands, and when seen from the tide it towers splendidly from its firm rock. Its gardens have for centuries been celebrated. We read from an old account written at least two hundred and

Set in the midst of bleak moorland country in Sutherland, the hamlet of Altnaharra attracts anglers for the fine fishing in Loch Naver and surrounding streams.

The atomic power station at Dounreay, Caithness. Experience in the operation of this fast fission breeder reactor will increase the efficiency of future power stations.

fifty years ago that:

"there be pleasant gardens planted with all kinds of fruits, herbs and flowers used in this kingdom, and abundance of good saffron, Tobaco, and Rosemary : the fruit here is excellent and chiefly the Pears and Cherries. There is in Dunrobin one of the deepest Draw wells; all of Aisler work from the ground to the top, called St. John's Well, which is within the Castle in the midst of the Court."

Fulmar petrels have evidently decided that Dunrobin Castle is a natural feature of the landscape, for these ocean birds during recent years have taken to nesting in niches high on the castle and the young birds sometimes fall to the ground. When one looks seaward from the rooms high in the castle one might imagine that one was on a large and very steady ship, looking out over the sea to the Black Isle where, at the onset of night, a high lighthouse shines. On the broad stairway of the castle are hung tiger skins and other relics of the hunt. I remember when I arrived at the castle with Dugie, the collie who at that time was our companion, he began the ascent of the stairway confidently enough. As he passed one tiger

QUINAG AND DRUMBEG

The little village of Drumbeg, on the coast road round Eddrachillis Bay, is overlooked by the long narrow mass of Quinag (2,653 feet). The lochan, which reflects the summer sky, is one of many hundreds that riddle this low, broken part of Sutherland.

BEN HOPE AND STRATH MOR

The green valley of Strath Mor and the proud heights of Ben Hope (3,040 feet) from the south. In the foreground are the remains of Dun Dornadilla, an ancient drystone tower which may have been built by the Picts. Loch Hope lies beyond the cliffs to the left of the picture.

Looking south-west across Dornoch Sands towards the hills of Easter Ross. The sands, caravan site and magnificent Royal Dornoch golf links make this a popular holiday place.

Chanonry lighthouse stands at the tip of a promontory of the Black Isle, opposite Fort George. It is named after the ancient chanonry of Ross, the medieval cathedral of which, now ruined, is at nearby Fortrose.

after another, on either side of him, his tail dropped and, when a few more steps would have taken him to safety, he suddenly turned and, in a panic, bolted down the stairs. On another occasion, this time during the Second World War, I was travelling to the castle, accompanied by a collie named Dara, on a goods train. The long goods train broke in two during a steep climb and Dara and I, in the guard's van, hurtled down the hill, propelled by thirty runaway wagons. On that visit I have memories of the gracious personality of Duchess Millicent, mother of the present Duke of Sutherland, who was staying at Dunrobin at the time. She listened with sympathetic interest to the narrative, at dinner that night, of my successful efforts to pull up the runaway train, and at the end she remarked quietly and musically, "You deserve the Albert Medal."

North of Dunrobin with its magnificent beech avenue is Helmsdale, where the Helmsdale river, noted for its salmon, reaches the sea. The railway follows the course of this river almost to its source before turning east at Forsinard. Following the coast road northwards from Helmsdale, one crosses the county boundary between Sutherland and Caithness at The Ord and in six miles drops down from nearly 800 feet to near sea level at Berriedale. Here, on a hill above the road, is the shooting lodge at Langwell, a residence of the Dukes of Portland. One of the chief heights of the deer forest here is Morven, a shapely conical hill, from which it was customary for seamen in old days to take their bearings. Beyond Berriedale is the Sinclair castle of Dunbeath, built at the edge of the cliff with the voice of the North Sea beneath it. In time the traveller arrives at the fishing port of Wick (the name is taken from the Norse original, which was *Vik*, "a bay") and so on to John o' Groats and the Pentland Firth.

The traveller can cross the Pentland Firth from the airport at Wick to Kirkwall in Orkney in half an hour's flying time. It is certainly quicker by air, but one sees more of the coast, and the varied bird life, if one crosses from Thurso by the mail steamer to Stromness. Stromness is a west port of Orkney : to reach it, one has to judge the strong tides, which on occasion may attain a speed of twelve knots, of the Pentland Firth, and a straight course is rarely possible. Hoy, the "High Island", is the first of the Orkney group to be reached. Its cliffs, at St. John's Head, reach the great height of 1040 feet. This precipitous and lofty coastline of Hoy supports a very large puffin colony, and when one is in a ship fifty miles west one can see parties of puffins, sometimes consisting of many birds, flying high and fast from their fishing grounds towards Hoy, at that distance scarcely visible.

Dunrobin Castle is one of the glories of Sutherland. Set on a natural terrace close to the sea, it was begun in 1275 by Robert, second Earl of Sutherland, and called Dun Robin after him. Originally it was a square keep with bartizan turrets at the angles, but enlargements in the Scottish baronial style were made by Sir Charles Barry in 1848. Further alterations were made by Sir Robert Lorimer in 1921, and the "extinguisher" roofs add to its appearance.

In Ben's *Orkney*, written in 1529, it is stated that white hares abound on Hoy and are taken by dogs. At a much later date ptarmigan were introduced here, but did not take kindly to the island, for its hills are not sufficiently high. On Hoy is perhaps the farthest south nesting site of the bonxie or great skua, a large and dark piratical sea bird, which has been seen to slay a greater black-backed gull at a single blow. The Old Man of Hoy is a remarkable pillar of red sandstone, 450 feet high, rising at the edge of the rocky coast, a prominent landmark from the mainland. The last time I crossed the Pentland Firth from Thurso, I travelled with a friend who took his Bentley across in the steamer. This distinguished car, with its bright red tourer body, attracted much attention in Stromness, and indeed throughout what is called the Mainland of Orkney but, whether it resented being left out in the open at night, or whether it was allergic to the damp ocean air of Stromness, it was never easy to start in the mornings. On the morning of our departure we had ultimately to be towed ignominiously to the pier, where the captain of the mail boat awaited us with well-controlled impatience.

From Stromness we made an expedition to the small

WHITEN HEAD

This splendid cliff, also known as Kennageall Head, lies at the north-east extremity of Loch Eriboll, reaching out into the Atlantic. It can be reached only on foot, but the journey is worth making as there is a fine series of caves to be explored.

CASTLE OF MEY

In 1952 Her Majesty Queen Elizabeth, the Queen Mother, purchased this castle which stands near Canisbay, on the Pentland Firth. It was originally called Barogill, and is a former seat of the Earls of Caithness. The Queen Mother renamed it Castle of Mey, and under her personal supervision it has become an attractive home.

At the end of the nineteenth century Helmsdale was a busy fishing village. Now the industry is less prosperous, but the drifters still tie up at the quay of its small harbour.

An unusual display of antlers against white walls catches the eye at Berriedale. The buildings, once the Berriedale Inn, became a smithy and are now a private house.

island of Eynhallow, the "Holy Island", which rises from the sound between Pomona (or Mainland) and Rousay. It is an isle of grass, short heather and, on the west side, of rocks. No one has lived on Eynhallow for more than a century. In the year 1851 a dangerous fever caused several deaths in the four crofting families who had their homes here and the survivors were persuaded to leave the island. It was then discovered that one of the houses had been originally a church or chapel, with Norman and Gothic arches. A Norwegian scholar, by name Professor Dietrichsen, thought the chapel was a Cistercian foundation. Other authorities think it more likely to have been a Benedictine chapel, perhaps of the early twelfth century. Near it are the ruins of small buildings, perhaps part of the monastery. Its Norse name, Holy Isle, makes it appear probable that long before the twelfth century the island had been the site of an older Celtic or Pictish church, and that therefore the Norsemen had named the island *Eyin Helga,* Holy Island. On a sunny morning of exceptional visibility my friend and I boarded a small motor boat at the Sands of Evie and, crossing the blue sound where terns daintily fished, in less than half an hour landed on the low south-east shore of Eynhallow.

The tide was high and we had walked only a few feet across that shore when we saw on the shingle a ringed plover's nesting scrape containing a single egg. On Eynhallow where, in keeping with the traditional sanctity of the isle, bird life is protected, the fulmar petrel, which usually breeds on the ledges of sea cliffs, lays its white, glossy egg on the ground, in a site such as an eider might choose. We noticed, also, fulmars nesting on the turf roof of a low, partly ruined building. Others, although it was mid-summer, were still courting, for it is a peculiarity of the fulmar that courtship takes place at least a year before an egg is laid. When we approached the building the brooding fulmars continued to sit, but the courting birds took wing. On a day of little wind ground-nesting fulmars have some difficulty in becoming airborne. One such bird, which I unintentionally disturbed when I emerged from the door of a ruin, scuttled with outspread wings across the shingle into the sea before it was able to rise. Because of the holy associations of Eynhallow it is said that no cat can live here, and the nesting birds are spared that enemy. As we walked along the low shore, arctic and common terns swooped at us with shrill cries. Small tern chicks, in dark down, crouched motionless near the nesting scrapes.

The ruined church or chapel is on the south-west side of Eynhallow. It is roofless, but the walls, and the gables of chancel and nave, are at full height. Three doors lead into the porch, that on the west

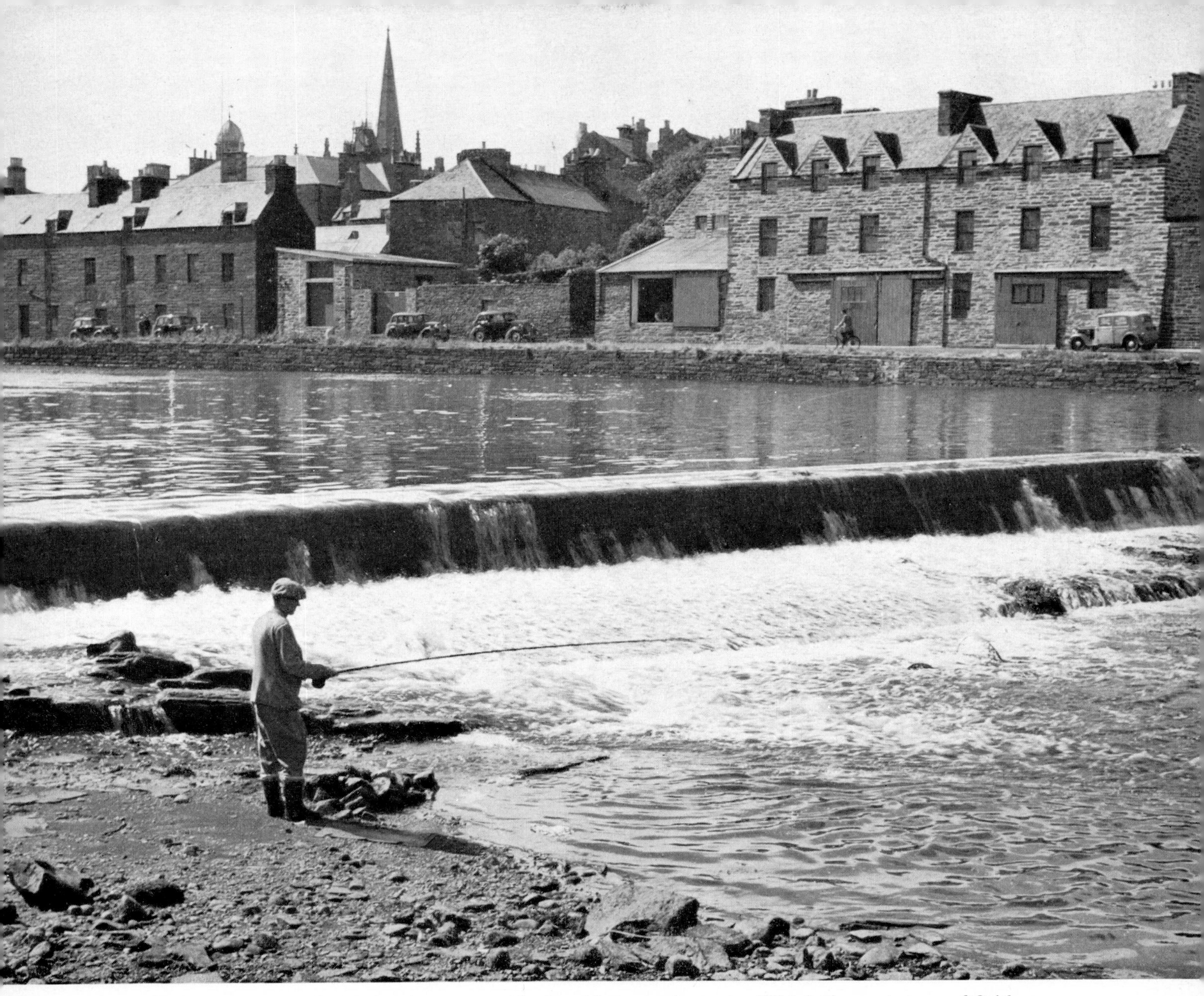

In Wick, as in Inverness, anglers can catch sea trout and salmon from a main street. Wick is the county town of Caithness, and has been a place of some consequence for at least eight centuries. It is an important fishing town, but has never developed as a port because, in spite of many expensive improvement projects, large vessels can only enter the harbour at high tide.

being probably the most ancient. Near the church are the remains of the monastic establishment, believed to have been the abbot's room, refectory and cloister. These stand on the gentle slope, rather higher than the church. The farm buildings of the monastery are commemorated in the place-names Upper Barns and Lower Barns, and these ruins are still visible. When we looked again at the sea the tide had turned. A great tidal stream, the Burgar Rost, was now flowing north-west through the sound against the cool, sharp, ocean breeze. This stream, of a more deep and intense blue than the sky above, had white, curling waves and seemed to radiate joy and power. A second tidal river, or rost, the Cutlar Rost, of almost equal size, surged through the channel between Eynhallow and Rousay. As the old Orkney saying has it :

> Eynhallow frank, Eynhallow free,
> Eynhallow stands in the middle of the sea.
> A roaring rost on every side,
> Eynhallow stands in the middle of the tide."

The deep song, or muffled roar, of these Atlantic rivers was an accompaniment to the shrill cries of the

CASTLE GIRNIGOE

On the cliffs near Noss Head, north of Wick, are the ruins of the adjoining sixteenth-century castles Girnigoe and Sinclair. Both were Sinclair strongholds, and withstood many attacks by their hereditary enemies, the Gordons. The song "The Campbells Are Coming" is said to refer to an expedition against Girnigoe by Campbell of Glenorchy in 1672.

LYBSTER HARBOUR

The fishing village of Lybster is situated twelve miles south of Wick. On an exposed and often stormy stretch of coast its well-designed harbour is a welcome refuge, and in fine weather the adjoining open spaces are used for drying nets. The name Lybster is a relic of the Norse invasion in the tenth century, as are many of the place-names along the Caithness coast.

terns—small white figures darting across the blue heavens above. The colouring was unusually lovely in the clear air, and far across the blue sea rose the lighthouse and cliffs of Noup Head on Westray. As the tide ebbed seals approached the shallows, one large bull watching us with curiosity. With a great splash he submerged, to thrust his long, sleek head above the surface a few seconds later, drawing long breaths and at the end of each breath closing his nostrils tightly. On the short heather above the ancient ruined church a pair of fulmar petrels were resting on the short heather. When they rose at our approach a white egg was exposed. The owner of the egg soon returned, flying low and gracefully up-wind, and then hovering above the nesting hollow. More than once the fulmar passed, each time flying more slowly, and at last alighted and brooded the egg. Not far off lay a sucked fulmar's egg, perhaps eaten by a gull. Eiders, too, were brooding on this gentle slope. One eider duck was just hatching her brood. She rose from her nest, but did not fly, and ran a little way across the short heather, where she crouched. While we were still near the nest she rose, hurried on foot back to her family, and brooded them closely.

Kirkwall, with over four thousand inhabitants, is the chief town of Orkney. Its narrow, stone-flagged streets and varied architecture make it a town of great character.

The Earl's Palace in Kirkwall, built by Earl Patrick Stewart in 1600-1607, is a good example of seventeenth-century baronial architecture with ornamental castellation.

Eider drakes (they take no part in rearing the family) were awaiting the coming of the summer "eclipse" plumage as they swam near the tidal streams. On the grassy crown of Eynhallow was a considerable colony of greater black-backed gulls, which are most destructive to the eggs, young, and even the parents, of other bird species. I have seen an almost full-grown young greater black-back disgorge, when alarmed, a downy fulmar nestling which its parent had evidently brought it for food. Uttering deep, barking cries, the greater black-backs sailed rather heavily overhead. Their young, large and fat, ran actively over the short vegetation. One of them unintentionally trespassed on a colony of common gulls. The gulls swooped at it and bowled it over. It rose each time to its feet, and ran at its best speed towards its own colony, which it reached apparently unharmed : it had avoided a number of vicious swoops by ducking at the critical instant.

On the north-west slope of Eynhallow blue scyllas were flowering. Here the ground fell away towards the sea in a slope literally covered with the bloom of sea thrift. One plant was remarkable by reason of its deep red flowers. The warm, sunlit air was perfumed by this splendid colony of sea thrift, which ended in a cliff of moderate height. Here I watched an unusually large colony of black guillemots, which rarely have a communal colony like the common guillemot. Eynhallow has long been a haunt of the black guillemot, and Duncan Robertson, its late owner, who loved the isle and its birds, placed it on record that for a number of years a black guillemot with a white ruffle nested here. Some of the guillemots were courting; beneath them the sea tangle glistened in the strong sun as it swayed gently in the ocean swell. Nests of oyster catchers were in the thrift, and an arctic skua patrolled overhead, its dark form and narrow wings sharp against the blue sky. In a small ruin, rock pigeons were nesting. The rock doves of Orkney show brown in their plumage; they have perhaps in them a strain of the homing or domestic pigeon and are not, like the blue rock doves of the Hebrides, pure bred. We passed the close-brooding fulmar, motionless except for her laboured breathing, an anxious look in her large eyes, fixed intently on us. As we waited on the shore we saw our boat put out from Rousay and cross the blue sound, where the strength of the ocean rivers was now abating.

On Pomona, or, as it is usually called, Mainland of Orkney, is the city of Kirkwall. Its cathedral was founded by Magnus, King of Norway. It is said to be one of the three cathedrals of Scotland to be preserved entire at the Reformation, the other two being St. Giles in Edinburgh and St. Mungo, the cathedral church of Glasgow. On New Year's Day,

1671, lightning struck the steeple of Kirkwall Cathedral and one of the historic musical bells fell to the pavement. It was damaged but was later sent to Holland and, being refounded there, had its music restored. It is fortunate that Kirkwall Cathedral escaped an excess of religious zeal, for it is of unusual beauty, both without and within. No one visiting Kirkwall should omit to visit, less than an hour's run by car, the ancient settlement at Skara Brae with its stone beds and cupboards believed to date from at least 2000 B.C. Not far from Skara Brae is Maeshowe, said to be the finest burial cairn of the Stone Age in Europe. Through a low passage one enters this large, grass-grown cairn and finds, in its depths, a round building with roof of stone. The sagas relate that early Norse raiders broke into the chamber, hoping to find treasure, but a night spent in the company of the bones of the illustrious dead so preyed upon their nerves that three of them went mad. Not far away is the little bay where King Haco, grievously wounded at the Battle of Largs, was carried ashore to die. His body rested in Kirkwall Cathedral.

Two wars have left their mark on Orkney. On Marwick Head is the tall memorial to Lord Kitchener, who lost his life in the First World War when the cruiser taking him to Russia struck a mine and foundered. During both wars the British fleet had its base in the great sea basin known as Scapa Flow. The Second World War resulted in a benefit to the island group, for the main island has now been joined to the South Isles by four remarkable causeways, to which the name Churchill Barrier has been given. After the *Royal Oak* had been torpedoed by a daring U-boat commander in Scapa Flow, these causeways were built across the channels to keep German submarines out. The first links Pomona with Lamb Holm; the second joins Lamb Holm with its neighbour Glimps Holm; the third connects Glimps Holm with Burray; the fourth joins Burray with South Ronaldsay. The work was done largely by Italian prisoners of war who laboured for months, dumping stones and blocks of concrete into Lamb Holm deep-water channel, before their labours showed any result. The Italians have gone, but their chapel, small, artistic and beautiful, remains as their memorial, although when I was last there no authority had agreed to be responsible for its maintenance. The Churchill Barrier makes life easier on the South Isles, for there is now a good road to South Ronaldsay, with a bus service several times daily.

Between Orkney and Shetland is Fair Isle, and it is a memorable experience to approach it in the dusk of an evening and anchor, beneath the rays of its strong lighthouse, at the edge of the tidal stream of North Harbour, where fulmars maintain ceaseless

The village of Skara Brae in Orkney is at least four thousand years old. The drifted sand which had concealed and preserved the remains was partly removed by a storm in 1850.

The force of the sea around Fair Isle is so great that it has eaten into the cliffs, leaving single, separate pinnacles of hard rock around the coast, like those near Malcolm's Head.

patrol. Thanks to the efforts of the National Trust for Scotland, Fair Isle maintains its small and hardy population, and in May, 1959 there was a pleasant ceremony here when the extension to the pier, finished in record time, was opened. One of the most influential families on Fair Isle are the Stouts. The island mail boat, *The Good Shepherd,* which weekly makes the hazardous crossing with mails, passengers and provisions to and from Shetland, is skippered by one of this family; he tells me that he is descended from one of three brothers who left Yorkshire to seek their fortunes in the North Isles. There were then no horses on Fair Isle : it was not until 1951 that the last of the bullocks which drew the plough was superseded by a small tractor. The Duke of Medina, Admiral of the Spanish Armada, was shipwrecked on Fair Isle in 1588.

Travelling by sea from Fair Isle to Lerwick in Shetland one passes Sumburgh Head with its high cliffs and strong tide, and navigates the Sound of Mousa, where is a celebrated "broch". If the wind should be blowing from south-east, there is a brief period of shelter here, to be paid for by heavier seas before Lerwick and its harbour are reached.

Here I can do no more than touch on the islands of Zetland, whose home port, it is said, is not in Scotland, but Bergen in Norway. Lerwick from time immemorial has been a fishing port and was much used by the Dutch—witness the old account which states that the name Zetland is from the name the "Hollanders" gave it, Hetland or Heathland, because of its heather. The ruined castle of Scalloway

Outlaw among the birds which nest on the cliffs and islets is the great black-backed gull, fierce, powerful and predatory.

FAIR ISLE

Fair Isle, which lies between Orkney and Shetland, now belongs to the National Trust for Scotland. It is a bird sanctuary, and the buildings above the beach are the bird-watching station of the Scottish Ornithological Club. The island has long been famous for the high quality and intricate patterns of its traditional knitwear.

Lerwick, on the east coast of Mainland, is the most northerly town in Scotland. It is the county town of Shetland, and although the town itself probably dates only from the seventeenth century, the harbour has been used from time immemorial. The houses reach out into the sea, like those in some Norwegian sea-ports.

The streets of Lerwick, like those of Kirkwall, are narrow, smoothly flagged and architecturally intriguing.

on the west coast is said to have been built by Earl Patrick Stewart in the year 1600. From Walls, also on the west coast, stores are taken to Foula, the most remote island of the group. Efforts are being made to maintain its small population and it is to be hoped they may be successful. The North Isles, Yell, Fetlar and Unst, are actually farther north in latitude than Bergen in Norway. Unst has a large sea-bird population and on the neighbouring rocks of Muckle Fluga there is an increasing gannet colony.

Few strangers visit the island of Fetlar. My wife and I left the rain-swept flagged streets of Lerwick on an October morning when sunshine alternated with sleety showers. At Mossbank the bus shed its passengers and we crossed the strong tide in the Sound of Yell where black guillemots, already in almost white winter plumage, swam and dived. Two miles of a sea passage brought us to Yell, where we found the mail steamer *Earl of Zetland* at anchor. The ship's wireless recorded a warning of a severe south-west gale, but this still had not risen when we dropped anchor off Brough Lodge on Fetlar and a rowing boat took us ashore. Later we were told the story of the sea eagle of Fetlar, which carried a baby from the neighbouring island of Unst to its eyrie on the high cliffs at the back of Fetlar. The child's parents, who had laid the baby down while they were busy lifting peats, had seen the flight line of the eagle. They followed with what speed they could in a boat and landed on Fetlar. There they met a lad of about ten years of age, who agreed to be lowered to the eyrie on a rope. The baby was found entirely unharmed; the two eaglets were partly resting on it, and this no doubt kept the child warm. When she had grown to womanhood she was wooed and won by her rescuer, in true fairy story manner. The tenth generation resulting from that romantic wedding lived on Fetlar at the time of our visit there, some years ago. They should, in order to commemorate the incident, assume as their crest a white-tailed or sea eagle in flight!

Two more stories of the sea eagle we heard in a

The "St. Ninian", one of several vessels which maintain a regular service between Leith, Aberdeen, Orkney and Shetland.

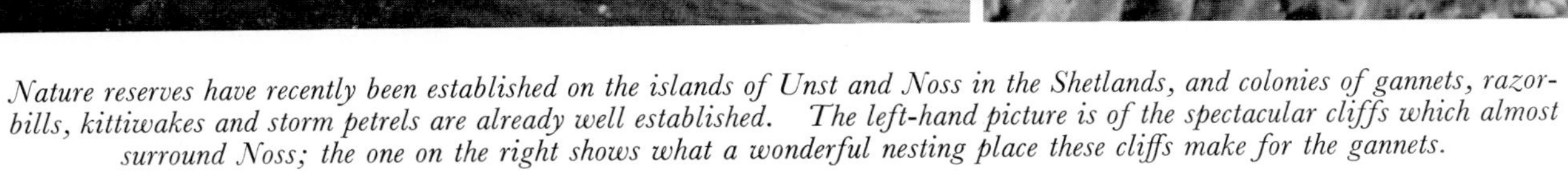

Nature reserves have recently been established on the islands of Unst and Noss in the Shetlands, and colonies of gannets, razorbills, kittiwakes and storm petrels are already well established. The left-hand picture is of the spectacular cliffs which almost surround Noss; the one on the right shows what a wonderful nesting place these cliffs make for the gannets.

remote house in which an old lady of eighty-eight was knitting a Fair Isle pattern jumper. In the first tale an eagle pounced on a large halibut swimming near the surface. It failed to lift the great fish from the water or to disengage its talons, and was dragged down and drowned. The bodies of the eagle and the halibut were washed up on Fetlar, the eagle's talons still sunk deep in the halibut's flesh. The second story was of a sheep's adventure with a sea eagle. The sheep, then four or five years old, was found to have an eagle's leg in its back, the talons gripping the wool. A dead eagle was later found, the talons of one foot grasping the heather, the other leg and foot missing. It was surmised that the eagle had attempted to hold the sheep with one foot, while it grasped the heather with its other foot, to hold back the animal. The eagle had under-estimated the strength of the sheep, which had torn its leg off.

As I draw near the end of this chapter on The North, I remember how Norway was once more brought near to Fetlar during the grim early years of the Second World War. One of the Fetlar Home Guard told us that he was roused, one night in 1941,

DUNCANSBY STACKS

East of John o' Groats is the cliff of Duncansby Head, 210 feet high and the north-east extremity of the Scottish mainland. A mile to the south are Duncansby Stacks, a group of jagged rocks which have become detached from the mainland by the action of sea and weather. The picture looks north-east, beyond Duncansby Head, to the Pentland Firth, with Hoy in the distance.

THE CLIFFS OF HOY

The island of Hoy, which lies between the Pentland Firth and Scapa Flow, is the loftiest of the Orkneys and the second largest. On the west coast the magnificent sandstone cliffs shelter Rackwick Bay and village, whose inhabitants are reputed to be descended from the survivors of a ship of the Spanish Armada which was wrecked nearby.

Puffins are colourful and prolific inhabitants of the nature reserves of Hermaness on Unst in the Shetlands. Hermaness is also a breeding ground for the great skua, arctic skua, red-throated diver, eider duck and arctic tern. The Shetland reserves have probably saved certain rare species from extinction.

by knocks at his door. He found four Norwegians outside. In order to escape from the Nazis, these men had crossed the two hundred miles of ocean in an open boat so small that he himself would have been doubtful of crossing to Unst in it, even in fine summer weather. The engine had broken down and the men had rowed most of the two hundred miles. When their oars broke they rigged a small sail made of blankets. They steered by a small pocket compass and reached safety after four days and nights at sea, yet many others were lost during that hazardous crossing. It is almost certain that many missed a landfall and passed to the north of Shetland. These thoughts may have been in the minds of some of the crew of the Bergen Line's vessel *Meteor* with whom I sailed on a cruise arranged by the National Trust for Scotland in May, 1959. These waters brought hazard, yet safety, to many of their countrymen.

THE NORTH-EAST

John R. Allan

THE North-East has a strange shape on the map, as if it had been drawn by a slightly educated ape or by a company director at a conference. Looked at on the ground it makes sense. It is the Lowland part that lies to the east and north of the Central Highlands. It is a narrow plain between the mountains and the sea, although the plain is difficult to realise because of the humps and hollows. The land is different from the Highlands: so are the people and their occupations. The Highland economy is based on raising sheep and cattle; the Lowland on arable crops and the fattening of beasts for the market. There are often no distinct borders between Highland and Lowland—some of our best farmlands are in the Central Highland area. But it is a rough generalisation that Highland farming means the dog and stick and Lowland farming the plough. One other great difference is that the North-East is an industrial country. It contains Dundee and Aberdeen, each with a population nearing two hundred thousand, and there are many small towns that have their manufactures. It is an industrial country, but one where the chief business is farming, which the other trades have not been able to spoil. The small manufacturing towns such as Forfar, Brechin, Montrose, Huntly, Elgin and Keith retain a modesty, sometimes a charming modesty, among the farmlands. And there are the many fishing villages; with Peterhead, Fraserburgh, Buckie and Lossiemouth, towns that have grown up with the herring trade. The fisher towns and fisher villages sit on the land but the sea winds and sea life possess them. They are like fishing fleets drawn up on the shore. So the North-East is a very varied country with a diversity of life; but, in spite of the diversity, there is much in common from Dundee to the gates of Inverness.

The people are a little different from those of the Highlands. That may be difficult to see, for mass entertainments and the ease of travel are wearing away local differences. But the differences remain. They are the results of a different environment, a different way of life. I would not say we work harder in the Lowlands, since the true aim and object of technology is to take the draught out of labour, but we take work more seriously. You might say we are more geared into mesh with the machines than people in the pastoral Highlands are. The pace of the Highlands is that of the shepherd taking long strides with monstrous boots through the bracken, even though the Highlander is only serving you a tartan doll, made in Japan, at the village post office. The pace of the Lowlands is quicker, more business-like, though it may get you no further by the end of the day.

It is unwise to make any great distinction between the Highlanders and the Lowlanders, for so many that now live in the North-East are of Highland descent. About two hundred years ago the population of the Highland glens increased too rapidly: it became too great a burden on a poor soil. In bad years corn had to be taken up into the glens at a great expense to keep the people alive. Then the new agriculture produced more corn on the Lowlands; that agriculture needed more hands, and the Highlanders began to move down. A little later the textile manufacturer became greedy for labourers. Work, wages and corn drew in a mass migration from the glens. Those who came down often had hard times in the early days of the factory system,

THE MEMORIAL ARCH, EDZELL

This arch, which is approached from the south by a long, straight tree-lined avenue, is a striking gateway to the village of Edzell, on the North Esk. It was erected in 1888 in memory of John, 13th Earl of Dalhousie and his Countess by tenants and friends.

GLAMIS CASTLE

Glamis Castle, in Angus, is the residence of the Bowes-Lyon family, to which the Queen Mother belongs, and Princess Margaret was born here. Glamis owes much of its present picturesque form to the first Earl of Strathmore, who supervised the building of the clusters of turrets, bartizans and "extinguisher" roofs from 1675 to 1687.

but they never went back to the glens. They settled into a new way of life and became throughout the generations a rather different people.

Another factor of great importance was the North Sea. We have become accustomed by the wars to think of the sea as a great defence, a great obstacle. But in earlier times that was not so. When the roads on land were often useless, the sea was the high road of the North-East—indeed of medieval Scotland. Almost all the royal burghs were on the coast; they were places of wealth and consequence and their trade was coastwise or across the sea. The foundations of the prosperity of Dundee and Aberdeen were on the sea. Montrose later had a very intimate connection with the Baltic. The sea traffic had gone on for a very long time; and, as always happens, more was exchanged than goods. There had been raiders from the Continent, there had been traders from the Continent. Norse, Danish, German and Dutch blood came into the North-East. This was a narrow margin of land where the Highlanders met and mingled with Scandinavian and Germanic people. By the interchange of ideas and of genes there has been a certain hybrid vigour. We are a mixed lot, but this hybrid vigour has kept us going in hard circumstances and through some very difficult times.

The North-East, in spite of its similarities, falls naturally into three divisions: those parts of Angus and the Mearns between Dundee and Stonehaven; the low country from Stonehaven to the Spey, with Aberdeen its eccentric centre; and the Province of Moray, of which Elgin is the capital.

It is not easy for me to write about the city of Dundee for I am an Aberdonian and it is traditional in Aberdeen to hold Dundee in rather low regard. It is probably a matter of the football, in which Dundee has given Aberdeen some hard knocks, but it influenced the atmosphere in which I was brought up; and, in spite of myself, I am inclined to think the

Looking from Law Hill, above Dundee, across the Tay to the shores of Fife. The picture shows how the town was crushed between the hill and the river by its rapid, uncontrolled expansion last century; but there are still fine views of the estuary, and the city itself looks very impressive when approached in the evening by the ferry-boat from Fife.

people of Dundee our natural enemies. That I get on with them very well is always to me a matter of a small surprise. But then I am no longer so passionately interested in the football.

Dundee sits on one of the finest situations in Europe, with the hills sheltering it from the north and the wide estuary of the Tay at its feet. Built on the slope of a hill, it looks over the shine of waters all day and in the evening there are superb sunsets beyond the hills and waters. There, if someone had planned a magnificent town, they could have built one, terraced up and up to some crowning glory on the top of the Law. It did not happen that way. Dundee grew slowly through the centuries, the often difficult centuries. The town must be very old and has been of consequence for a long time. Set on the wide firth with a safe anchorage, it was one of the great gates for trade with Europe. That trade was valuable. Merchants built themselves decent houses in the Scottish style and a town house for the council. That quiet burghal life seems very far away now and it is difficult in modern Dundee to recapture the spirit of those times. The old burgh enjoyed all the excitements of the industrial revolution and suffered many of its troubles. Towards the end of the eighteenth century and in the beginning of the nineteenth it grew very quickly by the textile manufacture. While coal and iron transformed the ways of life in Central Scotland, spinning and weaving were the great forces of change in the North-East. It had been the custom to take the yarn to the spinners and the weavers who worked in their own homes about the countryside—while the man worked his few acres his wife and children spun the thread, and another man in another cottage wove the linen. As power-driven machinery came in it was more economical to collect the workers around the machines, in a factory system. Capital had been used to put work out to the country: later, capital was used to bring people into the towns. So Dundee began to draw in people from the immediate countryside and then from the Highlands. The original town, the douce eighteenth-century town, began to be enveloped by factories and by cheap dwellings run up for the labouring poor. The linen trade got into difficulties about the middle of the nineteenth century but the Dundee manufacturers took to jute in a big way, for sacking and other coarse cloth. Very soon the manufacture of jute became the pre-eminent work in Dundee and remained so for a very long time. It was one of the curiosities of last century that the jute from India should have been brought to this one town, Dundee, and manufactured and sent all over the world, just as American cotton was brought to Lancashire. The town grew by the trade. Cheap houses spread up the hillside, degrading the magnificent site. But great fortunes were made. The new rich built themselves what they thought were beautiful houses in Broughty Ferry and out west by the Perth Road, or across the Tay Bridge in Wormit and Tayport. The houses remain, rather sad memorials of a great expansion. For the manufacturers of Dundee noticed that, however cheap labour might be in Dundee, it was still cheaper in Bombay. Instead of bringing jute the long sea haul to the labour, it might be a better proposition to take the machinery to the jute and to the millions of Indians who had not begun to hear of trade unions. Profits made in Dundee were invested in Indian mills. Families that had once been actively engaged in the jute manufacture in Dundee became more interested in drawing dividends from India. So Dundee raised up its own most dangerous rivals. It is a nice example of the free movement of capital. Even more, I think it is one of the fascinating accidents of history that Dundee and jute should have come together in such a big way. It did not last. In the twenties and thirties the trade contracted; and, because Dundee depended so much on it, the people suffered a hard time. The jute trade remains, but it is now not as important as it was.

Dundee over-specialised in jute, but there were other industries. The insistent demand for mill machinery encouraged engineering. The deep anchorage and the seaborne trade encouraged shipbuilding. There was also the making of preserves. It is said that marmalade was first made in Dundee, which is unlikely, but it has been made in Dundee on a large scale for a long time. Jam too, for the Carse of Gowrie, near at hand, is one of God's gardens. Dundee has given its name to that delicacy, the Dundee cake. Another and remarkable industry is the publishing of weekly papers for all ages, from coloured comics to that household institution, *The People's Friend*. Those diverse papers have one thing in common—although never denying that vice exists (and in Dundee that would be difficult) they are strong on the side of virtue: and they make money. The publishers applied the factory system to manufacturing wish-fulfilment as efficiently as others applied it to the manufacture of jute. Since the late thirties a great deal has been done to broaden the economy of Dundee. New industries have been encouraged by the government and by the town council. The new diversity is surely a good thing.

The city is being rebuilt. The worst of the old workers' tenements are disappearing. So unfortunately are the more gracious parts of the old Dundee. It is a city in a state of transition, with university buildings to balance the mills. The centre is being redeveloped—and redevelopment is something that gives one the chill of apprehension of the worst. Perhaps Dundee may be luckier than other places. But even if it is not, nothing can spoil the wonderful view from the hill over the firth, spanned by the railway bridge—the modest and seemingly insubstantial bridge—or out east where the big ships go slowly to the deep water.

East and north from Dundee there is a strip of good farmland and, by the seaside, the golf courses. The most famous is the championship course at

Anglers at Bridge of Dun, on the South Esk between Montrose and Brechin, fishing one of the best streams in Scotland.

Carnoustie, a public one where you pay your money and you take your chance. On this course lined with low sand dunes there is a feeling of great space. The white clouds billow in the blue sky, a light wind blows and the lark ascending sings. A man, squaring himself up on the tee, may feel he has the sky and the sea as well as the land to play on. That can induce a recklessness which ends in trouble, for the wide spaces of Carnoustie hold many cunning traps. These seaside courses, with their spare grasses and small herbs that scent the air, are to be found all round the north-east coast—at Montrose, Aberdeen, Cruden Bay, Peterhead, Fraserburgh, Spey Bay, Lossiemouth and Nairn: indeed nearly every village of any size has its course; and, if there are sometimes only nine holes, that is made up for by the whins, cliffs and other hazards. The course at Stonehaven is adventurously laid along the top of the cliffs and there have been gentlemen who tried short pitches with gulls' eggs.

Arbroath and Montrose are two interesting towns along the coast. Arbroath had one of the great abbeys of Scotland where Scotland's declaration of independence was drawn up during the wars with England. The abbey is now a magnificent ruin around which a textile and engineering town has grown up in a pleasant way, so that Arbroath is also a holiday place. It has a delightful miniature railway on which large gentlemen can ride in small carriages. Between Arbroath and Montrose, Lunan Bay has wide and little-frequented sands, a ruined castle for the imagination to play with and a hotel for more substantial refreshment. I must declare a great liking for Montrose. I would call it a douce town—and douce means sweet in a homely way, as ladies are who have come to a pleasant old age. It is douce with a touch of elegance in its eighteenth-century style houses and its wide High Street like a French place with its town hall and steeple. It was once a great place for trade with the Baltic. Now

it is a market town and a holiday resort. It has a delightful situation, having the sea on one side and a wide tidal basin on the other, so that it gives the illusion of being on an island. There have been plans to reclaim the basin but too many interests were involved and the scheme was given up. So the basin remains, a great placid stretch of water at high tide: and, at low tide, a landscape of sandbanks and shallows where fishermen dig for bait and seabirds stand on one leg waiting for whatever sea birds so patiently wait for.

A few miles back from the Angus coast there is a spine of high ground which continues into the Mearns—the Sidlaw and the Garvock Hills. Beyond them there is some of the best farmland and the fairest country in Scotland. Strathmore and the Howe o' the Mearns lie in a wide valley with the low hills to the east and the Grampians to the west. There are great baronial houses, large arable farms, woodlands for shelter and an air of long settlement and solid prosperity. The great houses, such as Glamis, Cortachy, Brechin, Kinnaird and Edzell, show what the land could bear two-three hundred years ago. Fenella's Castle at Kincardine was the home of a wild queen,

GOURDON

This small fishing village of about a thousand people lies half-way between Montrose and Stonehaven, in Kincardineshire. The picture shows the traditional kind of east-coast fishing boat, small, solid and stoutly-built like the town itself.

INVERCAULD HOUSE, DEESIDE

The River Dee rises in the Cairngorms, and flows through the Forest of Mar to Braemar, Balmoral and beyond. Invercauld House, seat of the Farquharson family, stands near the north bank of the river, between Braemar and Balmoral. On the south is Ballochbuie Forest, whose rich, various colours contrast with the snow and the water.

Arbuthnott House, near Inverbervie in Kincardineshire, stands on a site where Arbuthnotts have lived for eight hundred years.

half witch, in a much older time. There are many smaller houses—for instance Balbegno near Fettercairn, a decent example of the old Scottish style and The House of Dun near Montrose, an elegant eighteenth-century piece. These are just a few evidences of wealth being in the countryside for a long time, even though the wealth may have been not very well divided.

The countryside is still well-off. The large farmhouses with the ample steadings behind them, the fine herds of cattle, the heavy crops of corn and potatoes, the combine harvesters and pick-up balers are signs that the farmers in the Strath and the Howe are making the sort of living they have become accustomed to think their due. They have always been a little superior and despise those who scratch for a profit among the stones of Aberdeenshire.

It is a pleasant country in the summer, especially when seen from the top of Garvock Hill. All the land lies green below you in a blue haze of the sun and the Grampians stand up magnificently along the west. Another Eden, you might think—and not without a serpent or two.

The burghs in Strathmore and the Howe—Forfar, Brechin, Kirriemuir and Laurencekirk—were originally market places, with Brechin having a much superior importance with its cathedral. There were weavers in the burghs long ago and the factory system brought in the mills, except in Laurencekirk. The mills, and the people they attracted, changed the character of the old burghs but the growth never got out of hand. Today the burghs still depend a great deal on serving agriculture. Laurencekirk depends almost entirely on giving that service, in the way of selling and maintaining machinery, of moving goods and cattle by road, and of providing tradesmen for the rebuilding necessary to bring the farm buildings and houses up to date. In Laurencekirk it is easy to see the increasing importance of the town to agriculture and that the town is indeed the centre. Forfar and Brechin are equally important to farming but that is less easy to see because of the other industries. Though those towns have a variety of trades, and would like to attract more, they are not in the common sense industrial towns, and the wind off the cornfields blows down their streets.

North towards Stonehaven the foothills of the Grampians come nearer the sea. The cliffs stand higher, the soil becomes harder, until the ruins of Dunnottar stand on a crag that looks like the last outpost of the Grampians, as Dunnottar itself seems a last outpost of the Middle Ages. Beyond there is the second part of the North-East, the harder part, away from the ease of Strathmore, centred on the town of Aberdeen. To that new country Stonehaven is a proper introduction—the small, grey fisher village that grew up a little to become the county town of a small county and is now a holiday place of the quieter sort. It is easy to see that life was once hard in those parts and that its modest graces have been won always in hard work and often in danger. One may also get a sense of the wonderful endurance of these old communities: and endurance has been very necessary in this part of the North-East.

Somewhere hereabout a traveller may think he is getting to the bare edge of civilisation, but then there is the grand surprise. Ultima Thule and eternal darkness might be expected but instead there is the city of Aberdeen. It is a big place where nearly two hundred thousand people live, a big city to find anywhere so far north in Europe. And,

Aberdeen beach in winter, looking towards the lighthouse and harbour. In summer this stretch is gay with holidaymakers.

A panoramic view of Aberdeen from the south, looking across the River Dee. Most of the city is built of granite, which gives it a clean, handsome air. Aberdeen took its name from the river, at the mouth of which is the harbour on which its prosperity depends.

under skies blown clean by the sea winds, the silvery stone of the houses shines in the terraces built along the rise of the ground from the sea and the river, with many towers and steeples pointing the way to Heaven and factory chimneys that seldom look like the smoke vents of Hell. It is more than forty years since I first saw Aberdeen from the south and thought it wonderful, and I still get a touch of wonder from that aspect. Aberdeen has not the magnificent situation of Dundee but the people have done better with what they had.

Aberdeen stands on a shoulder of ground between two rivers, the Dee and the Don, and was once two separate burghs—Aberdeen on the Dee and the Aulton on the Don. The Aulton is now called Old Aberdeen which may be a pity since it is probably no older than its neighbour. The two are now one though still distinguishable. In medieval times Aberdeen had a strong castle. The Aulton had a cathedral and, from 1494, a university. Aberdeen prospered by trade with the Continent: the Aulton was devoted to learning. Aberdeen had a good anchorage on the Dee, the Aulton a poor one on the Don: so the trading went more and more to the former. The merchants of Aberdeen turned the anchorage into a harbour at great labour as their trade with Europe grew; and to satisfy that trade they developed the resources of the countryside. That countryside was poor in everything but people. The people, however, could be put to work in their

Balmoral Castle, the sovereign's Scottish residence, stands on a curve of the Dee at the foot of Craig Gowan. It is built in the Scots baronial style, of white Crathie granite.

homes, at the textiles, and especially in knitting stockings. Aberdeen stockings became famous, for they were knitted fine enough to grace the most elegant and the noblest legs in Europe. When the factory system came in, the merchants started mills in the town, which attracted people from the country parishes and from the Highlands. The town grew too big for its old bounds, and then a remarkable thing happened. The town council, inspired perhaps by the example of Edinburgh, made a grand town plan. They swept away a clutter of old hovels, removed a hill and drove a fine street westward through the middle of the town. This was called Union Street in celebration of the Union of the British and Irish parliaments in 1800. They were also fortunate to have two architects, John Smith and Archibald Simpson, who could design in the classical style; and the new street, and the squares laid out to the west of it, had a certain elegance. At the same time masons discovered how to dress the native granite. So a new and handsome Aberdeen arose.

Aberdeen has had three natural resources—the sea, the farm land and the industry of its people. The seaborne trade was the foundation of its fortunes. The development of the farmland added to that trade. The manufacture of linen and cotton led to great expansion in the late eighteenth century. Then a market was found for granite. First of all it proved a very durable stone fit for quays and sea walls; and then a method was discovered of polishing it in large slabs so that it looked to be of the semi-precious order, admirable for bank offices and gravestones. For a long time the working of granite was a major industry in the town, though it is not so now, as it is very expensive. When trawlers came in, Aberdeen, well situated for the fishing banks, became one of the great white fishing ports and remains so. Because there was an abundance of water, papermaking developed along the Don and by the Dee at Culter; and at Grandholm, also on the Don, there is perhaps the largest tweed mill in Scotland. In the town there are shipbuilders and engineers and a very large linen mill. I mention these to show the diversity of trades in Aberdeen, which has never depended too much on one thing alone. Again, it is worth noticing that a large part of Aberdeen's living comes from the resources immediately around it. The catching and handling of fish make a living for thousands and have made fortunes for some. So do the services the town gives to agriculture. As long as Aberdeen handles the chief parts of a fish supper there will always be some money in the town.

It is difficult to realise that Aberdeen is such a busy industrial town since the industries are not obtrusive. The buildings that dominate the town are Marischal College and the Town House, the former a rather

LOCH KINORD

Loch Kinord lies north of Dinnet, in Aberdeenshire. Apart from its beauty, it is famous for its "crannogs"—prehistoric loch dwellings of stones and logs — and on an island there is a castle where Edward I rested on his return from Lochindorb.

Burnside of Braco, near Pitcaple, is typical of the many small Aberdeenshire farms of about one hundred and fifty to three hundred acres, built up the hard way over the centuries.

A pleasant scene on a farm near Old Meldrum, Aberdeenshire, giving a glimpse of one of Scotland's most important industries —the rearing and exporting of valuable Shorthorn cattle.

startling exercise in tooled granite. The clean stone, the clear skies and the sea winds off the bay make Aberdeen stimulating and attractive. The long sandy beach with the golf links behind it suggests holidays, and Aberdeen has sold itself as a holiday resort which attracts hundreds of thousands of people. That, we old inhabitants think, is quite a master-stroke. It is by making so much of what we have that we have been able to carry on so long and so well.

The counties of Aberdeen and Banff are the rural background of Aberdeen. They can be taken in three parts—the fishing communities, the arable land and Deeside.

Deeside is rather a sport in this setting. It is a Highland glen with a clear river running over white stones, narrow bounds of light soil that run away to heather moors, and ranges of hills on each side that rise into mountains in the west. It is picturesque, it is historical and it is romantic. The picturesque is made up of shining water beyond silver birches, with the cornfields near, and beyond them the blue hills. A fairy tale sort of place. The historical adds to the picturesque. There is the square tower of Drum Castle. There is Crathes, a magnificent example of Scots baronial now owned by the National Trust for Scotland. There are Aboyne and Abergeldie and Braemar. At Kinord there are islands that carried lake dwellings; and, on the moors beyond, there are the burial places cf ancient men. There is also Balmoral, the private house of the reigning monarch. The presence of the Court has added greatly to the attractions of Deeside, which nature had made considerable. It has made Deeside fashionable and given it a Season, with sports meetings at Aboyne and Braemar for piping, dancing, tossing the caber and the wearing of the kilt. But west away from the piping and the dancing, lonely paths lead up into the Cairngorms over to Speyside and Donside. There, along those ancient paths, quiet is to be found, a commodity that elsewhere is too often in short supply.

The fishing communities of the North-East are near Deeside in distance but far away in spirit. On the Dee, fishermen catch salmon the hard way, with flies. The sea fishers get herring and white fish a harder way, at the risk of their lives. The sea fishermen live on land but they are different from the country people. They live in small tight communities in their villages by the shore; they are exclusive; and their ways of life and of thought are their own. Nowadays, although they live in their villages they fish out of the big ports—Peterhead, Fraserburgh, Buckie and Lossiemouth. Some fish out of Aberdeen. But they remain faithful to their own places, and there one can get a taste of an older and simpler society. Peterhead, Fraserburgh and Buckie have a great stir of life in the herring season when the drifters come in at morning with their catches and sail out again in the afternoon for a night at sea. There is a gleam of silver scales, a smell of salt, a rich smoke from the kippering yards and a talk and a clatter in the streets, with everywhere the gulls wheeling and squawking on the look-out for their dinner. At other seasons the harbours seem deserted for it was, and is, the custom that the drifters follow the herring down to East Anglia in the autumn. But the harbours are less deserted than they used to be, since the white fishing, especially at Lossiemouth, goes on all the time. The herring trade made the fortune of the ports. Now the towns look for other work. Engineering and food canning have been attracted to Peterhead and Fraserburgh. But let no one think Peterhead is a jumped-up sort of place. In the eighteenth century it was a fashionable health resort. It has still an afterglow of those times.

In the arable parts of Aberdeenshire and Banff there is mixed farming on a mixed lot of land. The remarkable thing is that so much has been brought under the plough and kept in cultivation through the worst of times. A tremendous labour went into the making of the ploughland—thousands of miles of ditches and drains had to be dug to run off the water; many many thousand of tons of stones had to be gathered off the surface before the plough could go in, and thousands of acres were trenched by the spade and the pick before there could be any hope of a crop. And when all that was done the poor land had to be fed and nursed, sometimes for generations, before it would give a decent return. The making of those farmlands is one of the great pioneering stories and what it cost in human fatigue is beyond all reckoning. But the fertility of the land has been built up slowly year by year. The basis of the improvement was stock, stock of any kind that feed the land while the land feeds them. The favourite cattle are the Aberdeen-Angus, the black-polled, that carry the best of beef. They are quiet, kindly and loveable beasts and most farmers have a soft side for them even though they do not have them on their farms. There have been and still are some very famous Shorthorn herds from which bull calves have been sold for many thousands of pounds. A deal of art has been exercised in the North-East in the evolution of these two breeds. Dairy herds of Friesians, Ayrshires and Jerseys have come in because dairying is profitable, as it should be, since it is much harder work than the feeding of beef cattle. The pig and the hen have become immensely popular during the last thirty years for they leave a profit and help to

North of Cruden Bay are the Bullers of Buchan, which Dr. Johnson called "a rock perpendicularly tubulated." In rough weather the waves breaking in the fissure at high tide make an awe-inspiring spectacle.

Salmon cobbles, with their nets piled high in the stern, make their way up the broad Findhorn estuary to the village of Findhorn after a profitable evening's fishing.

CROVIE BAY

Between Macduff and Fraserburgh, sheltered by the cliffs, lies the tiny fishing village of Crovie. It is away from all main routes, but is connected to the slightly larger village of Gardenstown, a mile to the west, by a path along the coast.

CRATHIE CHURCH

The little granite church at Crathie was built in 1895, and is attended by the Royal family when they are staying in Deeside. The churchyard contains a monument erected by Queen Victoria to her faithful old retainer, John Brown, who died in 1883.

THE OLD BRIDGE OF DEE

The Old Bridge of Dee was built in 1520-1527 by Gavin Dunbar, Bishop of Dunkeld. The seven ribbed arches bear inscriptions and coats-of-arms, and when the bridge was widened in 1842 the west face was carefully replaced to preserve its character.

feed the land. That matter of building up fertility, though it is not shown in balance sheets, is in the front of every good farmer's mind, perhaps a little behind the first consideration, profit. There are no very big farms, although one man with several may farm a two thousand acres or so. A big farm is three or four hundred acres. A common size is around one hundred and fifty acres. But the characteristic North-East farm, Aberdeenshire style, is the family one—enough to be worked by the farmer, his wife and their children in their teens. There are many hundreds of these farms, each with a tractor, two or three cows, a dozen young stock, a score of sheep, two or three breeding sows and two hundred laying hens, a break of turnips and two breaks of oats or barley. In good times those farms do very well; in bad times the farmers survive because their unavoidable expenses are low. Each one is the result of many men's work and forethought. They lie in a country that men have made fertile.

Every few miles there are villages with a kirk, a hall, a bank, an inn, a merchant's shop and a post office. Sometimes there are small towns—Kintore, for instance, an ancient burgh with a charming town

Cawdor Castle, near Nairn. Macbeth was Thane of Cawdor, and according to Shakespeare this is where he murdered Duncan. But the oldest part of the present building, the central tower, is fifteenth-century.

house; Old Meldrum with a town house and a distillery; Huntly with a magnificent ruined castle and a knitwear trade, Keith with its cattle markets and textiles. On the holiday coast of the Moray Firth Cullen has a wide sandy bay. Macduff has a swimming pool. Those are for quiet holidays. And Banff, the old county town at the mouth of the Deveron, has some fine old houses once lived in by merchants who traded overseas, or by country lairds in winter. On the edge of the town Duff House, like Gordon Castle on the banks of the Spey, is one of the stateliest homes, where everything is in proportion to the dignity of a Duke and no one less than a Duke could feel at home there.

Although so much of the farmland has been taken in from the rough in the last two hundred years, there is sometimes a powerful sense of time past here. There are many stone circles, as at Loanhead of Daviot. There are the ruined castles, as at Tolquhon and Huntly. There are the castles of Craigievar, in Leochel, and Fyvie, lovely examples of the baronial. In Buchan the ruins of the Abbey of Deer show what a small monastic house was like. And at Pitmedden in Udny there is a beautiful seventeenth-century garden where the fountain plays for visitors. But the unexpected treasures of this part are too many to mention here.

The Province of Moray is a kinder land than Aberdeenshire. It has ease and shelter where most of Aberdeenshire has not, and in some ways it is like Strathmore but on a lighter soil. Although it looks north it has the gentlest and the dryest climate in Scotland. It is fertile, too, for the land bears good cattle and good corn; and especially round Fochabers, the best of fruit.

The city of Elgin is the heart of Moray. There the softness, sweetness and grace of the province are most happily brought together. Elgin was a city long before many greater cities had ever been thought of. It had a magnificent cathedral which, though fallen into ruin, is still magnificent. Later it was a weaving town and it has still two mills turning out textiles of a very high quality. Much of the town is built of the local sandstone, a pale honey-coloured stone, and many of the houses are of the eighteenth century or at least are in that correct style. So there is some elegance in the houses; and, in the soft stone, there is the afterglow of many summers. The river Lossie runs through Elgin, winding in and out among the trees, and there sits the comely town, the mellow city of the north.

Elgin is for comfort, the indigenous comfort, malt whisky. The distilleries are round about, down towards Rothes and along the Spey. Barley, peat and soft hill water are transformed into an alcohol with inspiring essences. Those who have the time and the constitution to make long trial of the liquors—and each distillery produces a subtly distinctive one—can make as nice comparisons among whiskies as others do among wines, but fortunately they do not use as flowery language as the wine-lovers do, nor do they take up literary attitudes. Those who know the best malt whiskies make no song about them in case the generality drink up all the precious supply, drowned in soda or ginger ale.

Forres and Nairn are pleasant small towns with the moors behind them. They have the golf, Nairn has its beach and both are for holidays of the family sort. And around them there is the good farmland, with the hills of Ross across the narrow firth.

Down from Forres, at the mouth of the Findhorn, there is a remarkable country. The parish of Culbin was overwhelmed by sea sands which turned it into a desert. It was the sort of thing a ballad could have been made about—Culbin like an Atlantis, buried under the sand. But now the sands have been fixed by grasses and trees and a great forest stands with its roots many feet above the smothered kirk and houses. Culbin is worth a visit. It shows one way in which the deserts of the world can be nursed back to fruitfulness.

The hills and moors come nearer the coast as the Moray Firth becomes narrow towards Inverness. On Drummossie Muir there are the graves of the men who died fighting at Culloden. And there's a place to make an end. Culloden and all that was a Highland story.

THE CENTRAL HIGHLANDS

Tom Weir

To geographers the main topographical feature of Scotland is the Highland border fault, where from the Firth of Clyde to Stonehaven in Kincardineshire rise the maze of mountain peaks which ordinary folks know as the "Highland Line". Glasgow, Stirling, Perth, Dundee and Forfar lie along its brink. This great bulge of Scotland, topped by the opening of the Moray Firth, is the region we shall call the Central Highlands in our survey. It is separated from the rest of North Britain by another major topographical feature, namely Glen Albyn or the Great Glen.

Here is a diverse country with diverse climates. It includes the second biggest nature reserve in Europe, containing relics of the Ice Age and remnants of the primeval forests which followed its decline. It includes in Perth and Angus some of the best grouse moors and deer forests in the land, and its salmon rivers, almost impervious to drought where they are fed by melting snows, are legend among fishermen. It contains the best skiing grounds in Scotland, and is the most colourful hill country in the Highlands when the heather is in bloom.

Generally, in this area of the Central Highlands, the weather follows an east coast pattern, which means it is drier and sunnier than in the extreme west. Loch Tay in Perthshire is a good example of what I mean. Here, as you go from east to west on the loch, there is an increase of one inch per mile in the average annual rainfall, which means that at the west end the rainfall is twenty inches more than at the east end. And the little town of Pitlochry, near the centre of the area, has only a fraction of the rainfall of Glasgow.

So we will begin our explorations of the Central Highlands with the rainy country, the part closest to Glasgow and Stirling, namely the Trossachs—the "Bristly Country"—which historically extends from Loch Katrine to Loch Achray, but has come to mean in this century of travel the whole region of mountains and lochs extending from Aberfoyle northward and eastward to Callander. The charm of the Trossachs is its suddenness, the first abrupt rise of the Highlands from the green farmlands, the line of cleavage which inspired Wordsworth, Coleridge and Sir Walter Scott, not to mention the outlaw Rob Roy who used it as a springboard for cattle raids, using his great local knowledge of secret glens and caves to outwit his pursuers. The barracks built by the government to keep the Macgregors in check may still be seen at Inversnaid.

The approach I like best is from the Lake of Menteith, west from Thornhill by the goose-haunted expanse known as Flanders Moss, where the Forth winds sluggishly, though its source on Ben Lomond is not far away. There is a feeling of space here, an impression of being on the tundras of the far north, with the wild cries of the pink-footed geese and the whirling flocks of duck which make this their sanctuary from autumn to spring. Dotting the dun moor are green fields and farms reclaimed by the foresight of the Laird of Blair Drummond over a hundred years ago when he established families on the sour moss, giving them land at a small rent if they would dig out the moss and find the good soil beneath. The more land they reclaimed the cheaper became their rent. Reclamation is still going on, but this time it is the Forestry Commission who are doing it.

Indeed we are entering the domain of the Forestry Commission at the Lake of Menteith, though the main

plantings lie further over into the Trossachs. Menteith is Scotland's only "lake", and it is beautifully correct, for "loch" would be the wrong word for this English piece of scenery with its "Port" for sailing by motor-boat to the site of the ancient priory which was home to Mary, Queen of Scots for a short time when, as a child, she was taken there so that she should not fall into the victorious English hands after the Battle of Pinkie.

Aberfoyle is only four miles from the Port of Menteith and here you enter the Queen Elizabeth Forest Park which includes parts of the Trossachs and extends over the summit of Ben Lomond on one side to Loch Achray and Loch Vennacher on the other.

This is weekend country for Glasgow walkers and ramblers, with tracks wandering over moor and forest from one youth hostel to another, by Loch Katrine and Ben Venue or over Ben Lomond to Rowardennan. No need to breathe petrol fumes here or risk death on the busy west shore of Loch Lomond when the east shore north of the Ben is roadless and offers good camp spots in every bay.

The motorist can have his own thrill in the quick zig-zags of the Duke's Pass, each steep giving its own

LOCH ARD

About one and a half miles west of Aberfoyle lies the placid basin of Loch Ard. Islands near the south and south-west shores once held a castle and a chapel. To the west, as in this picture, the familiar peak of Ben Lomond rises above the wooded shores.

BEN VENUE AND LOCH KATRINE

The crags of Ben Venue and the neighbouring mountains have given the name to the Trossachs—"the bristling country"—a beautiful district made famous by Scott's poem, "The Lady of the Lake". The small steamer plies daily in summer between Trossachs pier, seen in this picture, and Stronachlachar near the west end of Loch Katrine.

Little Loch Drunkie may take its name from the illicit stills which used to operate in the district. It lies about two miles north of Aberfoyle and is seen from the Duke's Pass.

exciting view, such as that from the first rise above Aberfoyle when you suddenly look over Strathendrick to the great Lowland plain stretching to the Campsies across an expanse like a green sea dotted with white caps, each cap a farmhouse. Then on again to glimpse Loch Drunkie, to cross the topmost ridge and find beneath you the best view in the Trossachs.

Now you can appreciate why Scott wrote so ecstatically of the scenery, with the sharp rocks of Ben Aan thrusting through:

"Crags, knolls, and mounds confusedly hurled,
The fragments of an earlier world."

The Forestry Commission have been ingenious in their planting to fit their trees to the natural scene yet leave unspoiled the vistas of mountain, moor and loch which unfold as the road mounts to this greatest prospect, with Loch Achray below, hemmed by oaks, birches, hazel and beech jutting out at all angles as nature left them.

Whether the Trossachs scene is finer in spring or in autumn is something on which I cannot make up my mind. The loveliness of spring, when the oaks are yellow and the birches shimmering in new green, is unforgettable, especially so when the first brillance of primroses, violets and anemonies which form the woodland floors is replaced by the blue of wild hyacinths, making a haze on every glade and scenting the air for miles. But then I think of autumn, when the first September snows mantle the peaks, making the rowan berries glow more richly red against the burnish of bronze and copper from the fiery deer grass and the russet tints of the dying heather crowning every slope. One must see both to be convinced by each in turn.

The landscape has not changed so vastly since Wordsworth and his sister explored the region in August and September of 1803. They walked forty miles in two days, from the head of Loch Lomond by Glen Gyle to Loch Katrine, crossing the next day to Loch Voil and Strathyre. The big change the Wordsworths would see if they returned today would be the huge increase in the numbers of people who share their own love of nature, for the Trossachs is the happy hunting ground of fishermen, hikers, tourists, campers, caravanners and cyclists who find healthy recreation in the good countryside, and there is still plenty of room for all, especially off the beaten track into the Forest of Glenartney or west of Loch Voil where Ben More and Stobinian rise to over 3,800 feet amid a wild tangle of mountain tops blocking the northern sky.

Over these peaky hills lies Crianlarich, the railway junction for Fort William and Oban and the meeting place of three important glens, Glen Falloch, Glen Dochart and Strathfillan. Some people feel a sense of claustrophobia here, with steep mountain walls shutting them in from all directions. To a lover of alpine scenery it is a prospect which never fails to thrill, especially in winter when the snowy peaks may loom as huge as Himalayan giants, for altitude is a matter of scale.

I remember one such morning when, in November fog, we came by Perth and Crieff to find ourselves suddenly into thinner air in Glen Dochart. We were heading for Glen Coe, but it was eclipsed that day by the sight of Ben More and Stobinian towering above a veil of shimmering mist, their snow spires gleaming softly against a dark cloudbank. The drama of that sudden revelation is something that none of us who were there is likely to forget, accustomed though we were to views ranging from the Atlas Mountains and the High Alps to Everest.

We were following the western boundary of the Central Highland zone that morning, going by Tyndrum, where a train crossing the massive flank of Ben Lui looked like a child's toy as it puffed past the remnants of the old Caledonian Forest which grace this finest peak of Perthshire. Here, over six hundred years ago, Bruce was ambushed by the MacDougalls of Lorne in an action which gave them the famous Brooch of Lorne.

The route northward from here climbs out of Perthshire into Argyll, but only Duncan Ban Macintyre, who wrote the wonderful song in praise of Beinn Doireann, could have done justice to his favourite bit of country that morning, with hill slopes a mat of autumn colour, flaming into glens and corries to lose themselves in a thousand feet of snow. This is the point for getting a bird's eye view of Rannoch Moor,

Callander, with the railway station nearest to the Trossachs, is situated on the River Teith at its junction with the Leny. Here the first snows of winter cap Ben Ledi and the timber house in the foreground adds to the alpine effect.

cradled by high peaks, yet so uniform in height that it is possible to walk for ten miles across it and always be within fifty feet of the thousand-foot contour.

That day the triangular moor was like a scene in Tibet, with the enamelled blue lochs reflecting the snow-domes of peaks on crinkled ice, and not a breath of wind stirring an immensity of space. Strange to think that from this point so far west the main drainage of the moor is not into the Atlantic but into the North Sea by the River Ba and Loch Tummel and Loch Rannoch. Stranger still to think that only a few hundred years ago this was not a moor but a vast forest stretching bottle-green pine needles and red boughs from Glen Coe to Glen Lyon and the Braes of Mar and Strathspey. At the time of Bannockburn reindeer were still roaming the woods of Scotland.

The remnants of the old forest are still with us. You see them at Loch Tulla, and at Crannach on the railway line, but the greatest fragment left in Perthshire is at the "Black Wood of Rannoch". How many know it, I wonder? To get to it from the west end of the moor you would have to walk, for no road crosses the interior, and even the path from Kingshouse to Rannoch Station has partly disappeared. The traveller must take guidance from the telegraph poles that stride across bog and burn past great tree roots, like the bones of prehistoric animals, which lie part-buried in the bog as mute evidence that history does not lie.

It is a walk where you feel the pressure of history, in a country where man has hunted man, and wild boar, wolf, northern lynx, caribou and brown bear once abounded. In the sixteenth century the pine woods of Lochaber were so thickly infested with wolves that travellers dared not risk a journey unless it was absolutely necessary. The red deer that had its home in these woods was a third larger than the present animal outlawed to an unnatural habitat of bare hilltops. Banished from the woods, it has gone into decline. Local tradition has it that the forest was destroyed to extirpate wolves when organised hunts failed to keep them in check. Once the forest had been opened up in this way the action of wind storms would prove as devastating to the trees as the work of charcoal burners and other commercial exploiters of the time. The "Black Wood of Rannoch", like the Forest of Rothiemurchus in Inverness-shire, is a museum piece of this enormous Wood of Caledon which existed until the sixteenth century. It is now preserved by the Forestry Commission.

The "immense vacuity" of Rannoch Moor is not, however, going to waste in this age of hydro-electricity. Loch Laidon has a dam and power house, linking it with Loch Rannoch and Loch Tummel, and the waters of the moor, which cover three quarters of its surface, are being used for the first time in history. And southward across Schiehallion, from Glen Lyon to Loch Tay, man has harnessed even mightier forces by damming Loch Lyon and Lochan na Lairige to use the whole catchment area of "Little Switzerland", as skiers name the Ben Lawers region.

STRATHFILLAN

The West Highland Railway offers a wonderful variety of scenery. Between Crianlarich and Tyndrum it ascends Strathfillan, with pleasant prospects of Fillan Water. The river broadens to form St. Fillan's Pool, immersion in which was reputed to cure lunatics.

LOCH VOIL

Loch Voil is a long, narrow Perthshire loch in the heart of the Rob Roy country. The road to Inverlochlarig runs along the north shore of the loch, past the celebrated Braes of Balquhidder and Rob Roy's burial-place at the village of Balquhidder.

Motorists will find a new network of roads here, beginning in Glen Lochay where a cunning fish-pass enables salmon to surmount the previously impassable falls. Now they are hoisted up and rejoin the river by means of a little canal which is dwarfed by the gigantic pipes descending from the Tarmachans to the power house. Where was formerly a footpath into Glen Lyon there is now a first-class driving road, and it is easy to do a circuit from Killin to Fortingall, seeing the best of this long and beautiful glen.

And in Glen Lyon there is always something to see, where the river foams through rocky jaws and grey wagtails and oyster catchers bob on the stones. The stretch of the glen I like best is from Kenknock, where the Caledonian pines climb high on the slopes but give way to hanging forests of birch, by Bridge of Balgie to the narrows of the Pass of Lyon. Not the least of the charm of Glen Lyon is that it is lived-in. It is not a desert, like much of the Highlands, with only the ruins of crofts showing where a former people lived. White-washed cottages and prosperous farms with fine herds of cattle and sheep are the perfect accompaniment to the grandeur of the scenery. There can be few places more perfect to

Skiers enjoy excellent conditions on the slopes of Ben Lawers early in the season, and the snow sometimes lasts until April.

Water-skiing is an invigorating new sport, and the beauty of Loch Earn adds to its attractions. Sailing is also popular on this loch and there is a yacht club near St. Fillans.

try for salmon when the spring fish are running green-blue from the sea.

All the Tay, of course, is sportsman's country, and while angling enthusiasts are enduring the frosts of January to lure the first fish from the water, the skiers are out in force enjoying the slopes of Ben Ghlas and Ben Lawers. Bridge of Lochay Hotel is the headquarters of the Scottish Ski Club in this region, with close by the high climbing road to the Lochan na Lairige leading to the car park at 1500 feet. From there it is an easy walk to the hut at the ski grounds. Unfortunately the configuration of the hills does not allow them to hold the snow so well as in other parts of Scotland. Melting takes place all too quickly, so the best skiing here is in the early weeks of the season, though fresh falls and old drifts may provide good sport until April. At its best the skiing is superb, as bus-loads from Edinburgh and Glasgow discover every winter.

For the naturalist who is neither fisherman nor skier there is the Field Study Centre of Garth, which is a youth hostel just north of Fortingall of yew-tree fame. Pontius Pilate is alleged to have been born at Fortingall, and certainly there was a Roman camp in the neighbourhood. In the churchyard you can see the three-thousand-year-old yew, caged by iron railings. The bird life of Glen Lyon and the flowers of Ben Lawers are the attractions of Garth. The corrie known as the Allt Tuim nam Breac is the best place for alpine plants, and here you may see survivors of the ice age in full strength. You do not need to be a botanist to appreciate the feast of colour which carpets these upper slopes from April to July, when the mats of purple and yellow saxifrage and the blues of gentians and alpine forget-me-nots are in bloom. Visitors are asked not to pick the flowers, especially the very rare drooping saxifrage.

Water skiing is the newest sport to the region, but the centre for this is a little further to the south, at Lochearnhead, where narrow Loch Earn runs parallel to Loch Tay, with the peak of Ben Vorlich and the Forest of Glen Artney rising grandly above. Here at weekends and in summer evenings the enthusiasts congregate as a steadily increasing band.

I have mentioned the Forest of Glen Artney. This is not truly a forest within the accepted meaning of the term, since "forest" in the Highlands usually means a tract of uncultivated land used for sport. Around Loch Lubnaig and Strathyre, however, the Forestry Commission have restored the true meaning of forest by their considerable plantings and have given us some indication of what much of the Highlands is going to be like when their millions of little trees grow. By contrast the moors of Ben Chonzie and Glen Almond are bare indeed, but these uplands breed tremendous numbers of grouse and in good seasons give some of the biggest bags in Scotland.

The Earn valley opens eastward to a richer country, its river flowing by Comrie and Crieff to the great scoop formed by the trench of the Ochils. Crieff is deservedly popular with holidaymakers as a touring centre and a clean little town noted for sunshine. The view of the Earn I like best is from Auchterarder as you go north to Perth, when in autumn the huge sloping fields are busy with potato harvesters and wheeling over the corn stubble are the first winter geese newly arrived from Iceland. These are pink-footed geese, whose favourite loch is Carsbreck near Blackford, and anyone who travels by train from Stirling to Perth in winter cannot fail to see the wheeling gaggles or glimpse them feeding, head alert, in the fields adjacent to the railway. There is no other place in Britain that I know of where it is so easy to see wild geese.

Stirling for its castle commanding the bridges over the Forth, Dunblane for its cathedral and hydro, Gleneagles for golf and Perth for its Inchs are too well known for me to do more than make passing mention, but anyone with time to spare in Perth should take the walk to the top of Kinnoull Hill for its tremendous view over the windings of the Tay to Fife, and northward to the blue mass of the Grampians stretching from Schiehallion and Beinn a Ghlo to Angus and the Aberdeen Highlands, with the cultivated downlands called the Sidlaws rising beyond the fruit fields of the Carse of Gowrie. Out of sight, cradled between the Sidlaws and the Braes of Angus, is the fertile vale of Strathmore whose lowlands are so famous for oats, wheat, potatoes, fruit and cattle.

For the city that was once the capital of Scotland, Perth has a wonderful air of belonging to the country rather than the town. That is its charm, especially on market days when the tacketty boots and Scots tweeds proclaim that the farmers are in with a crop of lambs or a herd of good cattle beasts. The accent here is on quality, and if you would know the value the world buyers put on Scottish cattle you should visit the annual bull sales and hear the fantastic prices bid for prizewinners that are raising the standard of cattle breeding all over the world.

Even the name "Inch" has an association with the land, for it comes from the Gaelic *innis*, a long level grassland by the side of a stream. It was on the North Inch that the Battle of the Clans was fought, when sides were picked as in a football match and thirty men fought another thirty to the death. That was in the time of Robert III. Go to St. John's Kirk and history does not seem so remote when you see the place where John Knox preached such a fiery sermon in 1559 that some six thousand reformers ransacked the town for images to destroy. The church is the same, except that the tower is now topped by a spire.

Unfortunately the work begun by Cromwell when he destroyed the Mercat Cross in 1651 was carried out too thoroughly by town-planning reformers when they rebuilt the city in the nineteenth century. They built the new Perth by sweeping away the old buildings regardless of their priceless link with history. Modern Perth, with its fine shops and spacious layout, is a tribute to them, but the zealous searcher will have to be content with plaques marking the places and faces in Scotland's story.

This view to the east from Stirling Castle shows the tortuous curves of the River Forth and the wide spread of the Carse across to Abbey Craig and the Wallace Monument.

Kinnoull Hill is a south-western spur of the Sidlaws rising sharply above the Tay, east of Perth. The hunting tower was built as a ruin to add character to the view.

From Perth there are three main ways of exploring the Central Highlands. You may go north-west by Dunkeld, Pitlochry and Drumochter Pass to Speyside. You may go due north by the Spittal of Glenshee and over the Devil's Elbow to Braemar on Deeside, or

Loch Faskally is a new loch, created by the Tummel-Garry hydro-electric scheme in 1949-50. It is 2½ miles long, and its beauty, in winter as in summer, does much to compensate for the other glens which hydro-electric schemes have spoiled.

LOCH FASKALLY

you can take the Lowland road by Coupar Angus and Forfar through the rich lands of the Howe of the Mearns to Aberdeen, entering Deeside from the Granite City. None of these routes connects with the others because of the barrier of the Cairngorms and Eastern Grampians, whose granite plateaux offer only footpaths. A proposal to link Spey with Dee through Glen Feshie may one day become a reality.

How much variety Perthshire offers you can appreciate when you take the north-west route by Birnam Wood, following the Tay by the white houses of Dunkeld to Pitlochry and the Pass of Killiecrankie. Pitlochry, with its Festival Theatre and showpiece hydro-electric scheme at Loch Faskally, has justified the North of Scotland Hydro Electric Board's claim that vast engineering projects make the country more interesting to the normal run of tourists. Certainly it has made Pitlochry more popular, though not everyone will regard this as a blessing. Pitlochry, let's face it, is as "touristy" as a village in the Lake District. A talented theatrical company provides fine plays in the evenings. The brown trout fishing is excellent and cheap. Pitlochry, therefore, is a good place for a family man, with interesting tours to hand and the Pass of Killiecrankie close by. Loch Tummel, Loch Rannoch and the birks of Aberfeldy are all within easy reach by car or coach.

Killiecrankie is now the property of the National Trust for Scotland, and it can boast the most beautiful public convenience in Britain, with litter baskets placed at strategic points for descent to the Soldier's Leap. Scottish history is peppered with "leaps" where desperate men have braved death by taking to the air over gorges too wide for lesser mortals. The battle of Killiecrankie was fought in 1689 between General Mackay's troops and Jacobite forces under Viscount Dundee, and it was a Royalist trooper, fleeing from a Jacobite, who made the historic leap. Sceptics who doubted whether any man could leap this chasm had their ideas put right when in 1912 a visitor from Bedford, also a Royalist, cleared the river in a mighty jump from one rock to the other.

The main railway line to Inverness is carried on a huge viaduct which spans the Pass of Killiecrankie, cutting a narrow line through the hanging oaks and birches which are such a feast of colour in autumn. Both road and rail have to swing away westward at Blair Atholl to climb Drumochter Pass and outflank the high peaks. But the old roads go straight through the hills, by Glen Tilt and the Lairig Ghru to Aviemore, and it is a route capable of many variations.

One journey I remember well started one May weekend when two of us arrived in Blair Atholl at midnight and three miles up Glen Tilt spread our sleeping bags beneath a pine tree.

The "Fair City" of Perth was once the capital of Scotland. It has been a royal burgh since 1210, James I was murdered there, and in St. John's church John Knox preached the famous sermon which began the Reformation in Scotland. The picture shows the winding River Tay and the North Inch, where the famous "Battle of the Clans" was fought in 1396, and where the county team now play cricket.

To pop your head out of a sleeping bag in any Highland glen of a May morning is a breath of life, but in Glen Tilt the breath is a gulp. All nature seemed to exult among the crowding trees of that green glen, with shouting woodland birds mingling their songs with shrill oyster catchers and the thin "wheeting" of sandpipers.

That day we forsook the glen for the high tops, crossing the shoulder of Carn a Chalmain to drop to the Tarf Water. It was just the weather for fast moving, and in no time, it seemed, we were over the Perthshire boundary into Aberdeenshire on the top of An Sgarsoch and seeing ahead of us the high Cairngorms, covered in snow, stretching almost unbroken across the plateau.

We had intended to sleep in Glen Feshie that night, but after a brew of tea on a fire of bog pine a new plan presented itself. It was a magnificent night. Why not climb Beinn Bhrotain and spend the night on the summit in our sleeping bags? Unfortunately we were just too late for the sunset, but we did see the snow flush crimson beneath our feet, though the peaks were wan by the time we stood on the dusky summit. In a lee spot two hundred feet below the top we huddled together, warm enough in our eiderdown bags to appreciate the clear frosty sky of sparkling stars and the silence of the high tops.

The snows around us were tinted with sunrise when we awoke. But as we fried our breakfast over the Primus the corrie became flooded with scintillating light, each granule of snow and slender icicle shining like a gem among the warmth of bare rock and scree and green moss. The dawn chorus was a mingling of weird ptarmigan sounds. "Creakings" is the only word that describes the morning noises of these extraordinary mountain grouse.

Before us lay the longest high-level plateau in Scotland, and walking over it was like walking on a pavement, so firm was the snow. First we had to cross round the head of Glen Geusachan to gain the tops of Monadh Mor, and I wish I could convey the lonely splendour of the next few miles, over the great corrie edges that plunge sheer-down towards the Lairig Ghru. In these shadowy recesses the lochs were still frozen hard. The scene belonged to the Arctic, with no hint of the softer country of Spey until we crossed Cairn Toul and Braeriach and saw the great brown foothills dropping to the wide plain of Aviemore.

The route now was across the narrow neck of Coire Bennaidh and Sron na Lairig, then down the red screes which lead to the Lairig Ghru, and we held our hunger until we reached a certain place where the outpost pines are scattered on rocky knolls and birch trees cluster green in the gullies that drop to the plunging river. Sitting contentedly in the sunshine, drinking tea and listening to the willow warblers singing their songs, we felt as mellow as the wine-bark of the old pines themselves. Behind us was the granite and the shining snows, ahead the spreading forest and its track of pine-needles to Coylum Bridge. We had walked from Perthshire through Aberdeenshire into Inverness-shire in just thirty-six hours, covering the wildest country in Britain, yet in that exhilarating air we scarcely felt fatigue.

The more usual route across the mountains is by road and rail to Glen Garry and Drumochter, climbing the peaks by their 1,500 foot flanks. It is a rather featureless route in a bleak repelling countryside which improves on acquaintance, especially in winter. I have had some wonderful days here in January, when neither road nor rail was visible on the snow-plastered slopes of Marcaonich and Beinn Chaoruinn.

Driving over Drumochter you are travelling at right angles to the Spey on its tributary the Truim. This is the country of Clan Chattan, whose confederation comprised Mackintoshes, Macphersons and Macgillivrays, and if you speak to a native he will show you the crag known as Creag Dubh near Newtonmore where Cluny Macpherson lived, on and off, for nine years with a big price on his head. No member of the clan gave him away though all knew where he was hiding—an example of the true loyalty not uncommon in the Highlands.

Dunkeld is an ancient cathedral city on the Tay, hemmed in by wooded mountains. The twelfth-century cathedral was desecrated in 1560, but the choir is now the Parish Church.

An aerial view of Pitlochry, showing the Tummel dam and the end of Loch Faskally. At the south end of the dam is the power station and a fish ladder climbed by 5,000 salmon a year.

The mountains ahead of you now are the Monadhliaths, the "Grey Hills", in contrast to the Monadh Ruadh, the "Red Hills", which is the old Gaelic name for the range that has come to be called the Cairngorms in the twentieth century after the name of one mountain whose name means, literally, "Blue Peak". Westward over the Monadhliaths is the Great Glen, which General Wade linked to Speyside by building the famous Corrieyairack military highway from Laggan Bridge to Fort Augustus over a climb of 2,543 feet into Glen Tarff.

I have walked this interesting old road, past the stone barracks of Garvamore which is now a farmhouse. Just off the track to the south, the Spey has its source in tiny Loch Spey, a reedy pool backed by the 3,700 foot mass of Creagh Meagaidh. It is an unexciting chunk of roadless country however, except for its historical associations, which are plentiful. Prince Charles dodged General Cope's army marching on Inverness by crossing from Invergarry to Dalwhinnie, and Montrose used it to greater effect in 1645 to surprise the Campbells at Inverlochy in a double march, which reveals to anyone who knows the country how tough the Highlanders must have been.

The public road west of Newtonmore to the Great Glen is much more exciting than the Corrieyairack, threading Loch Laggan as it does beneath the cliffs of Corrie Ardair of Creagh Meagaidh. This corrie of the high wood has witnessed some notable feats of winter mountaineering of recent years on thousand-foot ribbons of ice. The climbing is not good in summer due to the dirty nature of the rock, but the walk up from Aberarder Farm is well worth while, and leads to a col in the ridge known as "The Window", a conspicuous pass which was used by Prince Charles on 28th August, 1746 when he crossed over from Lochiel.

Queen Victoria was so taken by this country that

GLEN LYON NEAR BRIDGE OF BALGIE

Glen Lyon lies west of Aberfeldy, and stretches almost to Tyndrum. It is the longest glen in Scotland, narrow and overhung, and the river rushes over rocks sparkling with crystals. In its confines a MacGregor force was almost exterminated in a fierce battle with the Stewarts of Garth.

BEN LAWERS AND LOCH TAY

Ben Lawers, which rises above Loch Tay to almost 4000 feet, provides excellent skiing and is an easy mountain to climb. It is part of the 8000 acres of Perthshire which belong to the National Trust for Scotland, and in summer has a profusion of rare and lovely alpine plants.

South-east of Fort Augustus the wild Pass of Corrieyairack winds through Glen Tarff to Speyside. Fine views of the surrounding Monadhliaths refresh the hiker on his journey.

she nearly bought the estate of Ardverikie, whose fine house stands in noble grounds that might be a fragment of the Canadian Rockies in their pine woods. Immediately behind the house is some of the best deer-stalking in Scotland, extending over the top of Ben Alder to Loch Ericht—another stretch of country untraversed by anything more than shooting paths. Only in the Forest of Mar will you see so many fine head of deer, and nowhere in Scotland is more attractive in winter. For walkers and climbers the youth hostel on Loch Ossian is the best centre, and it is easily reached from Corrour on the West Highland railway. Distances are long but the rewards are considerable for those who enjoy getting off the beaten track.

Now we shall return to the Spey valley, on the way to Inverness, which I mentioned as having the nearest approach in Scotland to a continental and alpine type of climate. This is among the best tree-growing regions of Scotland, owing to the dryness of the glacial drift which has only the thinnest layer of peat lying on top. On this sandy and gravelly soil grow the most elegant birches in Britain and the finest pine trees. To see them best I prefer the old road on the east bank of the Spey in preference to the faster main road through Newtonmore, Kingussie and Kincraig. For a flashback to the old way of life in Speyside visitors should go to the Folk Museum at Kingussie.

The extensive flood meadows by the ruins of Ruthven Barracks are testimony to the power of the Spey, which in time of flood has caused considerable havoc and loss of life. Nowadays the diversion of its headwaters by hydro-electric schemes has removed much of its destructive power, but this fastest flowing river in Scotland is still dangerous. Reclamation of its flood areas is overdue. Meantime the birds thrive on the waters, and ornithologists find the stretches of meadow and marsh rewarding for rare wading birds and all sorts of wild fowl. Thanks to pony trekking and facilities for field study at Newtonmore, more and more people are discovering the delightful country of Speyside, whose only rival is Deeside. It seems certain that, in the not too distant future, these valleys will be linked by a road across the mountains from Glen Feshie.

Beyond Loch Insh the rather flat scenery of the Spey suddenly changes as the wooded knoll called Tor Alvie and the heights of Craigellachie close in. The monument on top of the Tor commemorates the fifth and last Duke of Gordon, and at its base is buried the famous Duchess of Gordon who raised the Gordon Highlanders with the reward of a shilling and a kiss. The climb to the monument is worth while for the view of pine forest and granite mountains which are the Cairngorms and second biggest nature reserve in Europe. This is the most considerable tract of high country in Britain, and fortunately you do not need to be a climber to enjoy it.

Aviemore makes a wonderful centre for exploration. Loch an Eilean is only three miles away, but in the hour taken to walk round it you will taste the magic of the Cairngorms. Shut in by the vast forest or glimpsing the northward vista over pine, birch and loch you might feel yourself in Finland. Come to the ruins of the old castle on the west shore and you look on Cairngorm towering over Coire Cas in one leap of heather and rock. Everywhere are young self-sown seedling pines of the old Wood of Caledon.

Rothiemurchus is one of the few stretches of natural Scots pine forest which have been properly worked as a continual natural resource. On the whole the Scots have been poor foresters in that they allowed woods, by bad management, to be destroyed. Rothiemurchus, on the other hand, has been worked for probably a thousand years and it demonstrates that natural forest, cut intelligently and selectively, is probably the best use for much of the Central Highlands.

Nature Conservancy scientists are now making a close study of the Caledonian Forest which spreads its vast canopy of green boughs into Glen Einich and up the hill slopes to a height of 1,800 feet. But the trees

Glen Feshie is one of the seven natural deer forests which meet on the Cairngorm range. Since there are no fences or boundaries of any kind between the forests, the deer move from one to another according to the direction of the wind and the season of the year. The River Feshie runs through the glen to join the Spey near Kincraig.

which depend from the peak of Cairngorm are in Forestry Commission territory and are reached from Glen More, whose road runs due east from Aviemore. The region is a National Forest Park, with caravan and camp site on the fringe of Loch Morlich, whose sandy shore under the high peaks makes it one of the gems of Scotland.

This is the region which is being developed as Scotland's chief winter sports centre, with access road and ski lifts to make the most of the natural storage chests in the mountains which hold snow to mid-summer. It has taken a long time for people in the south of Britain to realise that here in March or April is a land to rival any for skiing, and where first-class tuition can be had at modest prices. Enthusiasts are even complaining that the slopes are getting overcrowded, but the man who wants solitude can find it with little trouble in tours across the 4000-foot plateau of Ben Macdhui or in remote corries where few ski marks have ever been made.

The great "trade route" for mountain walkers is, of course, the Lairig Ghru, the "Gloomy Pass", which cuts through the range at 2,700 feet, the highest hill pass in Britain. It is as well signposted as a public

highway, yet there is no house nearer than eighteen miles. The walk from Aviemore to Braemar is twenty-seven miles, and even if you do not contemplate going the whole way you should explore the first few miles through the forest to a point where the trees thin out and the thrust of Lurcher's Crag and Sron na Lairig form the cleft of the pass. The River Dee rises just beneath the crest, in little holes of water among the stones. Beneath you stretches Speyside, seen over the wrinkled mat of pine trees which is Rothiemurchus. Far beneath, hung with birch and alder, is the river by whose banks you may see crested tits, crossbills, siskins, redstarts, goosanders, oyster catchers and sandpipers. In the wilder flats the greenshank nests, and on the high tops you will find ptarmigan, dotterel and the golden eagle.

The narrow glacier lake of Loch Avon, birthplace of the river Avon, is perhaps the loneliest place in the Cairngorms, and above it is a great boulder known as the "Shelter Stone". This is a rock which has fallen from the cliffs above and come to rest on a nest of smaller boulders, forming a roomy weatherproof chamber within, a room with a view on a plinth of granite, sheer for 600 feet, which is still providing new routes for cragsmen. Using the Shelter Stone as a base for a few nights, the walker or naturalist can explore the highest tops of the Cairngorm Nature Reserve. Another shelter known as Corrour Bothy provides a perfect base for exploring the west side of the Lairig Ghru, whose corries of rock and snow are the fiercest in the Cairngorms. Anyone exploring here must be absolutely self-supporting in food and bedding for this is no-man's-land, where you are more likely to meet a deer or a fox or a wild-cat than a human being. There is plenty of scope for adventure in this arctic land.

One region of Speyside which few vistors ever reach is the heathery uplands stretching from the Braes of Abernethy to Tomintoul. In it is a unique gorge,

RIVER ALMOND IN THE SMA' GLEN

The Almond rises above Loch Tay and flows east to join the Tay near Perth. The Sma' Glen is the narrow part of Glen Almond, a few miles north of Crieff. In places there is barely room for the road beside the river, since the slopes rise steeply on both sides, with hills of nearly 3000 feet on the south-west.

LOCH TUMMEL

Loch Tummel lies between Kinloch Rannoch and Pitlochry, and is joined by the River Tummel to Loch Rannoch on the west and Loch Faskally on the east. The hydro-electric dam on the Tummel at Pitlochry, which created Loch Faskally, greatly enlarged Loch Tummel and again enhanced rather than spoiled the natural beauty of the scene.

Pony-trekking on Craigdhu, near Newtonmore. Pony-trekking is an exciting way of seeing lovely but inaccessible country, and is especially popular on Speyside.

Captain Tommy Edwards, chief instructor for the Scottish Council for Physical Recreation courses on angling, fishing the Spey near Grantown.

where the Water of Caiplich becomes the Water of Ailnack. When I went there I took the car from Nethy Bridge to Dorback Lodge and found myself looking on a new view of the Cairngorms, with the Pass of Ryvoan prominent beneath Beinn Bynack. The country here has a strange character by reason of huge exposures of alluvial drift where moraines and stream banks have been sheered away by erosion.

I went by the Allt Mor on a good track to the flat top of Geal Charn. Still I saw no sign of a gorge, until I struck south and found myself on the edge of a sudden drop with rock walls plunging below and the stream threading its way through a pure canyon with a fierce pinnacle called "The Castle" inviting a climb. You can follow the gorges down to Delnabo and so to Tomintoul, on the River Avon, which vies with Leadhills as being the highest village in Scotland, with plenty of good accommodation for visitors. Tomintoul is easily reached by car from Grantown and Nethy Bridge.

If you intend to follow down the Spey from Aviemore then I would recommend you to take the old road which goes by Coylum Bridge and Loch Pityoulish to Loch Gartan, now partly a nature reserve to protect the ospreys which are back again as breeding birds in Scotland after egg collectors had exterminated them from our native fauna. There are several eyries now, though not all are in use, and thousands of visitors have been privileged to watch them, thanks to the Royal Society for the Protection of Birds, whose officers keep a night and day watch but like to see people enjoy the spectacle of the great fish hawks swinging through the trees carrying pike, salmon or sea-trout.

From Grantown the most beautiful stretch of the Spey lies ahead, with the river enclosed by steep banks and woods as it plays a game of hide and seek to Craigellachie. There are wonderful places for salmon fishing here, and I know a man who fished a stretch every morning for twenty seasons and never once failed to land a fish.

The Spey, of course, stands not only for good salmon fishing but for the best of whisky, as the names Glen Fiddich, Glen Livet and Glen Grant signify. These are only three of the many distilleries which pepper the landscape hereabout on both sides of Ben Rinnes. Most of the fine whisky goes for blending and export but visitors to the neighbourhood can often pick up a bottle of the pure malt. Formerly the Spey was also used for floating rafts of timber from Rothiemurchus to the shipbuilding yards on Spey Bay, but the day of the "floaters" is past and will never return in this era of road transport.

To the west, in the triangle of country between the Spey and Inverness on the Great Glen, the most important natural feature is the Findhorn, whose course from the Monadhliaths to the sea is one of the most mysterious in Scotland. Few people have tried to follow it and none that I know have succeeded in exploring its many windings which lie out of sight of any public road, lost among forest and gorges of granite and red sandstone. The main Inverness road crosses it near Tomatin by a bridge of criss-cross concrete, but the finest stretches are lower down below Daltulich and Ardclach.

Indeed the "Bell Tower" of Ardclach is the place really to appreciate the transformation, as the Findhorn sweeps down from the moorlands to a defile with the green uplands and white dots of

Aviemore is a long, narrow village on the Spey in Inverness-shire. With the Monadhliaths on the west and the Cairngorms on the east, it is a wonderful centre for climbing, hill-walking, pony-trekking, skiing and angling, according to season. The railway lines go north to Forres and Inverness, and the town is also served by the fine road along Strathspey. Aviemore lies in the Grant Country; above it rises the rock of Craigellachie, from which the clan took its war-cry: "Stand fast, Craigellachie".

CAIRN TOUL AND THE DEVIL'S POINT

Cairn Toul (4,241 feet) is the white hump in the centre of the picture, and is one of the four main peaks of the Cairngorms; the Devil's Point is the nearer peak, and is considerably smaller (3,303 feet); on the right are the lower slopes of Cairn a Mhaim. These mountains overlook the southern end of the Lairig Ghru, the long defile which links Strathspey to Deeside. The Dee rises near Cairn Toul, and forms the tarn in the foreground.

THE RIVER TUMMEL AND SCHIEHALLION

Looking south-east across the River Tummel to Schiehallion from a point near Kinloch Rannoch. The snow makes the symmetry of the cone almost perfect, and heightens the contrast of the mountain, the river and the trees. Schiehallion is over 3,500 feet high and was used by Maskelyne for his experiments on the weight of the earth.

cottages perched above it. There is only a glimpse of the actual stream even here, but you can go down to the Wade bridge at Dulsie and follow down to Randolph's Leap, or on again to the woods of Darnaway, if you would get the true character of one of the finest rivers in Scotland. In time of flood when it bursts its banks it is one of the most terrifying of scenes, with the roar of its compressed waters crashing like thunder. Damage of former floods lies all along its course.

In this rapid survey of the Central Highlands I have tried to keep to topographical divisions rather than county boundaries. In order to cross the Cairngorms we have, therefore, to by-pass the Eastern Grampians which begin at Tullos Hill near Aberdeen and rise to Mount Battock, Mount Keen and Lochnagar on Deeside. Byron's verses do justice to their crowning glory:

England! thy beauties are tame and domestic
   To one who has roved o'er the mountains afar:
Oh for the crags that are wild and majestic!
   The steep frowning glories of dark Lochnagar!

Below the Devil's Elbow, where Glen Beag and Glen Lochy meet to form Glen Shee, stands the hamlet of Spittal of Glenshee. Ben Gulabin (2,641 feet) towers above the meeting of the waters and the hump-backed bridge is a familiar land-mark on the Perthshire approach to Deeside.

By purchasing the peak of Lochnagar as part of her Highland estate, Queen Victoria not only showed discriminating taste but rendered Scotland a great service by saving the old Caledonian Forest of Ballochbuie when it was due to be felled for its timber. It stands today as the most considerable fragment of the old forest extant and well merits Queen Victoria's description of the "Bonniest Plaid in Scotland". Further up, beyond the Linn of Dee in Glen Derry and Glen Quoich, are other magnificent woods, but none compares to the Forest of Ballochbuie. The golden eagle, which elsewhere in Scotland nests mainly in cliffs, uses these old trees, and in Glen Quoich, if you know where to look, you may find the largest eagle's eyrie in the world, occupying thirty feet of treetop.

The quickest route across the Grampians to Deeside from the south is by the Devil's Elbow, Glen Shee and the Cairnwell, which mounts to over 2000 feet and whose summit is sacred to the Dundee Ski Club. They have two ski-tows in the glen, a little one on Ben Gulabin near the foot of the pass, and another bigger one giving a lift just east of the highest point of the road. This lively club have races and meets every weekend in winter and they have greatly raised the standard of skiing in Scotland. The hills in summer have nothing of the beauty of Deeside but it is good grouse and deer country, though the best shooting is still farther east in the glens of Angus.

Kirriemuir, Brechin and Edzell are the springboards for exploring the eastern end of the Grampians. These are attractive old-world towns, situated in fertile country of golden wheat fields and turfy green hills beset with little glens leading in to the heather slopes which are such a blaze of purple in August. Strathmore carries the main road and rail to Aberdeen, but behind it, leading into the hills, are the little roads to lonely farms and shooting lodges. The feature of this part of the world is that all the glens which penetrate inland lie parallel to each other. It is the only similarity, because each glen has its own character. Take Glen Esk, above Edzell. It begins as a meek and sylvan strath rising to rounded heathery hills, not very exciting, until you come to Loch Lee and find the slopes closing in towards the 1,300-foot wall of Craigmaskeldie and the Water of Unich tumbling through a gorge.

Then there is Glen Clova, with Lord Airlie's castle

of Cortachy standing at its entrance. Clova is finer than the adjacent Prosen because, as you go up the glen, the mountains thrust down in wild rocky corries, two of them containing black lochans at over 2000 feet, Loch Brandy and Loch Wharrel. Among the rocks grow alpine plants of all descriptions, and botanists are still making new finds there. Both North and South Esk are fast salmon rivers, and both gather their waters swiftly from the high plateau, descending a full 2000 feet in only a few miles. There is prosperity and charm everywhere in the Braes of Angus, a charm that is sometimes missing from the more rugged and lonelier western seaboard.

For those who come to Scotland on the car ferry from London to Perth there is no better region than Tayside for exploring this fringe of the Grampians. Queen Victoria used to go to Balmoral from the Tay, and her coachman always knew to stop on the Sidlaws at the top of Tullybackart Hill for the vast view over fertile Strathmore to the blue wall of the Grampians which she loved so much. The hills have not changed since her time, but the farming regions have been revolutionised in the most properous times in the history of Scottish agriculture.

Sheltered by the Sidlaws and backed by the Grampians, you find in Strathmore a man-made landscape of huge fields dotted with cattle that are the pride of Scotland. Motoring over it last year on the way from Perth to Aberdeen, I was impressed by the development here, the new steadings, the fine fences and farm gates, and the sight of bulky combine harvesters sweeping up the golden crop of wheat, barley and oats. The pea crop was so heavy that it was an embarrassment to the canners. Instead of persisting in the innumerable crops of potatoes which served to make the land more and more acid, the farmers of Strathmore have dressed the fields with more and more lime to make possible greater fertility. Now they are busy reclaiming the northern slopes of the Sidlaws, thus giving the lie to the old saying that "poor times make good farmers." The truth, in these mechanised times, is that without a lot of money it is impossible to farm properly.

History, of course, is writ large everywhere in this district, with Scone and Huntingtower Castle not far away. Here was the capital of the old Pictish kingdom where the Kings of Scotland were crowned, a custom continued until the Stone of Destiny was removed by Edward I and placed in Westminster Abbey in 1296. Huntingtower is famous for its "Maiden's Leap", which recalls the occasion when the Earl of Gowrie's daughter, in the course of eloping, jumped a gap between two towers, sixty feet above the ground, to avoid being surprised by her mother.

Glamis and Kirriemuir provide focal points in Strathmore for those who like history and legend intermingled:

Canoeing is a popular sport in Scotland, but these naval ratings are surveying Loch Lee, in Glen Esk, as an exercise. The cliffs to the left are those of Craigmaskeldie.

> Glamis hath murder'd sleep; and therefore Cawdor
> Shall sleep no more—Macbeth shall sleep no more!

The haunted rooms and the secret stairways of Glamis Castle make Shakespeare's words ring with deeper foreboding. This ancestral home of Queen Elizabeth, the Queen Mother, is open three days a week to visitors. The museum in the Kirk Wynd, with its wonderful folk collection, is all too often overlooked.

The Kirriemuir that Barrie knew is not so different in this atomic age, though the little stone town with its narrow streets is more prosperous than it ever was in his lifetime, thanks to the jute trade. The cottage where Barrie first saw the light of day in 1860 is his museum now, and the little house he called "A Window in Thrums" carries an honoured label. "Thrum", by the way, is the local word for an end of thread hung on the loom to repair breaks, and is a reminder of the time when every house had its loom clacking from early morning well into the night. Changed days now, with the folks working normal factory hours and thriving on it.

From this fringe of the Grampians we shall skip across the Dee to the other fringe, "Where the Gadie rins, at the fit o' Bennachie," to quote the famous Aberdeenshire song. And all this corner down to Buchan is a land of song, full of bothy ballads and couthy dialect. The folks hereabouts are a farming people, among the most progressive in Scotland, but they have never become anglicised in any way. You do not get to know them easily. Some might call them dour, but this surface impression is false. Come to know them and you will find them full of fun and every one a real character.

The bothy ballads reveal their type of humour. Take *The Barn Yards o' Delgaty*:

Noo I ga'ed doon tae Turra Market,
  Turra Market for tae fee,
And I met in wi' a wealthy fairmer
  Frae the barn-yards o' Delgaty.

He promised me the twa best horses
  That were in a' the country roon'
But when I gae'd hame tae the barn-yards
  There's naething there but skin and bone.

The auld grey mare sat on her hunkers,
  The auld din horse lay in the grime:
And a' that I could "hup" and cry,
  They wadna' rise at yokin' time.

etc. etc.

Or *Drumgelgie*:

There's a fairm toon up in Cairnie,
  That's kent baith faur and wide,
It's ca'd the Hash o' Drumgelgie,
  On Bonny Deveronside,
It's five o'clock that we get up
  And hurry doon the stair:
Tae get wir horses corned and fed
  And likewise straught their hair.

Half an hour at the stable,
  Each tae the kitchie goes,
Tae get started tae oor breakfast,
  Which generally's brose.
We've scarcely got oor brose well-supped,
  And gi'en wir pints a tie;
Fan the Grieve he says "Hullo my lads,
  Ye'll be nae langer nigh."

And so on.

Read, or hear sung, a few of these bothy ballads if you would seek to know the people who live close to the soil from Bennachie to the Deveron. Ask them about the fertile countryside and they will tell you that:

Ae mile o' Don's worth two o' Dee
Except it be for fish an' tree.

Like the bothy ballads themselves, the Don's character is intimate, not aloof like the Dee, though these rivers flow parallel and enter the sea close to each other. Bennachie of Donside is better known

LOCH MORLICH
AND GLENMORE FOREST

Loch Morlich lies in the middle of the Glenmore Forest, east of Aviemore. Its sandy beach and sailing dinghies contrast strangely with the snow on the mountains. The forest is the home of a flourishing herd of reindeer, imported from Sweden in 1952.

A pine wood in Glen Derry, which is part of the Cairngorms Nature Reserve. Much of Scotland's Highland pine country has been devastated by indiscriminate felling.

Grantown-on-Spey was founded by Sir James Grant of Grant in 1776. It is well-planned and well-kept, with tree-lined streets, pleasant walks and a fine setting.

than Lochnagar because it thrusts further towards the sea and is in fact the last great projection of Highland mountain before the fertile sweep of Buchan. Its eye-catching peak is the Mither Tap, height 1,698 feet, whose summit crag gives it the character of a mountain twice its size. You can even go to "Paradise" here on the banks of the Don near Monymusk with great pines and larches making it indeed a heaven of peace worth seeking out. From Monymusk upwards is the most beautiful stretch of the Don, with variety of scene round every one of its numerous bends. Ancient castles pepper like boulders this landscape which has tales enough to fill several books of battle and adventure.

Westwards of the railway line to Huntly rise the prominent hills which give birth to the Deveron, where the Buck of Cabrach rises beyond Strathdon, and when I walk through the hills on one of the many footpaths which criss-cross them I like to think back to the times when every house had its private whisky still, until the act of 1820 made it illegal. Nowadays the only pleasure you get from the smoking chimneys of the distilleries which have replaced private enterprise is the thought that but for their enormous output your income-tax would certainly be higher than it is.

Over the Buck we are into Banffshire, but if you prefer an easier way than the footpaths there is the Cock Bridge road through Strathdon and over the Lecht at 2,114 feet, the highest driving road in Britain except for the Cairnwell. At the "Well of the Lecht" you may read an inscription dated 1754 telling that "Five Companies, the 33rd Regiment, Right Hon. Charles Hay Colonel, made the road from here to Spey."

Stories abound everywhere in this country, from the bonny salmon pools of Deveron to the "Laigh o' Moray" where they say they get forty more days of summer than the rest of Scotland. These are the fat lands of Moray where the "Brae o' Moray" drops to the sea, leaving behind for ever the wild lands where the cattle reivers of long ago had their howffs, ready to swoop and kill and steal from the people of the "Laigh". When not at the good sport of cattle reiving they were away at the wars fighting and dying as respectable soldiers. A good soldier is not always a good citizen, as any reformer will tell you.

Worse than any reiver, however, was the Wolf of Badenoch, illegitimate son of King Robert II, whose den was Lochindorb Castle in the wild uplands between Grantown and Forres. This black loch was the scene of Maurice Walsh's book *The Key Above the Door*. I like to think of the wild moor below it as the "blasted heath" where Macbeth and Banquo met the three witches, rather than the more civilised knoll near Brodie Castle on the Nairn road where the meeting is said to have taken place. Macbeth was a gentleman with clean hands compared to the Wolf, whose most notable gangster act in a history of burning woodlands and property was the sacking of Elgin Cathedral.

The blue peaks of Ross and Sutherland lie before your gaze as you descend from the peatstacks and dotted sheep of the Brae o' Moray towards Forres and the fat fields full of cattle along the Moray Firth. Westwards lie Cawdor and Drummossie Muir. The witches who haunted the moors about the time of Macbeth seem to have been firmly entrenched in the seventeenth century, for in nearby Auldearn they were said to go about in droves, changing themselves into the forms of cats, cows and hares and riding about on straws and beanstalks. One confession wrung out of a witch of the time said that they regularly met Old Nick and dug out dead bodies "to make salves and charms from the bones".

Drummossie Muir is only six miles from Inverness, and to the Scot it is a sad place because it includes Culloden. There the grass mounds of the slain lie round a large cairn marking the place where the battle raged fiercest. It was the end of the Jacobite cause, and it was the only occasion in battle when the charging Highlanders failed to break the English line. The date was April 16th, 1746, and it was a battle which should never have begun, not because the Jacobites were outnumbered two to one, but because they were dispirited, hungry and dissentient. The battle started at one o'clock, and half an hour afterwards Prince Charles was led off the field in tears, leaving a battlefield strewn with dead and dying clansmen. Cumberland's artillery had blasted them badly before the hand-to-hand fighting began, but it was not their principle to retreat. They fought on, and died. Grim days followed in Scotland, when it was an offence to wear the tartan, and a Scottish piper, James Reid, was executed at York for playing the bagpipes, "an instrument of war".

At Inverness small ships can enter the Caledonian Canal and sail to the Atlantic without having to make the long and often stormy voyage round by the Pentland Firth. The two seas are linked by the chain of fresh-water lochs which Telford joined to form the canal. Its total length is sixty-two miles, of which twenty-two miles are man-made channels, and it was completed in 1847 at a cost of £1,300,000. In this age of fast road transport it is little used, except by fishing boats and yachts, but it may well be very useful in the future for floating the timber of the Great Glen to the sea. The many miles of trees in the glen were among the first to be planted by the Forestry Commission and make noble woods today.

Loch Ness is over 700 feet deep, and never freezes. The bodies of people drowned in the loch are seldom recovered. Why? Perhaps strong currents below the surface? Huge holes in the banks? Or a hungry monster lurking in the depths? Divers who went down to look for a body a few years ago refused to go down again, nor would they tell what they had seen. Abandoned Urquhart Castle on the west shore of the loch is said to have a vault in which there is fabulous treasure. But the vaults are also said to hold plague. No one has yet risked the plague for the wealth, so here is another mystery, like the monster.

Kilchumein, at the head of Loch Ness, became Fort Augustus after the Jacobite rising of 1715. The fort was acquired by the Benedictine Order in 1876, and is now an abbey.

I have not seen "Nessie" myself, but there is little doubt that in this deep loch there is "something". The first to record it was St. Columba about A.D. 565. When preaching to the Picts he saw a huge creature in the river Ness. It has reappeared many times since then. You may doubt its existence, but if you were to speak to some of the Benedictine monks of the abbey at Fort Augustus about it they could find you several of their number who have seen it while going about their daily work. It has evaded television cameras and underwater searchers to date, and we are there-

fore left to speculate whether the monster is fact or some weird optical illusion.

The normal road for fast traffic up and down the Great Glen is by the west shore of Loch Ness, but the older route linking Fort William, Fort Augustus and Inverness was built on the other side by General Wade. It follows the loch shore to the gorge of the Foyers where, in spate, there is one of Scotland's really spectacular waterfalls. The beauty of the route owes much to the way the road climbs up and up until you are over 1,000 feet above the greatest cleft in Scotland, with nothing but mountains on either side. Here you can appreciate the cunning of General Wade when he spanned the Corrieyairack with a road over the Monadhliaths, connecting Speyside with this natural pass, with its branches to the troubled west and offshoots into Nairn and Moray. Without these roads the wild Highlands would never have been subdued by so few troopers. The old bridges still stand, showing how well his engineers built.

The alpine world of the Central Highlands is a constant revelation, and I shall never forget one January day in 1958, during a big freeze-up, when

LOCH LAGGAN

Loch Laggan, looking south-west towards Binnein Shuas, with the Ben Nevis range in the distance. The loch lies at the head of Glen Spean, and is skirted by the road linking the Great Glen to Strathspey. The south shore of the loch is being enhanced and developed by forestry schemes; ancient dug-out canoes have been found, preserved in the sand-banks.

CASTLE URQUHART AND LOCH NESS

The ruins of Castle Urquhart are strikingly situated on a bluff above Loch Ness. For four hundred years the castle was held by the Seafield Grants, who built much of the present structure, and incorporated interesting devices for pouring molten lead on assailants. The Monster has been seen near here; the dungeons of the castle are said to contain treasure and the plague.

An aerial view of the Cairngorms, showing three of the four great peaks. On the west, or left side of the picture, is the Braeriach plateau, with the summit of Braeriach slightly to the east. It is separated from Cairn Toul by a cliff and a deep corrie. The Lairig Ghru divides Cairn Toul from Ben Macdhui, on the extreme right. Cairngorm itself is further to the north-east.

the fog was so thick in Glasgow that all planes were grounded and passengers to Inverness and Aberdeen were flown out from Edinburgh, where the smog gave way to more genteel frost mist. Any misgivings I felt vanished once we were in the air, up into the golden sunlight, and in moments we were over the Tay, seeing the white roofs of Perth disappear in the first rise of the Grampians.

Over Edzell I looked westward on an incredible vision of the highest mountain mass in Scotland glittering in a huge ice-cap against the palest sky. I could pick out the long glens penetrating it, Prosen, Clova, Lethnot, Esk, smoothed out under immense snowdrifts, only the dykes and lonely houses showing that people lived in this world of frozen rivers where no tracks led. Drawn in pencil curves the pendulous snow cornices overhanging the shadows indicated the north-east whence the storm had come three days earlier, killing five hikers who had set off to cross from Braemar Youth Hostel to Glen Doll by Jock's Road.

In Aberdeen the Dee was frozen so hard that folk could walk on it, but as we flew over the mountains and headed for the Moray Firth there was a transformation. Ten miles from the water, the snow ended as neatly as a contour line on a map, giving the coastal villages of Buchan and Banff a look of summer warmth in contrast to the arctic vista of the interior. Cruising easily through the clean, cold air, with Scotland like a map below me, I felt a new intimacy with this splendid country. The parts were now a whole, with all the bits of the jig-saw fitting, from the green fields of Moray to the Cairngorms, with silver ridge upon silver ridge disappearing as far as the eye and imagination could follow.

EDINBURGH, FIFE AND THE BORDERS

Moray McLaren

EDINBURGH, as is another capital, is built upon, or at least around and on the slopes of, seven hills. From the summit of the north-eastern Pentlands (about 1,700 feet) you can see much of the terrain that gives the title to this essay. You can do more. You can look northwards and downwards upon Fife (not Fifeshire, please, as it is so often miscalled) as if you were an approaching airman. Turning southwards and eastwards, you can all but see into England, and catch a fine view of many of the Border peaks. You can do all this while standing with one foot in Edinburgh and the other in Border country, because the Edinburgh city boundary runs exactly along the topmost heights of this part of the Pentland Hills.

This is as it should be. Edinburgh, Fife and the Borders form something of a unit in the highly diversified country of Scotland. The Fifer, however admirably independent he may be, is racially a pure south-east Lowlander. So are the men of the Lothians and Berwickshire, so are many of those who live in the Walter Scott country in the Melrose and Selkirk direction. Edinburgh, of course, draws upon all Scotland for part of its personnel, but the strong unmistakable Edinburgh strain of the majority is the same—south-east Lowland. The south-east Lowlanders have a related speech, related architecture and related customs. The countryside may differ between hill and plain, the Firth of Forth may thrust itself like a wide but pointed sword into the heart of the unit, but it remains a unit; and Edinburgh by the shores of the Firth lies at that heart. Edinburgh (not without some dispute) is still the capital of modern Scotland. In a deeper and certainly undisputed way she is the capital of the south-east Lowlands, Fife and the Borders. It is proper, then, to begin the study of this terrain, this unit, at its heart and capital, Edinburgh.

R. L. Stevenson called Edinburgh "my precipitous city". He spoke of this quality in her when he lived in Edinburgh, but it was when he was in his last years in the South Seas, on the other side of the world, that he coined this phrase. It was a phrase uttered in a poignant mood of affectionate homesickness, and it has stuck; it is so right. Apart from the seven hills mentioned above, Edinburgh internally is full of sudden declivities and ascents. I mention this element in Edinburgh at the beginning because it is one of the first things the visitor to Edinburgh notices, especially if he comes from the south and from the plains of the less austere England. To the visitor it seems that he is always going uphill or downhill, that he is always raising his eyes to the rocky crags or small mountains that surround Edinburgh, or else that he is looking down a long vista to the sea. Precipitous is the word.

The true body of Edinburgh, the core and substance around which all else of it has grown, is the combination of the Old Town and the New Town. But though the Old Town is medieval in origin and has its beginnings over a thousand years ago, the New Town is not new in the modern sense of the word. It began to exist just about two hundred years ago and is eighteenth century, Augustan and ample in a style which has, alas, long been forgotten in the more ephemeral architecture of today.

The two towns, then, the New and the Old, are complementary. The Old is set high upon a rock overhanging all Edinburgh and visible from all parts

EDINBURGH FROM CALTON HILL

Looking west towards the Castle from the Calton Hill. On the left are the crown of St. Giles' and the spire of Tolbooth St. John's, in the High Street; on the right the clock tower of the North British Hotel, the Scott Monument, and Princes Street, with the New Town to the north.

EDINBURGH: PRINCES STREET

Princes Street, Edinburgh, looking west. In the centre is the Scott Monument, with the Royal Scottish Academy and the National Gallery behind. The gardens were made by draining the Nor' Loch and creating the Mound, which now leads up to the Castle rock. Princes Street has been called the finest street in Europe.

EDINBURGH: THE NEW TOWN

The New Town of Edinburgh, looking north from the Castle. The New Town, with its elegant squares and crescents, is a fine piece of Georgian town planning, and takes full advantage of its situation. Princes Street and the gardens are in the foreground, the Firth of Forth in the distance with the hills of Fife beyond.

of Edinburgh. The New is, if not upon a plain, far below. It begins on the last hill that steps down to the sea and occupies that slope. The Old Town is a jumble of romantic pinnacles, winding ways, rotting slums (in the process of being cleaned up), high tenements and occasional modern buildings which carry on the old style of Scots architecture. The New Town is an ordered massive piece of town planning constructed in the age of elegance. Despite all that our Victorian grandfathers and fathers and (let it be forcibly said) *we* have done to destroy its elegance, much of that elegance survives at the present time. The original project was too largely conceived, and was built of too permanent a stone. Nearly three generations of Philistinism have done no more than spoil parts of it superficially. It still remains, not only in site but in quality, the complement to the romantic disorder of the Old Town.

That Old Town has its crown and climax in one of the celebrated buildings of Europe, Edinburgh Castle. The castle is not so much perched as set grimly four-square on the top of the huge volcanic rock which juts out of the very centre of Edinburgh. In past centuries, even before Edinburgh began to be

The Palace of Holyroodhouse stands at the foot of the Royal Mile on the edge of Holyrood Park, with the slopes of Arthur's Seat behind it. Members of the Royal Scottish Country Dance Society performed in the forecourt of the Palace for the film "Scotland Dances".

a city, the castle was a superb natural fortress. Even now, it would take a fairly heavy non-atomic bombardment to capture it. Edinburgh Castle's original stones were there well over a millennium ago, and before Edinburgh was. When examined from within it is a strange jumble of the centuries in style, but this does not detract from its grim beauty. From without, that is to say viewed from anywhere else in Edinburgh, which it completely dominates, it has a heart-lifting rather than beautiful or romantic quality. Standing on its highest point you can see not only Fife and the Borders but the Highland hills and much else of Scotland as well. Whatever Glasgow and the rest of the country may think of the city of Edinburgh, all Scotland feels, and rightly, that it owns Edinburgh Castle. It is almost certain to be the first thing that the visitor to Edinburgh sees of Edinburgh. It will probably be the last thing he sees of it as he departs.

The castle always has been, and still is, a military building. The Old Town proper, in the sense of being a place in which people have their dwelling-places, depends or rather declines from it down the slope of a hill. The western face of the castle rock is sheer. On the east side a narrow strip of rock runs steeply down for the length of a mile. Throughout the last thousand years people have built upon this narrow rock under the protection of the castle. At one time these buildings were all that Edinburgh was. The capital of Scotland was a straggle of high-built houses running the "Royal Mile" between the castle and the Palace of Holyroodhouse where Scotland's kings and queens used to live. This "Royal Mile", high-perched, windswept, full of the tumult of life, is one of the historic streets of the world. It is certainly the most historic thoroughfare in Scotland.

Were this essay the length of a whole book, one could fill it with an account of the history of the "Royal Mile" and the Old Town of Edinburgh, and then feel that one had missed more than half what one had wished to include. Let it suffice here to say that nearly all the story of Scotland has eventually come to flow up and down this "Royal Mile". The Stewart kings and queens rode and walked here. The reformers lived here. A house is said to be one in which John Knox lived for a time. The turbulent seventeenth century was canalised in Scotland into this thoroughfare. The golden period of Scotland's eighteenth century, of David Hume, Adam Smith and "the fifty other men of genius" was concentrated here. Today few of the people who have the making of modern Scotland actually live in the "Royal Mile" or the Old Town; but activity of importance still goes on there. Here are the headquarters of Scottish Law, of the Scottish Kirk. Here are some of the finest libraries in Great Britain; and here are the City Chambers whence Edinburgh is governed. And yet those who still live in this antique place are now the poor. They are the Scottish and Edinburgh poor, full of character, and national character at that. In a sense they carry on a tradition, although they live where once the rich, the powerful and the noble once lived. The reason is that about 160 to 200 years ago a great movement, or flitting as we call it in Scotland, took place.

In the second half of the eighteenth century the small, historic little capital on the rock grew so piled up with more and more floors being added, and so crowded, that it became intolerable. The New Town across the Nor' Loch (now the site of Princes Street Gardens) was designed and began to be built. As it grew, those who designed it fled from the constriction of the Old Town to the amplitude of the New. The poor remained behind. But something more than the poor remained. That something was not only some of the old buildings. It was the sense of the past. Many of the old buildings began to decay and were gradually pulled down. Some have been recently re-erected in a sensible effort to preserve the old Scottish style of architecture.

A "sense of the past" may be vague, and impossible to define, but a man would indeed be imperceptive if he did not feel it as he walked down the half-foreign-looking length of the Royal Mile. He would be imperceptive if he did not notice it in the small winding "closes" off the main street and in such of the original buildings as remain. Finally, he would have to be a very dull person if he did not become aware of it when he reached the end of the Royal Mile and came to the Palace of Holyroodhouse. Again, one could devote a whole book to Holyrood. In this small palace the history of Scottish royalty is enshrined. It is in itself a pleasant enough, if not very impressive, building. In its setting, however, with the great bulk of the hill called Arthur's Seat immediately behind it, it takes one by the heart.

The New Town is, as has been said, the exact complement to all this. It was extremely fortunate for posterity that when the inhabitants of old Edinburgh decided to escape from the overcrowding of the Old Town, the classical style of architecture in the North was at its most elegant. It was fortunate that the genius of the Adam brothers and of other architects was available. It was fortunate that our forefathers, in their desire for spaciousness and graciousness, should have decided not to stint themselves, to give themselves all the space and grace that they could obtain.

The true backbone of the New Town as first designed is the still noble thoroughfare of George Street, but nowadays we think of this unique piece of Georgian town-planning as beginning with the famous Princes Street. The operative word above is "but". Princes Street, one of Europe's famous streets, is certainly among Great Britain's showpieces. *But* there is much controversy about it. It has been described as Britain's most beautiful street. Others more architecturally inclined have called it the ugliest. It is neither. It is a one-sided street, the actual houses and shops of which are neither better nor worse than those comprising the usual discordant nineteenth-century and Victorian mess which is presented by the main streets of most modern big towns. But (that word again) its site and position is superb. In this respect it has its rivals in Europe, but none surpasses it.

Walking along the north side of Princes Street, and keeping your eyes firmly away from the confusion of buildings that our immediate forefathers have left us, you have a truly noble sight before you. You look southwards and into the light. From the Castle almost down to Holyrood you can see the outline of medieval Edinburgh painted, as it were, against the sky like the drop-curtain scene of a theatre. Castellated towers, grim buildings, graceful pinnacles and old lofty tenements hang above you as if on canvas. All the imperfections of detail in the Old Town dis-

In the Canongate, modern shops and flats have been built in a style which blends with the old. It is still possible to ride between the Castle and the Palace in a horse-cab.

appear when viewed from Princes Street. As the day progresses the light changes, and what was grim is touched with the light of the setting sun. But the Old Town is not the only "noble prospect", as Dr. Johnson would have put it, from this celebrated thoroughfare. You can see Arthur's Seat towering like a mountain at the east end. From the west end you can catch glimpses of the impressive Pentland Hills. Whatever one may say about the architecture of the buildings in one-sided Princes Street, one's enjoyment in looking up, southwards and away from it into the heights of this "precipitous city" is thrilling.

But (and here the word is introduced with little reservation) when you approach the New Town proper it is a very different matter. Here too you will have occasional "noble prospects", sudden vistas of the sea and of the distant shores of Fife, but the buildings that immediately surround you are also admirable. They are more than admirable, they are deeply satisfying in a way that never palls and that grows with the years. The New Town of Edinburgh in these northern climes was the latest (and some would say the most successful) concerted effort in town-planning in the classical tradition in Europe, therefore in the world. It is surprising how late this classical style of building went on. It began in the 1760s and continued well into Queen Victoria's reign, even into the 1850s. It is partly, but only partly, this that helps to give the New Town its unique appeal. When, in the rest of the western world, and most certainly in Britain, men were putting up pastiches of mock-Gothic and other imitations of the past, the Edinburgh builders, without affectation,

THE OLD COURSE, ST. ANDREWS

On this famous course all the holes have names: this is the last, called Tom Morris after the legendary "Old Tom" Morris, and his son "Young Tommy" who won the Open Championship four times in succession before his tragic death, aged 24. Many a match has been lost in the dip to the left of the green, "The Valley of Sin"; on a summer evening, or at a championship, the fence behind the green is lined by the most knowledgeable audience in the world. Nearby is the Royal and Ancient Golf Club, where the rules of the game are made and interpreted.

DEAN VILLAGE, EDINBURGH

The Dean Village, Edinburgh's "artists' quarter", is only a few hundred yards from the centre of the city. Once its mills were busy, and the Water of Leith was polluted and foul; now the river is as clear as a Highland burn, and the village is a quiet spot in a noisy town. The picture shows the small bridge in the village itself; downstream is Telford's much larger, more famous bridge, which carries the main Queensferry Road. In the background is Belford Church.

were quietly continuing in the classical traditions of the Renaissance. They were continuing, let it be stressed, not imitating.

This is not a guide-book, and this essay is intended to be a general description rather than a compendium of travel information. I must, therefore, avoid the temptation of mentioning particular places in the still fairly ample terrain of the New Town. I have spoken of its style. Its general shape and growth, however, I must also mention. It is a progression of ordered terraces, streets, squares, crescents and other partly curved, partly rectangular places—a procession stepping down the last hill of this hilly town that leads to the shores of the Firth of Forth. This procession was sometimes made slightly irregular in the early days by the need to comply with the rights of property owners. In later years the Philistinism of wealthy and commercial generations has here and there interfered with details in the style of the buildings that form this procession. These are the only immediately visible faults that the present writer, a son of Edinburgh and of the New Town of Edinburgh, can find with it.

One adjuration, slightly in the guide-book style, I must permit myself. If you come to Edinburgh for the first time and stay for only a few days, you may find that your attention has been so taken up by the romantic and remarkable past set upon the rock and the hill above you that you omit to see the New Town. This would be a great mistake. Having enjoyed the Old Town, the castle and Holyrood, do spare a little time for wandering in the district north of Princes Street which leads down to the sea. It is an ideal place for urban meandering.

No one knows what the future holds for such an enclave of dignity and comparative peace. The traffic is still partly deflected from it, but who knows when the tide will burst in. It is inconceivable that

The Military Tattoo is perhaps the most popular item in the Edinburgh Festival. The Castle Esplanade is turned into an arena, the show is held in the evening, and the floodlit Castle makes a romantic backcloth. Troops from many countries take part, but the pipes and drums of the Scottish regiments are always the main attraction.

the buildings should in our lifetime be deliberately destroyed by civic effort, but we may yet see the gardens and wide spaces of this gracious remnant of a past age invaded. They might even be considered as parking places for the teeming cars of this motor-crowded island. Our forefathers were generous, one might say extravagant, in leaving us such a heritage of space and grace. We may have some respect for grace, but we are over-greedy about space.

One word more about the New Town, for it concerns parts of Scotland other than Edinburgh. Mention has been made of the unmistakable New Town style of architecture. It is a style which has spread far north and beyond the confines of the capital, and even when the capital had all but ceased to build in it. Somehow the impetus of this architecture moved up the east of Scotland. In Fife (which we shall shortly be discussing) especially at St. Andrews, in Perth, in Aberdeen and in many other and smaller towns there are squares, crescents and individual houses exactly like those of the New Town of Edinburgh. The last of these towns is Thurso on the northern coast of Caithness. The New Town style of Edinburgh is individual and unmistakable, but it is in direct succession to and derived from the Renaissance in Italy some 500 years ago. Thus upon the shores of the Pentland Firth and facing the Orkney Islands (known to the ancient Romans as *Ultima Thule*) there dies the last ripple of the mighty wave of the Renaissance begun in the Mediterranean centuries ago. It is there because of the New Town of Edinburgh.

So much for the great centre of Edinburgh, the Edinburgh of the slowly growing past. This is what those of us who live in Edinburgh mean by Edinburgh—the Old Town and the New. It is all the Edinburgh that nine-tenths of the visitors will see. Nevertheless, the capital, like every other city in Britain, spread vastly and amorphously in the nineteenth century and the first half of the twentieth. In such later buildings there is little town-planning. Apart from a certain satisfying solidity of stone building, it would be idle to pretend that this great urban and suburban growth of Edinburgh differs intrinsically from that of any other British, and particularly Scottish, city of the period. In the matter of site, however, this growth had great advantages.

Edinburgh only could, and indeed still largely only can, expand by marching down to the sea or up into the hills. It marched down to and joined the ancient and once independent port of Leith. It marched along the seaboard, taking in other ancient ports and seaside villages such as Newhaven and Granton. It also marched up and around the seven hills which are its present foundation and which were once its guardians. It has to the far south even begun to march well up the near mountainous slopes of the Pentland Hills.

The result is that there can be no large town in Britain and few, if any, in Europe that has suburbs in which there exist such splendid prospects, fine vistas and dazzling views. The sea, with its islands, the nearby hills with their crags, the one great volcanic rock of the castle with its embattled crown, and finally, the distant peaks of the real Highlands in Perthshire, with snow on them for much of the year—all these can be seen from the growing fringes of Edinburgh and without ever leaving the streets. The words "the suburbs" have a somewhat commonplace ring about them. In Edinburgh the houses of the suburbs are as suburban as are those of any other city. The people who live in them, the suburbanites, have the same virtues and failings as have other suburbanites, but they are surrounded by a beauty which is quite "unsuburban" in quality.

What of the people of Edinburgh? Walter Scott in a famous line of verse called the place "Mine own romantic town". And indeed, with its mixture of medieval and classical architecture, its sea coasts and its hills, it is one of the romantic cities of the world. But the people can hardly be expected to live up to such surroundings. We have had our considerable romantic figures from the past, culminating perhaps in Scott himself, but romanticism or even an eye for

Charlotte Square is a good example of the Georgian architecture of the New Town of Edinburgh. The houses are very fine individually, but the chief impression is of the perfect balance of the whole.

beauty is not one of the salient characteristics of the reserved yet kindly-hearted folk of Edinburgh. Long ago, in the reign of James IV, Edinburgh was a nest of singing birds. Not so long ago, in the late eighteenth and early nineteenth centuries, Edinburgh was the home of genius. Perhaps some virtue has now gone out of her. Perhaps it will return. But at present the beautiful city of Edinburgh is a difficult town for an artist to live in. Beauty is disliked here, the aesthetic sense distrusted. It is oddly appropriate that the science of surgical anaesthesia should have been launched in Edinburgh over a century ago. It remains (as far as the people are concerned) a city of anaesthesia in which art is put painlessly to sleep. Nevertheless the capital of Scotland, for all her greyness, for all her long winter nights, her piercing springs, her unpredictable summers, her predictable people, is a place of great beauty in which to live. Her light—changing, variable, sometimes grim, sometimes tender—is a continual joy. Her folk, once you have accustomed yourself to their ways, are as decent and kindly and friendly and dependable a people as you will meet anywhere.

From the highest point in Edinburgh you can look down upon and, in a sense, over Fife in that you can

see the hills beyond it. You cannot, however, see all Fife, for its northern shores by the Firth of Tay are hidden by its own small county uplands. It is a fine independent little county which, lying between two Firths (of Forth and Tay) and with its east coast on the North Sea, is all but three parts an island. It is this nearly separate quality in it that has encouraged people to give it its time-honoured title of the "Kingdom of Fife". It is only time-honoured, however; there is no real historical justification for supposing that this spit of land was ever an independent kingdom.

All the same, if you are to follow your eye and really travel into Fife from Edinburgh, the best way is to cross the water. It is still just possible to cross the Firth of Forth by boat from Granton or Newhaven. And indeed this is the time-honoured way of approaching from Edinburgh that land which James IV called "a grey cloth mantle with a golden fringe", the golden fringe being those beautiful sands which you can see from the capital with the southern summer sun upon them. Today, however, the customary route is by Queensferry. To cross the water is to feel at once the difference between Fife and its neighbouring county of Midlothian, which used for some time

THE TAY BRIDGE FROM NEWPORT

The Tay Bridge joins Wormit in Fife to Dundee in Angus. The original railway bridge collapsed while a train was crossing it in 1879, and ninety people were killed. The present low, curved bridge, which was completed in 1888, carries a double line of rails for two miles over the Tay estuary. There have long been plans for a road bridge, but cars still cross by the Newport ferry.

CARBERRY TOWER, MIDLOTHIAN

Near Inveresk, south-east of Edinburgh, stands Carberry Tower, the seat of Lord Elphinstone and a fine sixteenth-century building in pleasant grounds. It is near Carberry Hill, where Mary, Queen of Scots encountered her insurgent nobles in June, 1567; the troops deserted, Bothwell was forced to flee, and she was taken as a prisoner to Loch Leven Castle.

The Forth Bridge is a mile and three-quarters long and over 350 feet high; it is massive but curiously graceful. The new road bridge will make the ferry-boat a thing of the past.

on old maps to bear the name of "Edinburghshire".

The difference for one coming new into Scotland is not great, but those of us who live in the eastern Lowlands notice it at once. To begin with, Fife is flatter and slightly richer in appearance than is the land round Edinburgh and in the Border hills to the south. Fife has a long tradition, if not of great wealth at least of prosperity, as prosperity goes in our northern climes. Her farmland is good, the fishing from her coasts second only to Aberdeenshire, and the industrial age has drawn upon the plentiful coal that is to be found in her more inland and western parts. And Fife has a long tradition of rich trade with the Continent, conducted when Scotland was still an independent country.

This trade is ended now, but its traces remain. All over Fife you will find the influence of continental building and particularly building in the style of the Low Countries, which were the parts of Europe most traded with by this eastern projection of Scotland. The most celebrated example of this is the fascinating little township of Culross (pronounced "Cooros"). Before the Reformation Culross, with its Cistercian abbey, was a notable Scottish ecclesiastical centre. Even then it was something more; for the monks of those days were hard workers in the mines and in the salt pans. Culross flourished under the monks. But after they left the local industries were carried on, in the seventeenth and eighteenth centuries. To them and the prosperity they brought was added the benefit of European trade. Culross, lying sheltered and far up the Firth of Forth, was for Scotland a point of connection with the outside world almost as important as Leith or Aberdeen. Now, save for the antiquarian, the visitor and the lover of old Scotland, it is no more than a fascinating curiosity.

With all this long history behind it, ecclesiastical, industrial and commercial, Culross, as has been well said, "is a corner into which Time has amused himself by raking choice collections of architecture and character." The abbey with its massive Norman tower still stands in part and serves as the parish kirk. There are signs of the places where ships from Europe used to come in, and a pleasing and touching jumble of Scottish town "wynds" (that is, closes and causeways), ancient houses, many now preserved by the National Trust for Scotland, and standing remnants of Culross's one-time importance. No one could claim for Culross much of great architectural beauty, though there are elements here and there that are worthy of that description. But the little half-forgotten town has another quality. It speaks for the past and makes that past live. It is a past in which the fortunes of Scotland and the trading towns of Holland were mingled. All this is in the stones of Culross.

Culross is tucked away, an enchanting Scottish-Dutch remnant, in the western part of Fife. Today most of western Fife is devoted to coal-mining and to other modern industries. Here lies much of the wealth of the modern and still prosperous county, although even in the industrial royal burgh of Dunfermline we are once more forcibly reminded of the past. Let it be said at once that Dunfermline, the birth-place of the famous Scottish-American millionaire, Andrew Carnegie, is far from being a forgotten outpost (as is Culross) from past centuries. It is a comfortably-off county town and the shopping centre for West Fife.

Nevertheless, the past is inescapable here. The abbey founded by Margaret, Queen of Scotland and now Saint Margaret, a thousand years ago, dominates the town from the southern approaches. Here are buried the remains of the saintly Queen. Here also was placed the body of the immortal soldier, leader and king, Robert the Bruce. The ruins of the palace are impressive. They too date from the period of Bruce. Were it not for the presence of St. Andrews in Fife (and later on we shall be talking about that lovely city) Dunfermline would be the shrine of the past, not only for Fife but for eastern Lowland Scotland.

One cannot leave Dunfermline without mentioning another form of prosperity which hangs over the town. Perhaps it would be better to describe it as a chance for prosperity, a sense of opportunity at hand for any citizen to grasp. Andrew Carnegie left immense sums for the benefit of all Scotland. Much of this he canalised for the use of his native place. Dunfermline, for so small a town, is staggeringly rich in amenities for all its citizens. No child born in Dunfermline with the slightest aptitude for learning lacks the help which most generously endowed scholarships can give it. Is it out of place to draw attention to this in a book about the face and appearance of Scotland? I think not. Just as I said that you can feel the remote past in the Old Town of Edinburgh, so it is possible to feel this great Scottish-American's love for his country and birth-place.

It is with pleasure that I move now to the coasts and the inland parts of eastern Fife, where one may give a more general impression of a fascinating corner of Scotland. Save for a few coastal towns, and possibly the neat little county town of Cupar, the landscape and the buildings in general are of greater interest than names here.

Eastern Fife is still essentially rich in the traditional way. There are not many hills, save the Paps of Lomond, visible from Edinburgh, and Largo Law. By far the greater part of the land is flat and is used as farmland that has continued as a granary and as land for agricultural beasts. The small villages that lie inland have a charm all their own. They are connected by a multiplicity of winding and rather confusing roads; and even today not many motorists see them. They lie hidden away in the sea-surrounded corner of Scotland and must present much the same appearance as they did in the past, in the era before motors were invented.

Usually they consist of one small street of neat houses that may have been built in the eighteenth, nineteenth or sometimes seventeenth century. Here too, amongst the older houses and cottages, you will see the obvious influence of Low Country and Dutch architecture. The neat fronts, the crowstep gables are reminiscent of buildings you see in the old Dutch pictures. A feature of the village kirks is largely peculiar to Fife, certainly to the eastern Lowlands. This is the small steeple placed perkily on the top and centre of a thick four-square tower. Maybe the old seventeenth- and eighteenth-century rural builders of this eastern shire were copying certain Dutch churches, maybe they found that they had not the skill to build long thin steeples, or maybe they thought that this style of church architecture looked pleasing. It certainly looks pleasing today.

Let it be admitted that the usual Scottish remotely rural village has not the welcoming and pleasing atmosphere and aspect of the English village. Far too many of them are just grey gaggles of mean nineteenth-century houses with a forbidding church and one or two even more forbidding public houses. The Fife villages, though certainly more northern and bleak in aspect than their English counterparts, do have charm. It is the charm of the unspoilt, lingering on

Part of Culross, including the "Palace", which was built by a seventeenth-century coal owner and is one of the fine vernacular buildings now preserved by the National Trust.

Many Scottish kings are buried in Dunfermline Abbey, and Bruce's sepulchre is there. The nave of the abbey church was built by David I; the choir is nineteenth-century.

ST. ABB'S HEAD

St. Abb's Head is a bold, rocky promontory in Berwickshire, a striking feature on a splendid coast. Further north are the ruins of Fast Castle, "fitter to lodge prisoners than folk at liberty", which was probably the original of Wolf's Crag in Scott's "Bride of Lammermoor".

PRESTON MILL

Preston Mill at East Linton is probably the oldest water-mill still working in Scotland: it was built in the seventeenth century, and restored in 1760. The red pantiles suggest Dutch influence, and give it great character and charm.

from the past yet still living. Each of these villages is the centre of a fairly flourishing farming community, and a community that has lasted easily into the present, alive and without break. Always one is reminded of the old Scottish-Dutch links. But, having been reminded, it does not take one ten seconds in glancing around to know that one is in Fife and nowhere else in the world.

The southern coast towns of Fife, apart from the larger places, like Kirkcaldy, devoted to modern industrialism, are fishing ports in origin and continue to rely on fishing and the holiday trade for their support. There are those who regard this still unspoilt coastline that runs north-eastwards roughly from Leven to the enchanting fishing village of Crail (at the very easternmost point of Fife) as the most attractive part of Scotland. Certainly there is much to be said for their point of view. Elie, Anstruther, Crail, these and other places face south into the eye of the sun, and get as much of the sun as is going in Scotland. Indeed this part of Fife is known as the "Riviera of Scotland". Apart from the sunshine, the view from here is lovely. You look directly across the waters of the Firth of Forth to the noble silhouette of rock-crowned Edinburgh amidst its hills. Behind them there lie the Pentlands. To the fore there is the Bass Rock and the fine coast of East Lothian with North Berwick Law above it. The countryside around these little fishing holiday towns is unspoilt. So, indeed, are the towns themselves, for the holiday-makers who come here relish the district and return year after year. They are not the ones who would like to see the Fife coast change under the influence of modern "improvements".

The fishing villages now partly adapted to holiday purposes were never ports connecting Scotland with the Continent. The Dutch influence in their building does not leap out at the eye in quite the way it does at

Crail is one of the chain of picturesque fishing villages on the east coast of Fife; their wealth and importance have declined, but their charm remains. Crail harbour is sheltered, but when a strong wind meets a high tide the waves hurdle the harbour wall.

some of the ports further up the Firth or in the inland villages. These little towns were built primarily for the practical purpose of housing fishermen and their families. Nevertheless, the Low Country influence was too strong to have been resisted altogether. This is very much Scotland, and Fife at that. But the ornamentation of some of the houses reminds you that the nearest country across the sea is Holland. If the present writer may express a preference, the ultimate little town of Crail on the "East Neuk of Fife" is, in his eyes, the most attractive of them all.

The moment you turn the "East Neuk" and start your journey northwards into that part of Fife hidden from even the highest point in Edinburgh, you cannot but feel that you are approaching something important. You are right. You are approaching the ancient and venerable university city, and one-time cathedral city, of St. Andrews. All signposts from the East Neuk at once begin to bear its name; and when you breast the slight hill and see the old ecclesiastical capital of Scotland before you, you will understand why. It is a lovely sight; and all roads here lead towards it.

There is no town in Scotland, not even Edinburgh,

The Town House of Crail, like many buildings in Fife, shows strong Dutch influence. The House contains bulls granted by Popes Julius II and Leo X—a sign of Crail's former importance as a trading and fishing port.

Above: St. Andrews from the West Sands, with the ruined Cathedral, St. Rule's Tower and the College Tower on the skyline. Below: St. Mary's College, and the tree planted by Mary, Queen of Scots. The students are wearing the traditional red undergraduate gown.

where the sense of the past so hangs over, and all but dominates, a vital and living present as in St. Andrews. It got its name from the fact that the relics of St. Andrew, patron saint of Scotland, were first brought to this land at this point in Fife. It was in pre-Reformation times the first bishopric in the country. Its noble cathedral, now a shattered, gaunt and rather alarming spectacle, was one of the finest in northern Europe. Its university was celebrated overseas. Not only cardinals, prelates and churchmen lived here, but kings, queens and ministers of state. Nowhere in Scotland did the clash of the Reformation ring out more dramatically than in St. Andrews. Nowhere else did men suffer (on both sides of the religious struggle) more tragically. The Reformation, with its abolition of episcopal rule, all but killed St. Andrews, save in the outward and visible form of its buildings. It remained for the nineteenth and twentieth centuries to bring life back into it.

In the nineteenth century two things happened. The university revived from its long half-sleep of nearly two hundred years and became a living place of learning. At the same time a game then known only in Scotland, and the east of Scotland at that, became gradually more famous. The English became aware of it and then enthusiastic about it. It spread overseas to the Continent, all over the British Empire and finally, most potently, to America. The game, of course, was golf. There may be dispute amongst golfers as to whether the Old Course at St. Andrews is or is not the finest course in the world (I hold, as a cardinal article of belief, that it is) but there can be no doubt that it is the most famous.

Golf brought people from all over the world to

Scotland, but particularly to the eastern Lowlands of Scotland, and, above all, to St. Andrews. And yet again, modern though most people would hold this game to be, it is rooted in the past at St. Andrews. The links there are natural; and for countless generations the ordinary folk of St. Andrews have been playing golf on the course that nature has laid out for them. They may indeed have been playing at something like golf there when the first stones of the cathedral were being laid.

The great grey, towering skeleton of the more than half destroyed cathedral stands at the extreme end of the eastern part of the city. It is a landmark to sailors at sea, and is visible from far inland. It haunts St. Andrews, perhaps, rather than dominates it. It haunts it far more than the Old Town haunts Edinburgh. At the western end of the little city the Old Course stretches out by the shores of the bay, with its matchless turf and its lovely greens.

Between these two ancient things lie the partly modern but inescapably ancient town and university of St. Andrews, with ancient byways and Georgian architecture. Let the photographs on these pages lure you to the old ecclesiastical capital of Scotland and the

THE TWEED AT MERTOUN

The lands of Mertoun are on a winding, thickly-wooded stretch of the Tweed between Melrose and Kelso, near Dryburgh Abbey. The woods shelter Mertoun House, which was built for Sir William Scott of Harden in the eighteenth century, and is now the seat of the Earl of Ellesmere.

DRYBURGH ABBEY

Dryburgh Abbey was founded in 1150 for the Premonstratensians. It was sacked by English invaders in 1322 and 1385, and was completely destroyed by the Earl of Hertford in 1544. It was presented to the nation by Lord Glenconner in 1919.

ABBOTSFORD

Abbotsford was built by Sir Walter Scott in 1815-23, in the style of architecture since called "Abbotsford Gothic". The house is pleasantly situated by the Tweed, just off the main road between Selkirk and Melrose.

Falkland Palace was begun by James II, became a favourite seat of the Scottish kings, and owes its appearance to James V.

Kinross and Loch Leven, with the Lomond Hills beyond. Queen Mary made her famous escape from the castle on the island.

present golfing capital of the world to see it for yourself. St. Andrews is old, St. Andrews is young. Whatever age you are, and whether your sense of the past is stronger than your sense of the present, or the other way round, you will feel the attraction of this unique miniscule city set between the standing bones of the great cathedral and the most famous golf links in the world.

From the highest point in Edinburgh you may see, as I have said, some of the peaks of the celebrated Border hills due south and slightly westwards. You can, however, see more than peaks of the east Border country. Indeed you can look over East Lothian and into Berwickshire as easily as you can overlook Fife from the same place. These lands are what remain of that part of Scotland which used to be called Lothian. And though they do not have quite the romantic appeal of the Walter Scott country further inland, they are certainly of the true Border country between England and Scotland. It was up here to the east that the hammer blows of the English forced the one-time frontier to the north of the river Tweed. The essence of Scotland has packed itself very much into a unit in this district. It is perhaps not too fanciful to suppose that the persistence of the English hammer blows had something to do with this concentration of Scottishness in Lothian.

East Lothian, which is the shire immediately contiguous to Edinburgh, is a lovely county. I can never understand why it does not make a wider appeal to visitors. Maybe, lying so close to the capital and containing the main road to London and the south, it is mostly regarded as a "corridor county", the means by which one gets from one important place to another. This is most unjust. Near to Edinburgh though it is, it is a wide, unspoilt, rich and beautiful piece of countryside with some fine characteristic examples of rural Scottish architecture in it. It has an excellent coastline of romantic rock and good sand, good golf courses (after St. Andrews, some of the best there are), fine open inland farming country, and finally some of the loveliest hills in Scotland, the Lammermuirs. It is scenically considerably superior to Fife, but more neglected.

For the purposes of this essay it would be better not to regard East Lothian as a unit, but to treat it and Berwickshire as the district of Lothian. Despite small differences the two Lothian shires have much in common. To begin with there is the excellence of their farmland. You do not need to be a professional farmer to know that these ample fields, stout farmhouses and good grazing ground are the signs of agricultural wealth. Northern and exposed to the east wind as this countryside may be, it does the heart good to feel the fertility of it all.

Then there is the coast. Facing north and east, this determined promontory of Scotland, holding within it such rich land, has endured for centuries the onslaught of the sea and the storm. This has not affected the land, but it has built an attractive and, at places, romantic coastline. North Berwick combines, as few towns outside Scotland succeed in doing, the indestructible qualities of an old fishing village and those of a haunt of fashion. Its golf courses are famous, so are its sands. But along with these are the immemorial rocks of this battered coast, and a lovely old harbour in which the colour of pink predominates.

And with the mention of pink one must draw attention to the beautiful delicacy of colouring all over Lothian, especially in East Lothian. The farmlands are a rich brown, the roots fresh green, the sea and sky pale blue and the buildings the most charming and unexpected pink. This pink is not something imposed, but comes from the substance of the Lothian stone itself. There is nothing sentimental about it. Tantallon Castle, for instance, is, though now in ruins, as dauntless a bastion of the fighting days of the past as you will get in all Scotland. Facing the raging sea, and with the wide open inland behind it, it stands out boldly—yet it is built out of a stone in which the pink reminds you of blood. This combination of delicate colouring and fortitude continues all the way along the buffeted Lothian coastline. It goes through the ancient Dunbar, now a holiday resort. It loses its pink in Berwickshire, but keeps its pale blues and greens through St. Abb's Head, Eyemouth, and through the charming little fishing village of Burnmouth until it reaches the historic town from which Berwickshire takes its name. But, by an unexplained anomaly, Berwick, though on our side of Tweed, is in England, and outside the orbit of this survey.

A man might enjoy himself for a long time and spend many holidays on the invigorating, severe yet beautiful coast of Lothian, without penetrating much into the body of this district, but he would be missing much. He would, for instance, be missing some of the most charming villages in all Scotland. It is high praise from a Scotsman to say that that white and black carefully designed unit of a tiny township, Gifford, is as attractive as any English village. So is Dirleton, and other lesser hamlets lying between the Lammermuirs and the sea. Haddington, the county town of East Lothian, is a dignified self-contained burgh in which the beauty of Georgian architecture melts almost imperceptibly into a remoter past. Berwick (and I really cannot resist mentioning it, for it ought to be our Berwickshire county town) is also a fine example of this east of Scotland town building. It is most certainly worth a visit, even if you have, strictly speaking, to go outside Scotland by three miles to look at it.

The visitor who lingered by the lure of the Lothian coastline would also be missing much in the way of purely wild scenery. The Lammermuir hills are unlike any other range in Scotland. They have no peaks, no jagged defiances of the skyline. They are soft and rolling, yet rise to about 2000 feet. They are feminine hills, with soft contours. They are filled with little burns and lochs abounding in brown trout. From their rolling uplands you can obtain a noble view over most of southern Scotland. In their valleys and on the slopes of them there are tucked away some ancient villages which give the appearance of being untouched by time. The upland and inland part of Lothian may lie within easy distance of Edinburgh, its hills may be easy to climb, its aspect may be different from the traditional "grandeur" of the Highlands and even of some of the more famous Border mountains, but it is as remote and as timeless a district as you will find in all Scotland.

In the centre of Clackmannan stands an old Mercat Cross, the Tolbooth and the curious stone or "clach" of Mannan.

Part of the fortified Palace of Linlithgow was built by Edward I, but most of it by the Stewarts. Charles I was the last king to live there; it was burned by Hanoverian troops in 1746.

These eastern parts of Lothian by rock-girt coast

ST. MARY'S LOCH

Deep in the hills between Selkirk and Moffat lies St. Mary's Loch, the "lone St. Mary's silent lake" of Scott's "Marmion". The hills, as Wordsworth remarked, are perfectly reflected in the smooth water. Nearby, where the River Yarrow leaves the loch, are the ruins of St. Mary's Chapel, which is the scene of Hogg's "Mary Scott" and "Mess John".

NEIDPATH CASTLE

Neidpath Castle, an old tower with later additions, stands on the Tweed near Peebles. The family of Tweeddale acquired it from the Frasers, and the second Earl made a famous defence of it against Cromwell. It is beautifully situated, though Wordsworth denounced the Duke of Queensberry for felling the fine trees which surrounded it.

and with their mild lovely hills and little undisturbed townships may not be what is usually understood as the Border country, but they most certainly are a notable part of the Border between Scotland and England; and their history tells of it. It does not, it must be admitted, tell of it so famously as does the more central Borderland where Scotland begins to bulge southward into her sister kingdom. "The Borders" (I put the words into quotation marks to note the popular usage of the phrase) were made internationally famous by Sir Walter Scott. And the land that he made famous by writing about it and by merely living in it is the highland and the valley country lying due south of Edinburgh and away miles from the guardian Pentland Hills.

If the Highlands be the land of Scotland's grandeur, the Walter Scott country, "the Borders", is the land of romance. Even had Scott never written, never existed, there would have come down to us the magic of this ballad-haunted country in which so many of the wars between England and Scotland were fought out in forays. It is a land of tradition and magic, lingering on amidst immemorial hills and the ruins

In Kelso, a pleasant Border market town at the junction of Tweed and Teviot, is a fine bridge built by Rennie in 1803.

Melrose Abbey was founded in 1136 by David I. Like the other Border abbeys, it was often sacked during English invasions.

"Peebles for pleasure": a fine setting and attractive town. The fountain in High Street commemorates the poet John Veitch.

of abbeys and old fortresses in which the Border folk of Scotland lived and looked ever uneasily southwards towards their richer and more powerful neighbours.

This land is strictly speaking in the Lowlands of Scotland and those who have lived there through the centuries are Lowlanders. Yet it is a land of noble hills that would in England be called mountains. The folk of these hills and valleys, too, have shown in the past a capacity for song and poetry, for story-telling and simple music nearly as touching as the great Celtic tradition of the north and west and of the scattered islands of the Atlantic. As far as the power of imagination goes, you cannot just divide Scotland into the "poetic Highlanders" and the "practical Lowlanders". The central Borderers have contributed far too much to the story of Scotland's song for that distinction to be made.

The ordinary route from Edinburgh (the focal point of this essay) into the Borders is by direct southern road through or on one side of the Moorfoot Hills. As we have already gone deep into the eastern and less celebrated Borderland of Lothian, let us continue on our route from there and come up into the central Borders by following the historic valley of Tweed. It is on the banks of Tweed that much of Scotland's story has been told. The waters of Tweed irrigate its history. Tweeddale is the very heart of Borderland.

Until just west of Coldstream the River Tweed marks the boundary between England and Scotland. It meanders broadly through low-lying country with little of visible difference on either side. Those who think, however, that, humanly speaking, the north of England melts into Scotland, will be quickly disabused by making crossings and recrossings of Tweed at that north-eastern corner. They will find in speech, behaviour and in type a marked difference between the men who live on the southern banks and those on the northern banks of the river. Not only does Scots law prevail on one bank and English on the other; here are two distinct nations facing each other across a noble and still wide salmon river.

As the great hills of the Border country begin to show up on the west, however, Tweed makes up its mind. It plunges into the upland country and becomes a purely Scottish river on both banks. Just before it enters the hills it passes through the ancient town of Kelso, standing foursquare and undoubtedly Scots, away from the English border. By the lovely little town of Melrose with the ruins of its Cistercian abbey (destroyed not by the Reformers but in the English wars) Tweed becomes more Scottish in character as well as in geographical position. And as it mounts upwards into the beauties of Tweeddale it seems to become conscious of its nationality.

Here in the upper reaches is no fat pastoral southern

waterway, but a river that knows that its origin lies in the heather-covered hills, wide spaces and rocky configurations. It is a fascinating journey to walk or ride up Tweed from its mouth by Berwick to its remote beginnings in the wild neighbourhood of Tweedsmuir. You begin indubitably in Scotland, but in the rich farmland of Lowland Scotland; you end in open moorland and hills as obviously Scots in appearance as any landscape in the West Highlands. To travel up Tweed is not to take a long journey, but it is a journey in the most romantic manner possible, plunging straight into the heart of Scotland.

After Melrose (how beautiful is that name with its connotations of honey and flowers !) the only big or county town actually on the banks of Tweed is Peebles—and how uneuphonious is the name of that pleasant place. On either side of Tweed, in its valley or in the vales of its tributaries, there stand the towns of Borderland which have been famous in Scottish history. There is Selkirk, Hawick, Jedburgh and the rather more modern Galashiels. Today these bustling towns (small by English standards) are thriving places of the tweed industry and centres of agriculture. At one time they were bastions of Scotland's freedom.

These were the towns that withstood the force of the first blows from England. These were the towns that were bled all but dry of the blood of their young manhood on Flodden field. In Hawick there stands the statue of the one Scottish standard-bearer who returned, rescuing the Scottish flag from that fatal field where: "The flowers of the forest are a' wede away". These Border towns have their position appreciably away from the ridge of upland along which the Scottish-English border runs in this district. They stand there partly because of the fertility of the lowland and well-watered districts around them. It is perhaps not too fanciful to suppose that they also stand there for historical reasons, crouching behind the no-man's land of the ridge of hills between the two nations.

Apart from these towns the whole valley and neighbourhood of the Tweed Borderland is scattered with peel towers and old Border castles and fortresses. These were half dwelling-places, half fortified outposts. They are too many to enumerate here. They stand today, some in ruins, some refurbished, some empty, some converted into modern houses in which people live. They stand as reminders of a past that

Selkirk on the Ettrick is famous for its tweed mills, but shoemaking was once the chief industry, and natives of the town are still called "Soutars" (anglice: shoemakers).

Galashiels is one of the many Border towns noted for high-quality tweeds and woollens. There have been mills there for centuries, though the rich export trade is fairly modern.

The Hawick Riding of the Marches and this statue in the High Street celebrate the victory of local "callants" over an English force after Flodden.

was indubitably grim but from which there flowered the whole rich and moving tradition of the Scottish ballads in verse and song.

How much of that tradition still lives in the matter-of-fact prosperous farm folk and townspeople of the Scottish borderland of today? These people in their grey, attractive, but not strictly speaking beautiful towns, in their solid farmhouses, are the direct descendants of the heroes and heroines in the ballads of the past. Today they are, of course, mostly concerned with the commercial business of making a good living in a prosperous district of their native land. He would be a bold man, however, who claimed that all poetry, romance and emotion had been drained from them. You cannot live in the shadow of such beauty as is shown by the Eildon Hills, or in the loveliness of the upper Tweed valley, and remain unaffected by it.

The Border folk live in today but treasure their past. Such ceremonies as the annual summer "Border Ridings", where each town, township and district proclaims its individuality, are the occasions for outbursts of gaiety, song and dance which are dear to even the most practical Border heart. Their speech is of the eastern Lowlands, but in its tune has a kind of sing-song melody which makes it a suitable vehicle for the speaking of native poetry. Of course they do not speak (nor make) much poetry today. I have, however, had the good fortune to hear Border school children speak their own country's ballads at the competitions of drama festivals. Much of it was dry-as-dust, being learned by rote. Occasionally, however, a childish voice would speak authentically out of the Border past and with feeling. It was a moving experience, of a kind that one would be unlikely to enjoy elsewhere in Scotland, save in the Gaelic West.

The Borderers are a proud and independent people. The Border country in which they live has a kind of proud beauty of hill and dale, independent of, or at least different from, the beauty of much else of Scotland. Yet scratch a Borderer and underneath you will find that he is an intensely patriotic Scot first and a Borderer second. For all its unique quality on the face of Scotland, the scenery of the Borders could exist nowhere else save in Scotland. The Borders have attracted great attention from writers about Scotland. There are almost as many books about them as there are about Edinburgh. Let this essay but point the way to them. Better still, let it encourage the visitor to wander in this richly beautiful district of our diverse Scotland.

Diverse it is indeed. But I would close as I began, by asserting an essential unity in the south-east Lowlands of Scotland, of which Edinburgh is the

MELLERSTAIN HOUSE

Mellerstain House, near Earlston, is one of the stately homes of Scotland. It was probably designed by William Adam for Lady Grisell Baillie, the poetess, was finished by his son Robert in 1778, and now belongs to the Earl and Countess of Haddington.

From the highest peak of the Eildon Hills, Sir Walter Scott could "point out forty-three places famous in war and verse." The three hills used to be one, but were "cleft by the wizard Michael Scott." Within them, the Queen of Elfland imprisoned Thomas the Rhymer, otherwise known as Thomas of Ercildoune or Thomas Learmonth, from whom the Russian poet Lermontov claimed descent. Nearby, at Newstead, is the Roman fort of Trimontium.

capital and focal point. These south-east Lowlands are partly flat, as in much of Fife and by the coasts of Lothian, partly hilly to the point of being mountainous in the central Borders. The building, the architecture that the south-east Scots have put up here in the past centuries, is partly wild, and in our eyes romantic. It is also, under the influence of the New Town of Edinburgh, classical, either severely classical in the grey manner or graciously and spaciously classical. The folk from the north-east tip of Fife, through Edinburgh down to the shepherds on the great hills of the Ettrick Forest in the Borders, may vary in the details of their speech and outlook, but they are of the same stock. And the lands on which they live have an obviously related Scottish quality which you will notice the moment you come into them from England.

I cannot end these remarks about Fife, Edinburgh and the Borders without mentioning the wonderful quality of the light which is so much a part of the district's beauty. Sometimes that light is obscured in the eastern mists that come from the sea, but more often it touches the scenery both in town and in country with its remarkable soft delicacy. This is the first sight that the traveller from the south will get of the famous northern light, gentle and long-lasting through the summer days. Up in these regions the sun does not strike directly down but comes slantingly from the horizon. The effect is luminous in the most delicate manner. Thus this countryside of wildness and plains, of noble townscape and demure villages and hamlets, of fierce Border keeps and practical modern farms, is for much of the year illuminated by the subtlest and softest natural lighting in Europe.

Index of Place Names

A Supplementary Index dealing with people, pastimes and items of general interest follows on page 239. Asterisks (*) following page numbers denote illustrations.

Supplementary Index

ACKNOWLEDGMENTS. *The Publishers wish to thank the Trustees of the Killearn Trusts for permission to reproduce the photographs of Killearn village on page 45; also Messrs. T. & R. Annan for the picture on page 16.*

OVERLEAF: *The Tay at Kingoodie*

Yonder doun dwinis the even sky away,
And up springis the bricht dawning of day
Intil another place not far asunder,
That to behold was plesaunce, and half wonder.

GAWAIN DOUGLAS

SCOTLAND
NORTH
Scale of Miles
0 5 10 15 20 25
Flannan Is.
Butt of Lewis
Cape Wrath
Sandwood Loch
Kinlochbervie
L. Inchard
Rhiconich
L. Laxford
Fionne Bheinn 2980′
Handa I.
Laxford Br.
Ben Stack 2364′
Eddrachillis Bay
Oldany I.
Rhu Stoer
L. Carnban
Drumbeg
Kylesku
L. Nedd
Unapool
L. Glencoul
L. Assynt
Lochinver
Inchnadamph
Canisp 2779′
Enard Bay
Coulmore 2786′
Summer Is.
Achiltibuie
Ben Mor Coigeach 2438′
Sron na Caillich 370′
Caillich Hd.
Scoraig
Gruinard Bay
Lit. Loch Broom
L. Broom
Ullapool
First & Second Coast
Laide
Loch Ewe
Aultbea
An Teallach 3483′
Sgurr Eididh nan Clach Geala 3039′
Loch na Sealg
Poolewe
Gairloch
Gairloch
Loch Maree
Slioch 3217′
Lochaidh Bhraoin
A'Chailleach 3276′
Droma
L. Fannich
EAST ROSS
WESTER ROSS
CROMARTY
Ben Alligin 3232′
Upper L. Torridon
L. Torridon
Kinlochewe
Bran
Achnasheen
Shieldaig
Ben Damh 2958′
Meig
Glen Carron
Applecross
L. Monar
Farrar
L. Carron
Plockton
Cannich
Balmacara
Glen Elchaig
Glass
L. Long
Falls of Glomach
Lochalsh
Kyleakin
Broadford
Kylerhea
Kyle Rhea
Rattachan
Kintail
Ben Attow 3383′
Glen Affric
Glenelg
Shiel Br.
Gl. Lichd
The Saddle 3317′
Br. of Shiel
Cluanie Wr.
Cluanie
L. Hourn
Kinlochhourn
L. Loyne
Ladhar Bheinn 3343′
KNOYDART
Tomdoun
L. Garry
Glengarry
Invergarry
Inverie
Loch Nevis
Carn a Ghobhair 2454′
Sgurr na Ciche 3410′
L. Quoich
INVERNESS
Sgurr nan Coireachan 3125′
Mallaig
Morar
L. Morar
Gl. Dessary
Loch Arkaig
Loch Lochy
Glen Gloy
Arisaig
Borrodale
Sithean Mor 1970′
Gl. Pean
Gulvain 3224′
Achnacarry
Gairlochy
Br. of Roy
Beasdale
L. Nan Uamh
L. Eilt
Glenfinnan
Eilean nan Gobhar
L. Ailort
Drum Fiaclach 2852′
Banavie
Corpach
Spean Br.
Spean
Rois-bheinn 2876′
Beinn Odhar Bheag 2895′
Loch Eil
Inverlochy Cas
Fort William
Shona
Kinlochmoidart
L. Moidart
Shiel
Gl. Nevis
Ben Nevis 4406′
Aonach Beag 4060′
Cairn mor Dearg 3348′
Dhomhnuill 2915′
Sgurr a Mhaim 3601′
Ardnamurchan Pt.
Beinn na Seilg 1123′
Kentra
Acharacle
Loch Shiel
ARDGOUR
Garbh Bheinn 2903′
Ardgour
Mamore Forest
Kinlochleven
L. Eilde
Kilchoan
Salen
L. Sunart
Strontian
Glen Tarbert
Onich
L. Leven
Inverco
Ballachulish
Pap of Glencoe 2430′
Glencoe 3766
Buchaille Etive Beag 2547′
Altnafeadh
Sd. of Mull
Coll
Tobermory
L. Teacuis
ARGYLL
Creach Bheinn 2800′
Loch Linnhe
Ben Vair 3362′
Bidean nam Bian
3345′
Buchaille Etive
LEWIS
L. Roag
Uig B.
Callernish
Stornoway
Broad B.
Eye Peninsula
Stornoway Harb.
L. Erisort
L. Langabhat
Scarpay
NORTH MINCH
L. Seaforth
L. Shell
W. Loch Tarbert
HARRIS
E. Loch Tarbert
Shiant Is.
Vaternish Pt.
Sound of Harris
Pabbay
Heisker
OUTER HEBRIDES
North Uist
LITTLE MINCH
Kilmaluaig
Quirang 1779′
Monkstadt
Loch Snizort
L. Dunvegan
The Storr 2360′
Kingsburgh
Sound of Raasay
South Rona
Inner Sound
Raasay
Benbecula
Dunvegan
Macleod's Tables 1538′ 1601′
ISLE OF SKYE
Portree
Bracadale
L. Bracadale
Scalpay
L. Sligachan
Sligachan
South Uist
Ben More 2034′
CUILLINS
Sgurr Alasdair 3309′
Blaven 3042′
L. Allan
Daliburgh
L. Boisdale
Soay
L. Scavaig
L. Eishort
Sound of Sleat
Sound of Barra
Eriskay
Cuillin Sound
Canna
Rhum
Barra
Castle B.
Eigg
Muck